Python Data Visualization Essentials Guide

Become a Data Visualization Expert by Building Strong Proficiency in Pandas, Matplotlib, Seaborn, Plotly, Numpy, and Bokeh

Kalilur Rahman

www.bpbonline.com

FIRST EDITION 2021

Copyright © BPB Publications, India

ISBN: 978-93-91030-07-0

All Rights Reserved. No part of this publication may be reproduced, distributed or transmitted in any form or by any means or stored in a database or retrieval system, without the prior written permission of the publisher with the exception to the program listings which may be entered, stored and executed in a computer system, but they can not be reproduced by the means of publication, photocopy, recording, or by any electronic and mechanical means.

LIMITS OF LIABILITY AND DISCLAIMER OF WARRANTY

The information contained in this book is true to correct and the best of author's and publisher's knowledge. The author has made every effort to ensure the accuracy of these publications, but publisher cannot be held responsible for any loss or damage arising from any information in this book.

All trademarks referred to in the book are acknowledged as properties of their respective owners but BPB Publications cannot guarantee the accuracy of this information.

Distributors:

BPB PUBLICATIONS
20, Ansari Road, Darya Ganj
New Delhi-110002
Ph: 23254990/23254991

DECCAN AGENCIES
4-3-329, Bank Street,
Hyderabad-500195
Ph: 24756967/24756400

MICRO MEDIA
Shop No. 5, Mahendra Chambers,
150 DN Rd. Next to Capital Cinema,
V.T. (C.S.T.) Station, MUMBAI-400 001
Ph: 22078296/22078297

BPB BOOK CENTRE
376 Old Lajpat Rai Market,
Delhi-110006
Ph: 23861747

To View Complete
BPB Publications Catalogue
Scan the QR Code:

Published by Manish Jain for BPB Publications, 20 Ansari Road, Darya Ganj, New Delhi-110002 and Printed by him at Repro India Ltd, Mumbai

Dedicated to

My family and teachers

My wonderful spouse and the two angelic daughters who make me a complete human. A special dedication to all great mentors, teachers, professionals, and all the wonderful innovators, authors, and leaders who make this world a better place!

About the Author

Kalilur Rahman has a Master's Degree in Business Administration, preceded by an Engineering Degree in Computer Science and over two decades of experience in software development, testing, program/ project management, and management consultancy. Kalilur has been a developer, designer, technical architect, test program manager, delivery unit head, IT services, and COE/factory services head of varying complexity across telecommunications, life sciences, retail, and healthcare industries. Kalilur has advised CXO-level leaders in market-leading firms for testing, business, and technology transformation programs. As a thought-leader, Kalilur is a regular invitee at many industry events across technology and domains.

Kalilur is a firm believer in "knowledge is power" and is passionate about writing and sharing his knowledge. Kalilur is an active member of various technical and professional forums and contributed to internal improvement initiatives in the organizations he worked for. Kalilur has varied interests includes technology, testing in the digital world, artificial intelligence, machine learning, DevOps, continuous delivery, agile, mobility, IoT, and analytics. He is a regular contributor at LinkedIn – a site for professionals and has over 800,000+ followers at the time of publishing. He has published over 200 articles across LinkedIn, DevOps.Com, and other leading magazines.

Kalilur is also an active quizzing enthusiast who participates and contributes at corporate level quizzing at competitive and information levels.

Acknowledgement

First and foremost, I would like to thank my family for supporting me in this journey to write this book. I would like to thank everyone at BPB Publications for giving me this opportunity to publish this book and helping me keep focused on the goal, and supporting me along the way.

I would also like to thank my colleagues and extended professional community for giving me endless support and resources to write this book. My learning from all the teachers (upwards, peers, subordinates, and industry experts) has been phenomenal and helpful in quenching a little bit of my thirst for knowledge and sharing the same with extended readers.

I would like to thank all the life-long learners like me who have an insatiable thirst for knowledge that permits people like me to embark on a journey of knowledge sharing and wisdom searching and making ourselves better.

I would be missing my duty if I did not thank all the wonderful people at BPB publications who made this book a reality. This includes the management team (Nrip Jain and others), the acquisition Editor, who persistently reached out to me to get this book going, the content editor who was very methodical, meticulous, friendly, and strict to make sure that tasks were done on time and for brilliant inputs to chisel the book for the first draft. My wonderful technical editor's technical prowess and attention to detail made this a better book to read. The copyediting team did a fantastic job in building the final version of the book, and the entire marketing and management team from BPB made a wonderful effort to get the best out of this book.

Lastly, I would like to thank my critics, my mentors, and my guides. Without their criticism, feedback and inputs, I would never be able to write this book.

- *Kalilur Rahman*

Preface

Over the past Techade (a NASSCOM term for the decade 2011-20), data science has been very popular and has a key focus area for technologists. Leading technology giants, massively successful startups, and software product engineering companies have leveraged the power of data science to build great products and services. One of the key elements for the success of data science and big data analytics is the growth in the tools and features to make complex tasks simple and the growth in computing infrastructure. Data visualization is one key concept used for various core aspects of data science in a very intelligent and simple way.

Python has opened the doors for making data visualization simple by exponentiating resourceful libraries to automate various visualization needs. Complexities such as the need to visualize complex data sets and data types are addressed by various libraries efficiently using Python. With an easy-to-adapt framework and architecture, Python automation offers the capability to write good visualization with a few lines of code. Python offers several benefits when it comes to data visualization.

The primary aim of this book is to create a scholastically simple and easy-to-use guide that spotlights the core concepts of data visualization using Python. This book can be used to understand the data visualization concepts easily to prepare the professional reading this book to become ready to do their visualization on various datasets. This book contains many examples to showcase a particular concept and key principles that may get asked as a potential interview question. This book will be a good pilot to learn the basic concepts of data visualization using Python. This book is divided into ten chapters, and it provides a detailed description of the core concepts of data visualization.

Chapter 1 introduces the concepts of data visualization. It covers data visualization, key elements of data visualization, and the importance of using test automation.

Chapter 2 introduces the power of visual storytelling, covers some examples of powerful data visualization, reinforces the benefits of data visualization, and some starter recommendations on various resources and tools to use.

Chapter 3 covers the elements of data visualization and the tools available. It covers different types of charts and graphs used in data visualization, a recommendation on choosing the right charts, different methods to consider for choosing different visualization elements, and suggested implementation approaches. It also covers various data visualization tools available in the market to consider.

Chapter 4 covers the hands-on examples using the matplotlib library. It covers an introduction to the wildly popular matplotlib library, covers the introduction to the library's architecture, and covers 50+ examples for data visualization. It also gives a list of matplotlib resources for use.

Chapter 5 covers hands-on examples using NumPy and Pandas libraries. It covers an introduction to Pandas plotting and examples and case studies of various visualization elements using Pandas plotting functions, modules, and toolkits. It also gives a list of Pandas resources for use.

Chapter 6 covers hands-on examples using the Seaborn library. It covers an introduction to the Seaborn library. Using different datasets examples and case studies of various visualization elements of Seaborn is showcased. It also gives a list of Seaborn resources for use.

Chapter 7 covers hands-on examples using the Bokeh library. It covers an introduction to the Bokeh library, followed by examples and resources for Bokeh.

Chapter 8 covers hands-on examples using plot.ly, folium, MPLFinance. This chapter has case studies for Plot.ly covering interactive visualization capabilities, case studies using folium for geographic mapping visualization, and MPLFinance for stock market data visualization of some financial charts.

Chapter 9 covers case studies and hands-on examples and exercises for the reader to try out. This chapter has examples to work out using all libraries covered (matplotlib, seaborn, bokeh, plot.ly. folium) and Altair. This chapter is a complete hands-on guide for the readers to apply the learning from the first eight chapters.

Downloading the code bundle and coloured images:

Please follow the link to download the
Code Bundle and the *Coloured Images* of the book:

https://rebrand.ly/h9lvo5w

Errata

We take immense pride in our work at BPB Publications and follow best practices to ensure the accuracy of our content to provide with an indulging reading experience to our subscribers. Our readers are our mirrors, and we use their inputs to reflect and improve upon human errors, if any, that may have occurred during the publishing processes involved. To let us maintain the quality and help us reach out to any readers who might be having difficulties due to any unforeseen errors, please write to us at :

errata@bpbonline.com

Your support, suggestions and feedbacks are highly appreciated by the BPB Publications' Family.

Did you know that BPB offers eBook versions of every book published, with PDF and ePub files available? You can upgrade to the eBook version at www.bpbonline.com and as a print book customer, you are entitled to a discount on the eBook copy. Get in touch with us at :

business@bpbonline.com for more details.

At **www.bpbonline.com**, you can also read a collection of free technical articles, sign up for a range of free newsletters, and receive exclusive discounts and offers on BPB books and eBooks.

BPB is searching for authors like you

If you're interested in becoming an author for BPB, please visit **www.bpbonline.com** and apply today. We have worked with thousands of developers and tech professionals, just like you, to help them share their insight with the global tech community. You can make a general application, apply for a specific hot topic that we are recruiting an author for, or submit your own idea.

The code bundle for the book is also hosted on GitHub at **https://github.com/bpbpublications/Python-Data-Visualization-Essentials-Guide**. In case there's an update to the code, it will be updated on the existing GitHub repository.

We also have other code bundles from our rich catalog of books and videos available at **https://github.com/bpbpublications**. Check them out!

PIRACY

If you come across any illegal copies of our works in any form on the internet, we would be grateful if you would provide us with the location address or website name. Please contact us at **business@bpbonline.com** with a link to the material.

If you are interested in becoming an author

If there is a topic that you have expertise in, and you are interested in either writing or contributing to a book, please visit **www.bpbonline.com**.

REVIEWS

Please leave a review. Once you have read and used this book, why not leave a review on the site that you purchased it from? Potential readers can then see and use your unbiased opinion to make purchase decisions, we at BPB can understand what you think about our products, and our authors can see your feedback on their book. Thank you!

For more information about BPB, please visit **www.bpbonline.com**.

Table of Contents

CHAPTER 1

Introduction to Data Visualization

> "Human visual perception is grounded on a single set of biological and psychological principles, regardless of culture. Cultural differences should be taken into account but be aware that there are common foundations for what we do."
>
> *– Alberto Cairo*

Data **Visualization** and data storytelling have taken the world by storm. Visualization skills are one of the hot skills in the market. Like the introduction, the focus of this book is to give an introduction to data visualization using Python as a primary tool of choice. Specifically, coming to the objective of this chapter, the idea is to introduce data visualization and the difference between various aspects of analysis and the importance of data visualization to the world of business analysis, product management, and its correlation. The importance of data visualization is so big that it determines the winners and losers. Some of the leading technology companies are successful due to their ability to derive insights into their customers' data, products, and services. Some of the large companies with a goldmine are data are not as successful as they should be due to the lack of ability to generate actionable insights.

Structure

In this chapter, we will cover the following topics:

- What is data visualization
- Key elements of data visualization
- Importance of data visualization

Objective

This chapter aims at giving a good amount of introduction to what data visualization is about, why data visualization is important, how it evolved over time, and its key elements. This chapter will set the context for approaching data visualization from atechnology solution point of view using Python later in the chapters.

Data visualization is a visual art of storytelling with an intent to share insights with a meaningful purpose. Data visualization leverages graphical elements such as graphs, charts, maps, and other elements to produce a meaningful graphical representation of data and information. It is a powerful way to share insights on trends, patterns, and outliers in a set of data. The users can analyze the patterns and gain an insight into the data shared. It can be said that visualization is an art due to the creative aspects involved. Data visualization is a very powerful concept in today's world and an important skill to imbibe to succeed.

What is data visualization?

Human brains are trained to spot patterns through our experiential learning throughout life. There is a popular adage - *A picture is worth a thousand words*. Our eyes are attracted to patterns and colors. In combination with the brain's cognitive abilities, we are attracted by visuals that make an impact. It could be an image, scenery, or an image in a movie or a TV advertisement.

Visualization is a process that transforms the representation of real data from something into something meaningful in a visual representation. The key is meaningful rendering in a simple visualization, even for complex data. Similar to the quote, *a picture is worth a thousand words*, a good visualization tells a story simply and efficiently, like a good painting. It is visual art that can be used as a powerful storytelling tool.

> **In literature, I can't say that story A is better than poem B; I have to compare stories with stories and poems with poems, despite being all literature. The same applies to data visualization.**
>
> *- Jorge Camões*

Data visualization, in a metaphorical way, is one way to leverage the visual art of storytelling. Visualization is an intent to share insights with a meaningful purpose. Data visualization leverages graphical elements such as graphs, charts, maps, and other elements to produce a meaningful graphical representation of data and information. It is a powerful way to share insights on trends, patterns, and outliers in a set of data. The users can analyze the patterns and gain an insight into the data shared. It can be said that visualization is an art due to the creative aspects involved.

Data visualization is both an art (visuals) and science (the method of rendering the data) combined. Data visualization can be leveraged to display insights of both quantitative and qualitative data under analysis[1].

The scientific part of data visualization is done using software or libraries available for rendering graphical visualization. This book is primarily dedicated to this aspect, focusing on a particular language we've chosen – Python.

The French cave paintings, at Chauvet-Pont-d'Arc Cave in France, albeit an art form, showcase some inspiring elements of visualization. Some of the themes used in data visualization were, in a way, let's say, inspired by some of the visual art forms that followed for years. It progressed further with abbreviations used for tax notifications by governments to simple graphs of a line graph or a bar chart before graduating to mind-boggling real-time interactive visualization.

Brilliant use of data visualization in history

Some of the greatest visualization examples include the following:

1. Visualization of the cholera deaths by John Snow, known as the father of epidemiology, is a study of disease and patterns to identify measures to solve the issues. He visualized the cholera deaths for a London borough. While visualizing the outbreak in the city, he noted that the number of deaths at a particular street (Broad Street) near a water pump was high. This led to an insight that cholera was caused by germ-contaminated water than particles in the air. This changed the course of medicine and treatments for outbreaks.

2. The brilliant use of wonderful data visualization by Florence Nightingale to record the causes of mortality during the Crimean war. Her fact-oriented visualizations proved that more soldiers died due to infections than that of actual fatality in the war. Her visualizations proved the power of inference of data. Data visualizations thrive on the power of insights and inference, and Nightingale's visualization brought the idea of a single picture being more powerful than thousand words to the fore. Florence Nightingale also produced other data visualization charts to prove a point to the government,

---

[1] We shall cover the specifics of different data types a bit later in this book.

healthcare professionals, and the public that sanitation is key for healthy lives. Florence Nightingale, also known as "The Lady with the Lamp," was a pioneering icon in statistics and data visualization.

Data visualization has transformed many organizations to become wildly successful and has helped governments make decisions to improve the lives of the citizens. Some of the data used are sales and profit numbers, market coverage, employee productivity, etc. It could be budget and revenue figures, health indicators for citizens, employment data, and education data to make policy decisions for governments. For humans, one major use case of impactful contribution by data visualization is the efficient usage to expand the average lifespan.

- By helping the healthcare professionals to do the right type of diagnosis and analyzing to understand the patterns and outliers

- By focusing on statistically important aspects to build procedures, discover and develop medicines, and choose treatment

- By giving an insight into the trends, progress, and to make an informed decision for the betterment of business

Data visualization is a powerful way to tell a visual story that can help determine outliers, patterns, trends, and correlations of data available and make meaningful decisions.

Key elements of data visualization

In the 21st century, data visualization has picked a lot of momentum with the advent of increased use of artificial intelligence and data science. The use of data visualization for research and development, education, and commercial usage have expanded exponentially using interactive dashboards, infographics, and other data rendering tools. It is used in every aspect of our daily life. It is a lot easier to generate powerful visual stories, and I see at least 5 to 10 data visualization elements daily.

One of the keys to the success of the popularity is the evolution of data visualization as an art and science discipline. If you take the examples of visualizations by Florence Nightingale and John Snow, both took a considerable amount of manual analysis and attention to details and great application of key data visualization elements to make them ground-breaking. There are many definitions of key elements that vary from designer-to-designer and author-to-author. From a simplicity standpoint, let us see some of the key elements of data visualization.

Elements of data visualization

There are plenty of guides available covering the key elements and themes to be considered for effective data visualization. We shall cover some of the essential elements to focus on and consider while designing data visualization. Let us see the key elements for data visualization in a diagram. We can call this *DUSSSS – Data, User, Strategy, Structure, Style, and Story.*

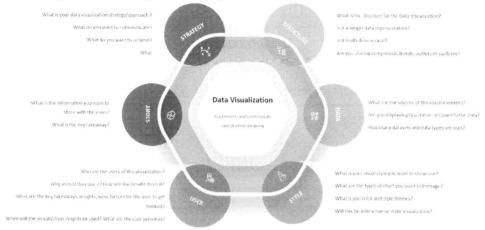

Figure 1.1: *Elements of data visualization*

Figure 1.1 shows the key elements in a simple visualization in the form of a pictorial. We shall cover each of the elements in detail. We shall explore each element in a question-and-answer format. At a high level, the six key elements to focus on are:

- **Strategy**: What is your data visualization strategy?
- **Structure**: How are you planning to structure your story?
- **Data**: What type of data are you planning to use? How many datasets are you planning to use?
- **Style**: A key element on your visualization style, choice of visualization elements such as graphs and charts, choice of colors and other visual elements, use of qualitative and quantitative information to convey a message
- **User**: The key to the success of the data visualization exercise. Who are your users? Why should they be using your product? What is the key takeaway for them?
- **Story**: Most important aspect of the exercise. What are you trying to convey, what would the key insights, messages, actions, inspirations they can take away to implement actions?

Let us delve into a bit more detail on these elements.

Strategy

Having a good strategy for your visualization exercise is very important. This is because the visualization outcome is purely based on the data being used. Like bad content or a theme could derail a movie or an advertisement, bad data can result in poor outcomes in story, elegance, insights, etc. Having a good strategy is important for a visualization exercise. This includes data strategy, design strategy in terms of user persona and visual elements, etc.

- Having good data capturing, data extracting, data cleansing, data integration strategy is very important. This strategy is especially important for planning interactive, real-time, update-oriented dashboards and data visualization. There should be a data strategy for the visualization exercise

- Another element to consider is the user experience and design thinking strategy to address the needs and wants of the users. Using a persona-based design of visual elements can help in designing better visualization elements.

  o As one size fits all does not exist, a designer bias can be avoided by taking the user requirements, and user needs into consideration through the empathy-based user-centric design of elements.

  o Design elements, style elements, visual themes, templates, messaging, colors, form factors, devices, and gesture-based themes and actions can all be thought in advance.

  o Having a clear structure, simplicity, better visibility, and consistency in design could be thought through before the design is done.

Story

Data visualization can be used for two purposes when it comes to stories and messages for the users. The best stories (or visualizations) are not used only to share information or create a user reaction. They can influence and inspire people.

- Some of the advertisements on TV have very strong visuals that tell, inspire, motivate and connect with the viewers at a deep level. Similarly, a good data visualization output should connect with the users. It should cater to the needs of the user. It should address a specific need or wants they have while viewing the data visualization product.

- A simple run-of-the-mill output may not appeal to everyone. This is one reason why the current set of successful data visualization tools gives the end-users many choices to play around with and customize the data visualization outputs to suit their needs.

- We need to be very clear in what we want to communicate and how the users and viewers will interpret it.

- A key takeaway message – be it an executive summary, call-for-action, insights should be included in the story getting told

Style

Style is very important for a data visualization element. This is similar to branding exercises carried out by various firms. This gives a unique association of the product with the style and a very consistent expectation, and a potential wow factor for the users. The use of essential styling themes will help convey the message in a brilliant and highly influential manner to the users / viewers. There are numerous techniques available for styling. Some of the tips are:

- Have an aesthetic element that hooks the users. The style should be impressive and beautiful but simple to connect with the users quickly

- Have a simple, easy to understand and decipher structure rather than a complex one. You can choose to have an intricate style depending on the audience.

- Have a better, simple, effective, and efficient design element that is used in a modular fashion across the board

- Have a style guide for the following:

  o The basic structure of the visualization

  o Text styles – for header, section, axes, messaging, legend, etc.

    ▪ The text used with context will explain the data visualization story in a better manner

  o Colors

    ▪ Background colors and images

    ▪ Colors to be used for data display

    ▪ Colors for special elements such as maps, density, outliers, highlighting patterns and trends

    ▪ It is advisable to minimize the variations in different colors, such as dark and lighter shades

    ▪ It is advisable to use color palettes available in the software or charting libraries

    ▪ It is better to use standard colors (recommended by most tools and libraries) for ease of use and readability

Structure

Data visualization, as mentioned earlier, is an art and a science combined. Every aesthetic art has a structure to it, and so does a scientific experiment, and it's the outcome. Hence having a structure for data visualization is an important aspect in deciding how the data can be presented by determining the structure of data to be used, structure of the data and insights presentation, the structure of data formatting, structure of how data will be presented. The presentation of the final data step of the data storytelling design journey including data collection, curation, format, visualization, and presentation. It would also include the frequency of data collection.

- Having a good data visualization structure also corresponds to keeping the user experience, needs, and wants in mind in delivering a design that matters the most.

- Structuring the content to be displayed in the visualization is important – such as what, when, how the users see.

- Structuring the timing of data collection and visualization, including the update frequency (if it is one-way visualization; and the data refresh in case of an interactive visualization).

- Structuring the approach for data analysis (such as exploratory data analysis used in data science), cleansing, the grouping of data, and most importantly about visualization structure and elements–as per the style and strategy adopted.

- The structure would also entail the amount of data to be rendered and the depth and breadth of analysis (mainly in the case of interactive visualization) to be performed.

A structured approach helps build data visualizations that will be cherished forever, like the examples of John Snow and Florence Nightingale discussed earlier in the chapter.

Data

Most of the successful firms in the world know how to use their data well. For effective data visualization or storytelling with data, you need to have good data, and you need to know how to use them, build a flow, and convey the message. A story can be boring, mediocre, average, exciting, intriguing, inspiring, motivating, depending on how it is told. Similarly, data can also be visualized in the same aspect.

Do you want to tell an exciting story, or do you want to tell a story that no one is interested in? Due to this important aspect, it is advisable to focus more on the data aspects. We have structured data sources such as tables, flat files, etc. We also have unstructured data in the current context. Plans to use them need to be understood and well thought.

It is also important to understand different data types such as:

- Qualitative data (data that cannot be measured quantitatively but is subjective data such as gender, exam results (pass/fail), categories (feedback, happiness, temperature groups, height groups, satisfaction, etc.), color, tastes, preferences, interests, etc.)

- o   Qualitative data can also be called categorical data

- o   Qualitative data are primarily non-numerical and text is used most of the times and can be binary-style (yes/no, pass/fail, male/female, blue/brown/black/green, cold/warm/hot, high/medium/low, highly satisfied/satisfied/neutral/dissatisfied/highly dissatisfied etc.)

- o   Qualitative data can be further categorized as *nominal scale data* or *ordinal scale data*
  - •   Nominal scale data is typically named or labeled data type mentioned above (male/female, hot/cold, and pass/fail, etc.)

- •   Further classifications include:
  - o   Dichotomous – having two possibilities –
    - •   Gender - male/female
    - •   Response - yes/no
    - •   The result - pass/fail
    - •   Temperature - hot/cold
  - o   Nominal with order –
    - •   Coffee temperature - cold/warm/hot
    - •   Probability - high/medium/low
    - •   Customer satisfaction - highly satisfied/satisfied/neutral/dissatisfied/highly dissatisfied
  - o   Nominal without order – such as
    - •   Colour of eye - blue/black/brown/green
    - •   The blood type of a person – O/A/B/AB +ve/-ve
    - •   Political inclination – left/liberal/central/right
    - •   Type of house – apartment, independent house, villa, trailer, homeless
    - •   Gender – male/female/other
  - o   Quantitative data are typically numerical, and they are measured with an accuracy such as height, distance, length, width, speed, profits, salary, duration, etc.
  - o   Quantitative data is ordinal data that can be of two types – namely discrete and continuous numbers.
    - •   Discrete data are typically whole numbers that can't be divided, and they are typically a count of occurrence – This is like many

wins, number of houses, number of computers, etc. You can't have a decimal value in a discrete data

o Continuous data can be further fine-tuned and broken into subunits within a range

- Example – the distance between the office and home – 7.27 KMs, weight – 72.5 kg

o Continuous data can be either interval scales or ratio

- Interval scales are numeric scales where the values between intervals are the same. For example, in some thermometers, the intervals are typically 10 degrees. Similarly, in some types of scale, the intervals are typically in 5 centimeters

- Ratio scales are similar to the interval scale except for the fact that zero does not exist. Examples are age or weight, or a normal room temperature of zero does not exist.

Additionally, it is paramount to use the right data and understand the data to be used. It is also important to decide the number of data sources to use. Deciding qualitative vs. quantitative data for visualization and how to represent the data helps. Better handling of data will result in outstanding data visualization results.

Additionally, it is important to explore the data to pick the right strategy to visualize data. This would include steps such as

- How to build a model for visualization
- Strategy to address the missing data and the exceptions and outliers
- How to plan and choose the right data elements for analysis
- How to run an exploratory data analysis
- How to plan the visualization approach
- How to represent or build a simple data visualization

Let us see the next element from the list to focus on – User.

User

A final key element to focus on is the *user*. When we deal with users, it always starts with the end in mind. We can develop better visualization relevant to the users by:

- Having a connect – by giving user-centric insights
- Giving good insights to the user through the data visualized

- Motivating the user by connecting them with the data

- Giving some actionable insights for the users

Using the elements highlighted above – strategy, story, structure, data, and design, a good programmer doing visualization should understand the audience, have a good framework, use the right tools, and empathize and connect with the user. This will result in the visualization to cater to the audience's needs better. It will help balance the design better and allow for better outcomes that will certainly imbibe a wow factor!

Importance of data visualization

To paraphrase a famous quote – *A picture is worth a thousand words* again, a lot of data and numbers can consume more time from humans than a picture. Data visualization makes humans understand the big picture of big data using a small, impactful visualization.

- Visualization makes it easier for humans to detect trends, patterns, correlations, and outliers in a group of data.

- A simple and powerful data visualization built with credible data with good analytical modelling can help businesses make quick business decisions.

- A good visualization

    o Does the difficult job of communicating a piece of complex information in a simple, clear, and concise manner to top business leaders in an easy to grasp manner

    o Can lead the users to focus on actionable insights that need their attention

    o Provides insights and story to establish a business goal by giving previously unnoticed patterns and correlations

    o Identifies the gaps, errors and helps businesses make corrective actions for better outcomes

    o Can help businesses set business goals to drive growth and address any problem areas easily

    o Helps users identify emerging trends and use them for any actions in the business or personal sphere (such as learning new technology trends, etc.)

    o Helps businesses such as investment banking and stockbroking to make real-time decisions to make a profit or cut losses o   Can help executives run better operations. A good executive dashboard with brilliant data visualizations with actionable insights helps executives make quicker and better decisions

We shall see more details in upcoming chapters, and a lot of importance and focus areas have been covered in the earlier subsections in this chapter.

Conclusion

In this chapter, we covered the introduction to data visualization, its importance, and the key elements to be aware of. We also looked at the key features one needs to be aware of to build data visualization from a storytelling perspective. Good data visualization is like a blockbuster movie or an enthralling ad. It needs a lot of planning, strategy, and messaging skills that will make a huge impact.

We covered the six key elements: strategy, structure, story, data, design, and user. The ability to create a brilliant visualization is a niche skill and helps one propel a career. It is advisable to structure data visualization clearly to get your message across. Adapting the style and content to the occasion and the context relevant to the users is also important. A strategy to the design can be outlined with structured thoughts with end-users in mind before starting the data visualization design. Having a good handle on the data and how to use them is key.

Most importantly, involving the users by highlighting the information that will excite them in the visuals is key. To boost the impact of engagement, it is important to improve the skills to visually convince the audience. It is important to seize the user's attention by removing distractions such as jarring colors, text, and information overload. The user feedback can also be leveraged to strengthen the visualization skills.

Over the next few chapters, we will see how to address the elements discussed in this chapter in a practical manner. The examples provided in this book will be in Python but can be extended to other languages.

Questions

1.   Why is data visualization important?

2.   Why is user experience important while conducting data visualization?

3.   Why are design elements important for good data visualization?

4.   What are the challenges in dealing with data for data visualization?

5.   What are the key benefits of using data visualization?

6. What is the difference between storytelling and data visualization?

7. Why is having a good strategy for data visualization a good thing?

8. What is the need to have a good structure for data visualization?

9. What is minimalism in terms of data visualization? How is it helpful?

10. Why should data visualization have a story element? Why can't we just have a graphic displayed?

11. What is the benefit of giving interactivity to the users? What are the benefits of dynamic data visualization products such as dashboards and applications?

CHAPTER 2

Why Data Visualization?

> "To find signals in data, we must learn to reduce the noise - not just the noise that resides in the data, but also the noise that resides in us. It is nearly impossible for noisy minds to perceive anything but noise in data."
>
> — *Stephen Few*

We covered a high-level introduction to data visualization and key elements to consider and keep in mind while designing data visualization. The objective of this chapter is to showcase some benefits of data visualization and how it leverages the power of storytelling. We shall see some brilliant examples of usage of data visualization that has been very powerful in communication, decision making, and entertaining storytelling, to name a few. This chapter will also give some good resources for further knowledge building.

Structure

In this chapter, we will cover the following topics:

- The power of visual storytelling
- Brilliant examples of data visualization
- Benefits of data visualization
- Recommendations and resources

Objective

This chapter aims at giving an introduction to how powerful visual storytelling is and how good data visualization helps in achieving the same. We will explore some good examples available in the public domain and how benefits were realized. The most important objective of this chapter is to give a list of good resources to explore and leverage and recommendations to read and upgrade knowledge on visual storytelling, data visualization and become an excellent visual communicator by leveraging data power visualization.

The power of visual storytelling

The power to connect - Humans need to connect, interpret, learn, understand to debate and accept, and cognize the facts to connect with data or a visual being presented. Most of us connect better with visuals and stories than numbers and text. Hence, good visual storytelling fulfils a basic human need: the eagerness or a hardwired interest for stories.

The power to derive insights - Good visualization stories help the audience uncover the messages and stories you are keen to share. They may even uncover some untold stories. A powerful message that conveys untold stories makes the visualization vivid and colorful to remember and understand. Finally, it leaves the audience wanting more information and messages.

The power to influence - Good communicators who can tell compelling stories rule the world, and so goes the adage that goes, "Those who tell the stories rule the world." The art of visual storytelling in business is absolutely important as humans get connected at an emotional and psychological level better than at a cognitive level. For example, marketing is no longer a discipline to communicate about the products you sell; but it is about the stories you want to tell and influence.

The power to inform and make quick decisions - Human beings are trained by the brain to handle visuals better, quicker, and impactfully as the cognitive effort is lesser than processing text or voice-based information. Author - Ekaterina Walter, in the book "The Power of Visual Storytelling: How to use visuals, videos, and social media for marketing your brand," says that

> **"Visuals are processed 60,000 times faster than text by the human brain, and 90% of information transmitted to the brain is visual.**
>
> **Humans evolved over millennia to respond to visual information long before they developed the ability to read text. Images act as shortcuts to the brain: we are visual creatures, and we are programmed to react to visuals more than words."**

Taking A picture is worth a thousand words; a visual story is probably worth more than that. This is why visual information in social media is much more powerful than any media in the world currently due to the reach, impact, and power it possesses. The benefit of good design for visual storytelling is summarized as the *design is about solving problems and providing elegant solutions. Information design is about solving information problems* - as per a brilliant quote from McCandless in his wildly popular TED speech.

The "Gapminder" website – **www.gapminder.org,** the brainchild of Hans Rosling, covers some of the brilliant visualizations delivered. One of the key points outlined by Hans Rosling is that our mind filters what is most dramatic and easy to associate with as the key essence. This means that to connect well to get user attention, content with emotional value add is paramount. Visual connect is much more than facts being passed verbally and is a great connect. Some unerasable memories about movies seen decades ago are an example of this.

There are plenty of examples of compressing tons of information into a single, powerful infographic and outline the power of visual storytelling. One brilliant example is available at **https://www.gapminder.org/tools/** that showcases various trends of the progress of nations in terms of animations, maps, trends, ranks using various types of charts and graphs. While we shall be covering most of the technical aspects of these graphs in the rest of the book through program snippets, it is a good idea to check this tool.

Another powerful summary of how data visualization has evolved and helped over the years can be understood from how the financial summary is shown in famous print media powerhouses such as New York Times and The Wall Street Journal. With the introduction of simple graph/visual elements, they've reduced stock-related pages by 7-8 pages with very powerful indicators. One can visualize stock performance with dots showing the range and trend for the highs/lows of the stocks. A good visualization can compress 1000s of pages, inputs, billions of data points into a meaningful insight that helps top leaders make big decisions easily.

Good examples of data visualization

Now let us see some examples of good data visualization. To showcase this, let us revisit the two examples we covered in *Chapter 1* - The Broad Street cholera outbreak and that of Florence Nightingale's chart. Why did they make a huge impact? They were simple and factual – using good data, represented a lot of data in a single picture, and conveyed a very clear, actionable message. Over the last 20 years, the usage of brilliant information design, computing power, availability of tools has helped in the explosion of multiple ways to render brilliant visualizations.

Let us take an example of a KPI or a metrics dashboard. This sample gives some key metrics. However, the data visualization for business needs could have a myriad of metrics across functions and industries. This dashboard gives some operational statistics for ecommerce websites, such as page views, time spent, visitor locations, etc., that can help the team take action.

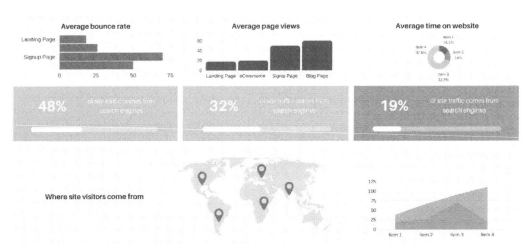

Figure 2.1: *A sample dashboard created using data visualization Tools – ecommerce site statistics dashboard*

What we looked at is a simple usage we may see in a business environment.

Let's take another visualization. This example is explained in detail in Chapter 8 of the book. Is there a possibility of using the words used in a book as a map? We shall check how to do this with the code and explanation later. This code uses Rabindranath Tagore's Gitanjali and a map of India to generate the visualization as in *Figure 2.2*.

Figure 2.2: *A visualization of Tagore's Gitanjali in an India Map using Python*

Finally, another brilliant visualization of all the Oscars awards over the last 90+ years represents a simplified representation graphically. The insights are very simple for what one needs to have in a picture to win the best actor or actress awards. One intriguing story told is that no sportsperson character wins an award unless the role is a boxer. This visualization can be seen at the following URL - **https://iibawards-prod.s3.amazonaws.com/projects/images/000/000/391/page.jpg?1403858126**

The examples given above are just a few of the good examples of brilliant visualization. There are thousands of such brilliant visualizations available. Now let us see some of the benefits of good visualization.

Benefits of visualization

We covered some of the benefits in earlier sections in this book. As mentioned earlier in the chapter, the book The Power of Visual Storytelling: How to use visuals, videos, and social media to market your brand says that the human brain processes visuals faster than text (up to 60000 times) and that our brain transmits more visual information than other forms (more than 90%). From the same source, we also infer that the human brain is capable of processing images in a period of fewer than 13 milliseconds.

Let us see some of the benefits of good data visualization.

- The first benefit is **rapid/quick decision making** - For rapid decision making, we need to compress the data, narrative, and visuals simplistically, which is aided by data visualization. This results in quick actions being made.

- The second benefit is a **better analysis summary** – Good data visualization can share outstanding summary analysis in a very simple manner. It avoids the need to analyze millions of records of data or thousands of pages of text or data. A picture of the data visualization can simplistically tell all the summary.

- The third benefit is **better business insights** – One of the main areas where the visualization is used is for the measurements of key business indicators, operational metrics, etc. This gives a better view of the key business focus areas: sales, marketing, finances, operational metrics, and other key parameters.

- The fourth benefit is **identifying trends, patterns, and gaps** – Another important benefit of visualization is displaying trends, patterns, and gaps in various visualized parameters. This would help identify the reasons and take actions to improve better outcomes – be it business, operations, or any other areas.

- The fifth benefit is **telling a powerful story** – Good data visualization can be leveraged to tell an impactful story in a timeline or based on trends and patterns. This is a very good way to tell stories in a very simple manner.

- The sixth benefit is **building a brand image** – Some businesses have built a reputation for telling very powerful stories through their brilliant visualizations. In a way, telling a good story also helps in building an outstanding brand value. There are some great examples of Coca-Cola being attributed to red and attributed color.

- The seventh and final benefit is the ability to **telling more with less -** A lot of information and messages can be shared with a simple visualization. This may be impossible to achieve in a narrative or using tons of data. A story can be narrated brilliantly with a single visualization.

Recommendations and resources

There are plenty of resources to refer to and benefit from. I am including some of the brilliant resources to read available on the internet.

Let us start with some brilliant data visualization resources

- Information is Beautiful website (**http://informationisbeautiful.com**)

- Data is Beautiful website (**http://dataisbeautiful.com**)

- Data visualization Catalogue (**https://datavizcatalogue.com/index.html**)

- Statista website (**http://www.statista.com/https://www.statista.com/chartoftheday/**)

- Flowing Data (**http://www.flowingdata.com**)

- Storytelling with Data website (**http://StoryTellingWithData.com**)

- Tableau Public Data visualization Gallery and Datasets (**https://public.tableau.com/**)

- QlikView Data visualization Demos - **https://demos.qlik.com/qlikview**

Excellent Trend Analysis

- Google Trends (**https://trends.google.com**)

Excellent Data Sources

- Our World in Data (**https://ourworldindata.org/**)

- Broad Institute's Datasets – (**http://portals.broadinstitute.org/cgi-bin/cancer/datasets.cgi**)

- Amazon Web Services – Datasets – **(https://registry.opendata.aws/)**

- World Health Organization Datasets – **(https://www.who.int/data/gho)**

- Pew Research Centre Datasets – **(https://www.pewresearch.org/internet/?post_type=dataset)**

- Google Public Datasets – **(https://www.google.com/publicdata/directory)**

- US Government's Open Data – **(https://www.data.gov/)**

- Europa Open Data – **(http://open-data.europa.eu/en/data/)**

As we coast along with the book, we shall see more resources for our learning.

Conclusion

In this chapter, we covered a good amount of introduction to data visualization, its importance, and the key elements to be aware of. We also looked at the key features one needs to be aware of to build data visualization from a storytelling perspective. Good data visualization is like a blockbuster movie or an enthralling ad. It needs many skills, excellent planning, strategy, and messaging skills to make a huge impact.

The six key elements we mentioned in *chapter-1* were strategy, structure, story, data, design, and user. The ability to create a brilliant visualization is a niche skill and helps one propel their career. It is advisable to structure the data visualization clearly to get your message across. Adapting the style and content to the occasion and the context relevant to the users is important. A strategy to the design can be outlined with structured thoughts with end-users in mind before starting the data visualization design. Having a good handle on the data and how to use them is key.

Most importantly, involving the users by highlighting the information that will excite them in the visuals is key. To boost engagement, it is important to improve the skills to visually convince the audience. It is important to seize the user's attention by removing distractions such as jarring colors and text and information overload. The user feedback can also be leveraged to strengthen the visualization skills.

Questions

1. Why is data visualization important?

2. What are the important needs while doing data visualization?

3. Why are the design elements critical for good data visualization?

4. What are the challenges in dealing with data for data visualization?

5. What are the key benefits of using data visualization?

CHAPTER 3

Various Data Visualization Elements and Tools

"By visualizing information, we turn it into a landscape that you can explore with your eyes, a sort of information map. And when you're lost in information, an information map is kind of useful"

—*David McCandless*

In the first two chapters, we got introduced to the "what" and "why" aspects of data visualization. In this chapter, we shall broach the topic of how albeit briefly. These topics are covered in detail in the rest of the book. These are the most important aspects and are almost uniform across applications, tools, and libraries to develop data visualization. Understanding the key elements of visualization elements is key to building a successful strategy. A good strategy and approach, and design elements are essential for good storytelling through data visualization, as discussed in the earlier chapters.

Structure

In this chapter, we will cover the following topics:

- Different types of charts and graphs used in data visualization
- When to use charts in data visualization

- Different methods for selection of the right data visualization elements

- Suggested implementation approaches using different software and tools available for data visualization

- Categorization of data visualization tools for various purposes and business needs

Objectives

This chapter aims to give a basic introduction to various data visualization elements such as charts and graphs. We will also touch upon how to choose the right type of element for various needs. We shall complete the chapter to understand the approach through a mind map on approaching the selection of various types of data visualization elements.

Different types of charts and graphs used in data visualization

The graphs, charts, and visualizations have come a long way from very simple beginnings. Ever since *William Playfair* published a simple bar graph in 1786, the usage has increased slowly and steadily. We have hundreds of charts to choose from, and innovations continue, and new styles of data visualization charts get created regularly. In this chapter, we shall cover some of the key charts to know (including the ones we shall visualize using Python in the later chapters).

The first question we need to answer while choosing a chart or any data visualization element is – "what is the purpose of the element/chart?" This will allow us to address further queries such as "what are we trying to address, how would it form a part of the story we want to tell," etc. The purpose plays a key role in determining the type of chart we would like to use. A chart helps in achieving the purpose. It can fully satiate the purpose or part of the solution to satiate the purpose with other elements.

A purpose could be to inform about data in a way that is easy to understand. This could be to show comparisons, or to show changes over time, to show relationships between variables, to show organized data visually, show distributions, show geographic data points, financial parameters, key performance indicators (KPIs), trends, the composition of data, the ranking of data, correlations, spatial data, shows a part of a whole set of data, the flow of data, etc. For simplification, we shall use the following types for this book.

- **Distribution**: This shows the entire distribution of data, or it could be a count of occurrence of data as well (as in histograms)

- **Time-oriented trends**: This shows trends of data movement over time – this could be by second, minutes, hourly, daily, monthly, yearly, etc.

- **Comparison**: This shows the composition of the data element or to compare two or more set of data of the same type
  - o **Spatial data**: This is to showcase maps and location-specific data to be displayed using various charts
  - o **Flow data**: This is to showcase movement or change of data from one point/position to the next to show how a data element flows in a sequence – such as the flow of funds, immigration data, etc.
  - o **Relationship data**: This shows any relationship between two or more sets of data/variables
  - o **Part of a whole data**: This shows the composition of data elements that make up the whole data (100%)
  - o **Deviations**: This shows how the data varies from a fixed point of reference to show the trends
  - o **Other types**: This shows financial data charts, KPI charts, word clouds, etc.

Table 3.1 covers types of charts, their purpose, and where they could be used.

Chart Type	Purpose / Usage / Description
Bar chart/ Graph/ Column chart 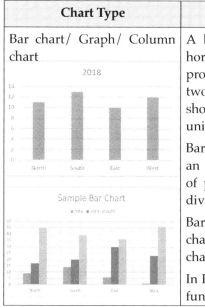	A bar chart is a visual representation of values in horizontal or vertical rectangular bars. The height is proportional to the values being represented. Shown in two axes, one axis shows the element, and the other axis shows the value of the element (could be time, company, unit, nation, etc.). Bar charts can also be combined for multiple values of an element over time to show the relative correlation of performance (such as annual revenues of different divisions within a company/competitor firms over time.) Bar charts rendered vertically are also known as column charts, and horizontal bar charts are referred to as bar charts in some tools such as Microsoft Excel. In Python, we have a bar chart and horizontal bar chart functions. We shall be covering it in future chapters.

Line chart/Graph 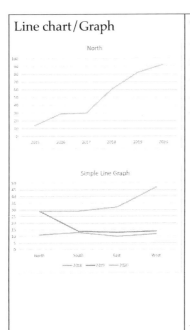 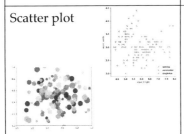	The line chart is a two-dimensional plotting of values connected following the order. Values are displayed (or scattered) in an ordered manner and connected. Line charts show the trend of an element in comparison against time. Line charts can be • A simple line chart (showing value of one element over a reference – such as time) • Multiple line graphs – showing multiple values over a similar reference point – such as stock prices of multiple companies over time (shown in different colors) • Splines – line graph that shows the curved connection of points instead of a straight line • Stepped line graph – where connections between points are shown in a step Line charts are typically used in combination with other types of charts to impact visualization.
Scatter plot	A scatter plot is a two-dimensional chart showing the comparison of two variables scattered across two axes. The scatter plot is also known as the XY chart as two variables are scattered across X and Y axes. A scatter plot can be displayed without connecting lines or being displayed with smooth curved connectors or connecting lines. To distinguish characteristics, a marker can also be used to make it effective.
3D scatter plot	3D scatter plot is an extension of the scatter plot and adds a third variable to show three dimensions by adding additional axes. An additional axis – Z is added to show the value of the third variable against the two variables compared in a standard scatter plot.
Bubble chart 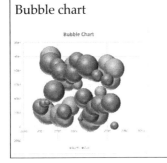	A bubble chart is built on a simple scatter plot, so the first two variables can determine the bubble's position on the Y-axis. A third variable represents each data point in a bubble, the value of which determines the size of that point, and the second by the number of data points in that bubble. The second variable determines each point's height and position and the amount of space between them. A bubble chart can be extended to a 3D bubble chart by adding additional axes as well.

Histogram 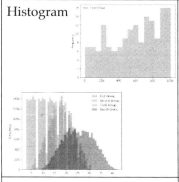	A histogram is a way to represent the distribution of numerical data elements (mainly statistical) in an approximate manner. A histogram uses a "bin" or a "bucket" for a set or range of values to be distributed. A histogram is discrete and need not be a contiguous one. Based on the bins and the values of the data, it can be skewed either to the left or to the right of the visualization. In a traditional statistical representation, as per the central limit theorem, data distribution over a large volume tends to be gaussian.
Pie chart 	A pie chart shows the proportion or percentage of a data element in a circular format. The circular chart is split into various pies based on the value/percentage of the data element to highlight. The pies represent the "part-of-the-whole" data. The overall sum of pies corresponds to the 100% value of the data being visualized. Pie charts are a very effective tool to show the values of one type of data. They can be further expanded into a pie of pie charts if a particular category of a pie can be shown using the subcategories making the pie (as an example – a pie can be the percentage of the population of a nation, and a pie-of-pie can show the population of states/provinces of a nation chosen to highlight)
Doughnut chart	A doughnut (or a donut) chart is an extension of a pie chart. The center part of the doughnut chart is empty to showcase additional data/metrics or expanded compositions of a pie or showcase another data element. A doughnut chart addresses the criticism of pie charts that it is difficult to compare pie charts due to the central area by deemphasizing the central portion. A donut chart is efficient in using space and can easily compare charts using the space effectively. A pie chart is useful for very simple visualization.

Area charts 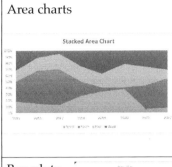	Area charts are used to plot data trends over a while to show how a value is changing. The area charts can be rendered for a data element in a row or a column of a data table such as the Pandas data frame. An area chart can show the part-of-the-whole by stacking the values of various elements making up 100% through a stacked area chart. An area chart can also be shown in a 3D shape. Some good examples can be the GDP summary or population summary of nations and sales by departments over time.
Box plots 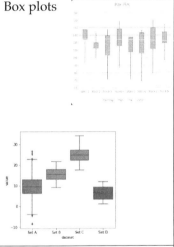	Box plot is a commonly used chart for business, professional aspects and extensively in data science-related visualizations. It is used to show the distribution of two or more data elements in a summarized manner. The key part is a box with a line shown at the median value. The area above the box is the upper quartile, and the area below the box being the lower quartile. The outliers are shown outside the box using an extreme line for both highest and lowest values. The number of values is typically not shown (unlike histogram, where we can define the buckets or bins) Box plots are used typically for two variables, and the wide format of a boxplot is typically used for three or more variables
Violin plot 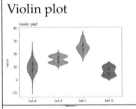	A violin plot is handy when the number of data elements is very high in number and where a box plot, histogram, or scatter plot may not showcase very meaningful insights. Violin plots give a better visualization of the density of the data elements and how closely they are interrelated in a distribution.
Density plot 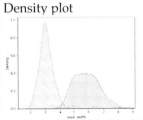	The density plot is closely related to a histogram and takes one set of numerical values as inputs. The output of a density plot is the display of the distribution of data. The distribution can be in the format of an exponential or a bell curve-like format. The chart can be skewed either to the left or right based on the volume of data for a particular data range.

Heat maps 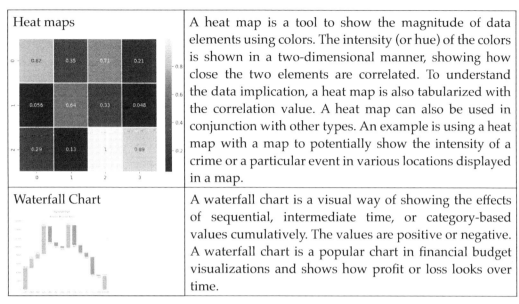	A heat map is a tool to show the magnitude of data elements using colors. The intensity (or hue) of the colors is shown in a two-dimensional manner, showing how close the two elements are correlated. To understand the data implication, a heat map is also tabularized with the correlation value. A heat map can also be used in conjunction with other types. An example is using a heat map with a map to potentially show the intensity of a crime or a particular event in various locations displayed in a map.
Waterfall Chart	A waterfall chart is a visual way of showing the effects of sequential, intermediate time, or category-based values cumulatively. The values are positive or negative. A waterfall chart is a popular chart in financial budget visualizations and shows how profit or loss looks over time.

Table 3.1: *Various types of visualization charts*

Other types of charts and diagrams used for visualization

Let us see some of the other charts and diagrams used (and sometimes referred to by various names) in a tabular format.

Types of Charts and Diagrams used for Visualization		
2D density Plot	Barcode plot	Bee swarm charts
Binary decision diagrams	Box and whisker charts	Bubble map
Bullet chart	Bump chart	Candlestick chart
Cartogram	Chord diagram	Choropleth map
Combo charts	Connect scatter	Connection map
Contour map	Control charts	Correlogram
Dendrograms	Diverging bar chart	Dot density plots
Dot map plots	Dot strip plot	Error bars
Fan charts	Flow charts	Function plots
Funnel chart	Gantt chart	Gauge charts
Graph visualization chart	Grid plot	Grouped bar plots

Grouped symbol chart	Hexbin plot	Hierarchy diagrams
Hyper tree diagram	Icicle diagram	Kagi chart
Kaleidoscope charts	Mandelbrot set chart	Marimekko chart
Mosaic charts	Multi-level pie charts	Network chart
Ohlc chart	Ordered bar chart	Ordered column chart
Ordered proportional symbol	Org chart	Pareto chart
Pert chart	Pictograms	Point and figure chart
Polar area chart	Population pyramid chart	Pyramid chart
Radar chart	Radial bar chart	Radial column/bar chart
Regression fit scatter plot	Sankey diagram	Scatter line combo
Seismogram	Space tree charts	Spaghetti plot
Sparklines chart	Spider charts	Spiral plot
Stacked bar plot	Station map chart	Stem and leaf plot
Stock charts	Streamgraph	Sunburst chart
Surface plot	Tally chart	Timeline chart
Tree chart	Treemaps	Trellis plots
Trellis line charts	Venn diagram	Vertical timeline
Voronoi chart	Word cloud	Word trees

Table 3.2: Types of charts and diagrams used for data visualization

Different methods for selection of the right data visualization elements

As discussed in the previous chapters, the selection of the right visualization element depends on various aspects. One of the major aspects to consider is the purpose and the data type you are using. We can have a logical approach to selecting the right visualization element. The type of chart to visualize may also be dependent on the type of data, the number of variables, and other aspects. Using these important identifiers, we can categorize various charts and diagrams.

A mind map is a graphic diagram that is used to organize information visually. It usually follows a hierarchical approach and shows relationships between various pieces of data as a whole.

We shall leverage a mind map to see how to visualize the charts. The key question we want to address that becomes the central node of the mind-map is the purpose of data visualization. Based on the hierarchical decision tree-like mechanism, we reach the terminal node that gives us an option to visualize the data for a particular purpose.

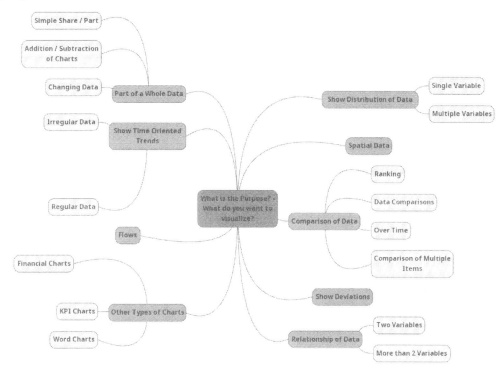

Figure 3.1: A mind-map of data visualization approaches and chart selection

There are numerous ways to group or categorize the charts, and all approaches are equally amenable to a good visual representation. A decision tree style table has been constructed to show how we can decide on the key data visualization elements. Suppose we expand the concept or idea further. In that case, we can build a comprehensive mind-map of or a hierarchical table that we can look for various data visualization purposes like *Table 3.3*.

Data Visualization -> What is the purpose? - What do you want to visualize?				
No	**Purpose**	**Criteria-1**	**Criteria -2**	**Chart**
1	Show distribution of data	Single variable		Bar histograms Line histograms
		Multiple variables		Scatter plots

2	Spatial data			Static maps
				Proportional bubble map Flow maps
				Contour maps
				Dot density maps
				Choropleth maps
				Heat maps
3	Comparison of data	Ranking		Ordered bar charts
				Ordered column charts
				Ordered proportional bubble charts
		Data comparisons		Slope charts
				Lollipop charts
				Bump charts
		Overtime	Cyclical data	Circular area chart
				Line chart
			A cyclical data	Bar chart
				Line chart
		Comparison of multiple items	Many items to compare	The variable width bar chart
				Table with charts
				Trellis charts
				Trellis line charts
4	Show deviations	Single category		Diverging bar chart
				Spline charts
		More than one category		The diverging stacked bar chart
				Surplus/deficit chart

5	Relationship of data	Two variables		Scatter plots
				Data tables
				Connected scatter plots
				Column + line combo charts
		More than two variables		Bubble charts
				Line charts
				Data tables
				Heat maps
6	Part of a whole data	Simple share/part		Pie chart
				Doughnut charts
				Arc diagrams
				Venn diagrams
		Addition/subtraction of charts		Waterfall charts
				Marimekko charts
				Grid plots
				Waffle charts
				Treemaps
				Venn diagrams
		Changing data	Some time-based data points	Bar charts / column charts
				Lollipop charts
				Pictograms
				Waffle charts
			Multiple time-based data points	Line charts
				Paired bar charts
				Proportional bubble charts
				Radar charts
				Spider charts
				Parallel coordinates

7	Show time-oriented trends	Irregular data		Line chart with markers
		Regular data	Single variable	Line charts
				Column charts
				Bar charts
			Multiple variables	Column + line charts
				Slope charts
				Area charts
				Connected scatter plots
				Heat maps
				Circle timeline
				Vertical timelines
				Streamgraph
				Seismogram
8	Flows			Sankey charts
				Chord diagrams
				Waterfall charts
				Network maps
9	Other types of charts	Financial charts		Candlestick charts
				Ohlc charts
				Renko charts
				Heiki Ashi charts
				Point & figure charts
				Sharp charts
				Seasonality charts
				Performance charts
				Market charts
		KPI charts		Thermometer charts
				Dial/dashboard chart
				Numeric chart
				Meter chart
				Big numeric chart
		Word charts		Text summary
				Word cloud
				Word trees

Table 3.3: A hierarchical decision-making tree table for data visualization chart selection

Let us see the different types of data visualization tools available.

Grouping and categorization of data visualization tools

About two decades ago, only a few standard data visualization software tools were popular. One of the most popular tools is Microsoft Excel. Statisticians used packages such as SAS and programmed using R. With the growth of the Internet and computing power; many new avenues opened up. Due to increased popularity and the need for data visualization, there are plenty of choices available. There are applications, libraries, APIs, and language-specific options available for visualization.

Some visualization libraries are specific for a particular purpose, such as statistics, machine learning, and financial reporting. Most of the popular libraries have common visualization options and elements for usage. For Python, we have a good number of libraries available. We shall be covering some of the popular tools (Matplotlib, Pandas, Seaborn, and Plotly) in detail and cover the basics of some of the emerging tools. We shall be leveraging some of the charting libraries implicitly in some of the programs we shall discuss.

The following diagram will be very handy to refer to summarize the tools available for data visualization. We will group them into commercial software, visualization applications (with commercial and free options), and visualization libraries. The mind map below covers them in detail:

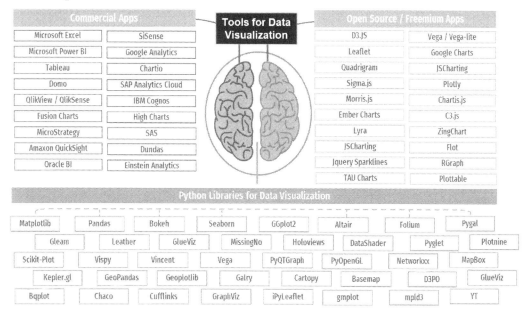

Figure 3.2: *A representation of the grouping of data visualization tools*

Let us see some of the details of these key visualization tools for consideration. For this book, the scope is primarily on Python as a choice for visualization language. Hence, a separate category on the use of Python-specific libraries is included. We can see the details in the next section.

Software tools and libraries available for data visualization

Let us see some additional details about the tools we covered in the data visualization tool mind-map above. This can be very handy if you would like to explore learning and programming, in addition to the libraries we cover in this book through examples and exercises. The following table covers some of the most popular data visualization tools and corresponding references:

Product / Library Name	Link
Altair	https://altair-viz.github.io/
Bokeh	http://bokeh.pydata.org/en/latest/
Cartopy	http://scitools.org.uk/cartopy/
D3 JS	https://d3js.org
Datashader	https://github.com/bokeh/datashader
Folium	https://github.com/Python-visualization/folium
GeoPandas	https://geopandas.org/
Geoplotlib	https://pypi.Python.org/pypi/geoplotlib_
ggplot2	https://pypi.org/project/ggplot/
Graphviz	http://www.graphviz.org
Holoviews	http://holoviews.org
Leather	https://pypi.Python.org/pypi/leather
Matplotlib	http://matplotlib.org
Missing No	https://pypi.Python.org/pypi/missingno/
Networkx	https://networkx.github.io
Pandas	http://pandas.pydata.org/index.html
Plotly	https://plot.ly
Pygal	http://pygal.org/en/stable/
Seaborn	https://seaborn.pydata.org/
Vega	https://vega.github.io/vega/
Vega-Lite	https://vega.github.io/vega-lite/

Vincent	https://github.com/wrobstory/vincent

Table 3.4: A table of popular Python centric data visualization tools

Some of the libraries were created due to Python's open-source nature and flexibility to be extended, and some features were non-existent in existing libraries. Once mastered the language and libraries, you can write your extensions and features that can be leveraged globally.

Product / Library Name	Link
D3.js	https://d3js.org/
Google Charts	https://developers.google.com/chart/
Excel	https://office.live.com/start/Excel.aspx
FusionCharts	http://www,fusioncharts.com
Google Sheets	http://www.google.com/sheets/
Illustrator	http://www.adobe.com/products/illustrator.html
Tableau	https://public.tableau.com/s/

Table 3.5: A table of popular data visualization tools that are not Python-based

We shall cover the purpose of the top libraries we shall be covering in this book, such as Matplotlib, Bokeh, Plotly, Pandas, and Folium, and other key libraries we shall be using in the respective chapters planned in the book. If you are keen to leverage some of the tools highlighted for learning and example coding, please refer to the links provided above.

Conclusion

In this chapter, we covered a good amount of introduction to data visualization elements and got introduced to the key elements of a data visualization – charts and graphs. We also delved into choosing the charts and graphs to support the six key elements we covered in the preceding chapter: strategy, structure, story, data, design, and user. We built a mind map and a decision tree for visualization purposes. The decision tree can be used to decide what we want to use for our visualization needs. We also covered various tools available for data visualization and focused primarily on the tools available for Python.

Over the next few chapters, we shall see how to use the libraries and tools mentioned in a hands-on and practical manner. The examples will be in Python, but if you want to extend your skills in other languages, there are plenty of choices that are covered with relevant information. The sheer volume of the ever-expansive tool list highlights the importance and popularity of data visualization.

Questions

1. Why is choosing the right visualization element important?

2. What are some of the benefits of pie charts?

3. What will happen if there are too many variables to display? What will be your approach to visualization?

4. How will you decide what type of chart to use for time-centric data?

5. What are the top commercial tools for data visualization?

6. What are some top applications for data visualization?

7. What are some of the top Python-based Visualization libraries?

8. What would be your choice for map-based visualization in Python?

9. What would be your choice to handle missing data for data visualization in Python?

10. What is the benefit of having a dynamic dashboard as a data visualization?

CHAPTER 4

Using Matplotlib with Python

> **"Most of us need to listen to the music to understand how beautiful it is. But often that's how we present statistics: we just show the notes, we don't play the music."**
>
> *- Hans Rosling*

So far, we've covered aspects of data visualization in a theoretical manner. In this chapter, we shall have some real practical examples of how to build them. We shall take one of the most widely used libraries to do data visualization - Matplotlib. We shall be covering the key features of Matplotlib and cover some of its core functions and features for using it with Python. As Matplotlib has a good number of features that can run into a voluminous book, we shall cover the key essentials to understand how to use Matplotlib for data visualization using Python.

Structure

In this chapter, we will cover the following topics:

- Introduction to Matplotlib
- Definition of figure, plots, subplots, axes, ticks, and legends
- Matplotlib plotting functions

- Matplotlib modules

- Matplotlib toolkits

- Examples of various types of charts

- Exercises and Matplotlib resources

Objective

This chapter aims to give a basic introduction to Matplotlib for experimenting with various data visualization elements such as charts and graphs. We will also touch upon details of how to use Matplotlib elements for effective visualization. We shall start with simple examples of Matplotlib and explore the libraries and toolkits available before trying out some of the important charts and graphs covered in earlier chapters. We shall conclude the chapter with some examples to try out and resources to consume.

Introduction to Matplotlib

Figure 4.1: *The Matplotlib logo*

Matplotlib is the most widely used Python library for various visualizations - static, dynamic, or animated. It is one of the most comprehensive libraries that exist in the Python tool landscape. A good number of libraries have extended Matplotlib for advanced features. These include BaseMap, Cartopy, Mplot3d, and Seaborn, to name a few. Visualization programs using Matplotlib can be done using Python scripts using an IDE, Python Shells, Python Notebooks (such as Jupyter), Web Application servers, and GUI tools.

John D. Hunter originally developed Matplotlib as an experiment to visualize some of the medical images of epilepsy patients. Matplotlib, along with the power of NumPy, SciPy, and iPython, became very popular over the last decade to become the most widely plotted library. The influence of MATLAB is very highly visible in the name of the library and how the interfaces are developed and named. MATLAB heavily influences Matplotlib's interface.

> **Note:** Before we try the examples, there is an assumption that the readers have basic knowledge of the following areas in Python
>
> - Python syntax
> - Variable types

- Basic operators
- Loops (while, for, nested loops, etc.)
- Conditional statements (if, if-else, etc.)
- Python data types - numbers, strings, lists, tuples, dictionary
- File I/O
- Exception handling
- Python functions (defining a function, calling a function, etc.)
  - o Arguments handling (required arguments, keyword arguments, default arguments, variable length arguments, etc.)
- Python classes and objects
- Ability to set up Python environments

  Additionally, it is assumed that the reader has a basic knowledge of using some of the key libraries such as:

  - o NumPy – Array handling functions
  - o Pandas – Data handling functions

  It is also expected that the reader has knowhow of

- Setting up a Jupyter Notebook environment for execution of the exercise

  or

- Setting up an integrated desktop environment (IDE) such as Visual Code, PyCharm, Spyder, Atom, or any popular IDE of choice by the reader to set up Python for running the exercises

To install matplotlib and the dependencies (libraries it refers to), we can use the following command in the command prompt or a shell. We need to make sure Python or pip utility is in the environment variable or the path.

Note: Let us see how to install* matplotlib using Python installer in various operating systems:

In Windows:

```
python -m pip install -U pip
python -m pip install -U matplotlib
```

Or simply

```
pip install -U matplotlib
```

In Ubuntu Linux:

sudo apt-get install python3-matplotlib

In macOS:

sudo pip3 install matplotlib

(*** There is a difference in the installer names of Python installer across operating systems. Suggest you refer to the right version. Ensure the dependent packages are installed before or during the installation of MatPlotlib.**)

The *matplotlib* depends on the following packages to function well. The above commands can ensure dependent packages (*Python, FreeType, libpng, NumPy, setuptools, cycler, dateutil, kiwisolver, and pyparsing*) are downloaded and installed.

Once the installation is completed, we are ready to do programming in Python with *matplotlib*.

> **Note:** One of the key requirements for visualization plotting and programming is data. For the examples used throughout the book, we shall be using the following types of data.
>
> - Random data generated using random functions in Python (primarily for numeric data)
>
> - Sample hard-coded data (for simplicity)
>
> - Open datasets available in the public domain (such as IRIS dataset, titanic passenger data)
>
> - Realtime datasets available (such as data from stock markets)
>
> For each chapter, we shall introduce the type of data we use for the examples in the chapter.

Let us start with a simple example. In this example, we will create simple **Sine()** and **Cosine()** waves.

```
1. import numpy as np
2. import matplotlib.pyplot as plt
3. plt.style.use('default')
4.
5. x = np.arange(0, 10.5, 0.2)
6. y = np.sin(x)
7. z = np.cos(x)
8. plt.plot(x, y)
9. plt.plot(x, z)
10. plt.show()
```

This program produces the following output:

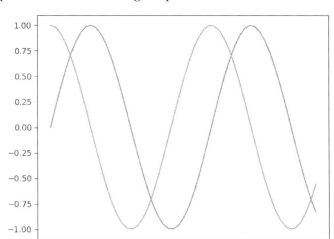

Figure 4.2: *A Python code output for displaying simple Sine and Cosine waves*

As you can see, it is very easy to build a visualization with very few lines of code in *Python*. We shall see the details about various functions used and parameters as we progress along in this chapter. At a very simple level, it uses the *pyplot* library from *matplotlib* to build a simple mathematical line chart based on trigonometric values for *sine* and *cosine* waves.

We import the libraries, set the data configuration, define the parameters, initiate the plot/graph, call the functions for various settings, and draw the plot. This is a simple structure of a *pyplot* visualization.

The next section shows how we can define the figure, plots, subplots, axes, and other parameters needed to define a matplotlib plot.

The definition of figure, plots, subplots, axes, ticks, and legends

Let us take the previous example of how the plot is built. This is done systematically, and every visualization element follows a process for the generation of the plot. This includes the figure, axes, the plotting type, title for the figure, x and y-axis label, ticks, and further segregations of the axis elements at a very high level. There are legends and other aspects to consider that we shall cover in the upcoming sections.

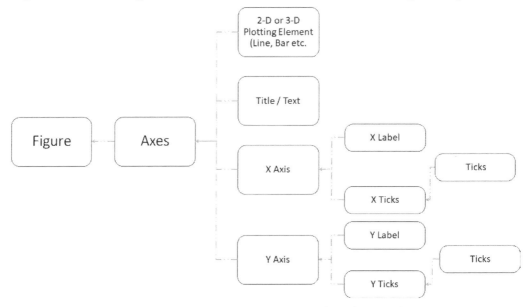

Figure 4.3: Matplotlib Plot – Architectural representation of a Python visualization interaction

In this diagram, the **Figure** is an element containing one or more than one axes or plots for visualization. An **Axes** can contain mostly one or more axes for rendering the plots. In some cases, it can have more than two axes to plot 3D elements and objects. Typically, each **Axes** has a combination of X-axis and Y-axis with a title, **ticks,** and label. Each axis handles the graph/plot limits that are rendered. Each axis has ticks to define the axes parameters. Finally, each plot is rendered through **Artists** tied to axes and render any text or visual objects rendered in a plot. **Artist,** like the name says, renders visual elements to a canvas. It takes care of the representation of figures, texts, axes, and lines on the canvas.

Let us take the anatomy of a plot in *pyplot* in *matplotlib.* To do this, let us get all the commands that exist in matplotlib. We can do this using the following line of code. We need to understand these key parameters as they form most of the visualizations we will be doing over the next few chapters. Even the extensions of matplotlib refer to some of these core functions implicitly. If we execute **plt.get_plot_commands()** in the python console, we get all the commands used for various plotting aspects of the matplotlib library in the console.

Out: ['acorr', 'angle_spectrum', 'annotate', 'arrow', 'autoscale', 'axes', 'axhline', 'axhspan', 'axis', 'axline', 'axvline', 'axvspan', 'bar', 'barbs', 'barh', 'box', 'boxplot', 'broken_barh', 'cla', 'clabel', 'clf', 'clim', 'close', 'cohere', 'colorbar', 'contour', 'contourf', 'csd', 'delaxes', 'draw', 'errorbar', 'eventplot', 'figimage', 'figlegend', 'fignum_exists', 'figtext', 'figure', 'fill', 'fill_between', 'fill_betweenx', 'findobj', 'gca', 'gcf', 'gci', 'get', 'get_figlabels', 'get_fignums', 'getp', 'grid', 'hexbin', 'hist', 'hist2d', 'hlines', 'imread', 'imsave', 'imshow', 'install_repl_displayhook', 'ioff', 'ion', 'isinteractive', 'legend', 'locator_params', 'loglog', 'magnitude_spectrum', 'margins', 'matshow', 'minorticks_off', 'minorticks_on', 'new_figure_manager', 'pause', 'pcolor', 'pcolormesh', 'phase_spectrum', 'pie', 'plot', 'plot_date', 'polar', 'psd', 'quiver', 'quiverkey', 'rc', 'rc_context', 'rcdefaults', 'rgrids', 'savefig', 'sca', 'scatter', 'sci', 'semilogx', 'semilogy', 'set_cmap', 'setp', 'show', 'specgram', 'spy', 'stackplot', 'stem', 'step', 'streamplot', 'subplot', 'subplot2grid', 'subplot_mosaic', 'subplot_tool', 'subplots', 'subplots_adjust', 'suptitle', 'switch_backend', 'table', 'text', '+', 'tick_params', 'ticklabel_format', 'tight_layout', 'title', 'tricontour', 'tricontourf', 'tripcolor', 'triplot', 'twinx', 'twiny', 'uninstall_repl_displayhook', 'violinplot', 'vlines', 'xcorr', 'xkcd', 'xlabel', 'xlim', 'xscale', 'xticks', 'ylabel', 'ylim', 'yscale', 'yticks']

Figure 4.4: Matplotlib plotting functions displayed through the get_plot_commands() command

Let us see various aspects of these libraries in a tabularized fashion.

Matplotlib plotting functions

Let us see all plotting functions available in *Matplotlib*.

Note: The commands are like a library reference. Only some of the plots and functions are used in the examples showcased in this book. The number of functions is too many to cover. Readers are requested to glance through or use the section as a reference.

Plotting functions

We shall cover them in various categories serving distinct purposes such as plotting, sub plotting, axes, legends, and general features. The majority of the types of charts were introduced at a high level in *Chapter 3*.

- **Plot - plot(*args[, scalex, scaley, data])**
    - Creates a general plot of y values versus x as lines. Additionally, parameters can be passed for line markers.
- Bar charts
    - **bar - bar(x, height[, width, bottom, align, data])**

- Used for a bar chart plotting. Additional parameters specify the height and other parameters.
  - `barh` - `barh(y, width[, height, left, align])`
    - Used for a horizontal bar chart plotting. Additional parameters specify the width and other parameters.
- Pie charts
  - `pie` - `pie(x[, explode, labels, colors, autopct, ...])`
- Other key charts/plots
- `boxplot` ⇒ Used for box plots
- `hexbin` ⇒ Used for hex bin plots
- `loglog` ⇒ Used for logarithmic charts
- `polar` ⇒ Used for polar charts
- `step` ⇒ Used for a step plot - A variant of line plot where two connecting points are shown in a step
- `violinplot` ⇒ Used for a violin plot to show data density
- `hist` ⇒ Used for a histogram chart
- `hist2d` ⇒ Used for a 2D histogram
- `matshow` ⇒ Used for an array of matrix display in a chart
- `specgram` ⇒ Used for a spectrogram chart
- `scatter` ⇒ Used for a scatter chart
- `quiver` ⇒ Used for a quiver chart
- `contour` ⇒ Used for a contour chart
- `stackplot` ⇒ Used for a stack plot - for plotting a stacked area chart
- `stem` ⇒ Used for a stem and leaf plot representation
- `streamplot` ⇒ Used for drawing a streamplot
- `imshow` ⇒ Used to show data as an image

Subplot functions

Subplots are used extensively in Matplotlib, and the two key functions to be aware of are as follows.

- `subplot(*args, **kwargs)`

  o Adds a subplot to the current figure in the display

- `subplots([nrows, ncols, sharex, sharey, ...])`

  o Create a figure with the specified number of subplots specified as per rows and columns

Coloring functions

The following are some of the coloring functions to use for **Matplotlib**:

- `set_cmap(cmap)` ⇒ Sets a colormap style

  o We can set various colormaps using the available functions -> `autumn()`, `bone()`, `cool()`, `copper()`, `flag()`, `gray()`, `hot()`, `hsv()`, `inferno()`, `jet()`, `magma()`, `nipy_spectral()`, `pink()`, `plasma()`, `prism()`, `spring()`, `summer()`, `viridis()`, `winter()`

- `colorbar` ⇒ Adds a colorbar to the image

Config functions

matplotlibrc is a configuration file used to set properties by **matplotlib.rc settings** and **rc parameters** are used to set default values of a figure size and DPI (dots per inch), line width, color, and style, axes, axis and grid properties, text, and font matplotlib. This is a useful feature to leverage, and the following functions are key for this purpose. The configurations for plotting are set using

- `rc` ⇒ Set current RC parameters

- `rc_context` ⇒ get context for changing current RC parameter

- `rcdefaults` ⇒ restore rcparams to matplotlib defaults

Understanding the core functions of *matplotlib* is important as it would form the basis for all our exercises in this book. Like mentioned earlier, even the advanced libraries build on these foundations. Now that we have seen all the functions comprehensively let us pick some practical examples of using matplotlib to draw some visualizations.

Matplotlib modules

There are other extensions available in the form of modules for Matplotlib that can be leveraged for various features that are not a part of the core *matplotlib* library. Some of the major modules and their features are as follows:

Function	Purpose
matplotlib.artist	Abstract base class for all the objects that are rendered in matplotlib through in a FigureCanvas. Every visible element is a subclass of this.
matplotlib.axes	The Axes contain most of the figure elements rendered, such as Axis, Tick, Line2D, and Text. It is used to coordinate system management in matplotlib.
matplotlib.axis	This contains the class to set X and Y-axis ticks.
matplotlib.cm	Color Maps and Color Map Utilities.
matplotlib.colorbar	Has functions to map scalar values into colors for visualization.
matplotlib.colors	Has classes and functions to set various color-related elements and themes in Matplotlib.
matplotlib.contour	Functions to support contour plots.
matplotlib.figure	Implements the top-level Artist Class that manages all the plotting elements in Matplotlib.
matplotlib.gridspec	To build a grid-like figure using multiple axes to plot a complex visualization.
matplotlib.image	Supports basic image operations.
matplotlib.legend	Useful for the creation of legends for the plots.
matplotlib.markers	A function to define and use various marker types.
matplotlib.patches	Contains utility functions such as different polygons etc.
matplotlib.pyplot	The core library is used extensively for plotting in Matplotlib.
matplotlib.quiver	Used for plotting quiver plots.
matplotlib.rcsetup	Has features to customize the default rc settings of Matplotlib.
matplotlib.style	Used for setting various styling themes for the plots.
matplotlib.text	Functions for text usage in a plot or figure.
matplotlib.ticker	Used for ticks formatting and locating.
matplotlib.tight_layout	Used for layout formatting and beautifying the subplots in a figure.
matplotlib.widgets	To build and use GUI neutral widgets.

Table 4.1: Matplotlib key modules

Matplotlib toolkits

There are other toolkits available in Matplotlib that can be leveraged for 3D plotting and similar features. They are application-specific extensions that include a collection of functions for plotting. One of the top toolkits available is *mplot3d*. The extension *mplot3d* toolkit is used for leveraging the 3D plotting to extend matplotlib capabilities. This is done by adding an axes object to create a 2D perspective of a 3D perspective using the functions.

Examples of various types of charts

Line plot

Let us see a simple example (Exercise 4-2 below) of plotting a line plot by generating random numbers using the *NumPy* random function. We assign the random numbers generated using the **randn()** function to a 1-dimensional array using the **cumsum()** function in *Numpy*. The **cumsum()** function is used to compute the cumulative sum of array elements over an axis. This is shown as the line.

This example code has two parts. The first part of the code produces a default line chart displayed based on a 1-dimensional array of random values. We generate 15 random numbers using the *NumPy* function and assign them to a 1-dimensional array. The second part covers some of the plot features such as marker type, markersize, markerfacecolor, linewidth, linestyle, and label, along with the color of the lines.

```
1.  # import the libraries
2.  import matplotlib.pyplot as plt
3.  import numpy as np
4.  # create data - 1 dimensional array of 15 elements using Random Numbers
5.  # Use Numpy cumsum() function for  array and random.randn() for randomization
6.  oneDimArrayValues=np.cumsum(np.random.randn(15,1))
7.  # basic plot function
8.  # Following line gives simple chart
9.  plt.plot(oneDimArrayValues)
10. plt.title('Simple Linechart')
11. # Matplotlib Plot - Exercise 4-2 Output-1
12. plt.show()
```

```
13.
14. #Following gives a bit more detailed features
15. plt.plot(oneDimArrayValues,          marker='*',          markerfacecol-
    or='red',markersize=10,
16.              color='green', linewidth=3, linestyle='dashdot', la-
    bel="Simple Line Chart")
17. plt.title('Simple Linechart with Markers')
18. #Matplotlib Plot - Exercise 4-2 Output-2
19. plt.show()
```

The code produces the following output shown below in *Figure 4.5 and Figure 4.6*. The first one is a simple chart, and the second one is a line chart with markers.

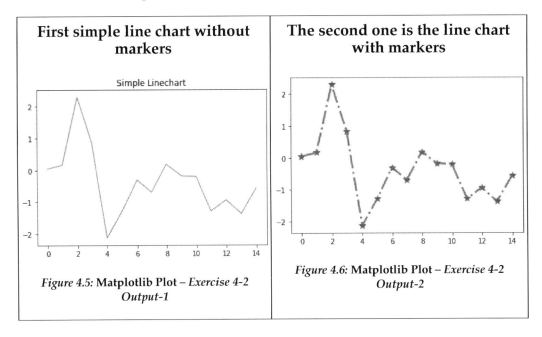

Figure 4.5: Matplotlib Plot – Exercise 4-2 Output-1

Figure 4.6: Matplotlib Plot – Exercise 4-2 Output-2

Exercise 4-3

How do we add multiple lines in the same chart? Let us take it a bit further to plot multiple lines in the same chart:

```
1. # Import the libraries PyPlot, numpy for random numbers, pan-
   das for dataframe
2. import matplotlib.pyplot as plt
3. import numpy as np
4. import pandas as pd
```

```
5.  # Define the Data using a Pandas Dataframe using NumPy random num-
    bers
6.  df=pd.DataFrame({'x': range(1,21),
7.                   'yy': np.random.randn(20),
8.                   'zz': 2 * np.random.randn(20) + range(1,21),
9.                   'ww': 4 * np.random.randn(20) + range(1,21),
10.                  'aa': 8 * np.random.randn(20) + range(1,21),
11.                  })
12. # Create a multiple line plot by calling 3 plot func-
    tions with various markrs
13. plt.plot( 'x', 'yy', data=df, marker='p', markerfacecol-
    or='blue', markersize=8,
14.          label="Pentagon", color='skyblue', linewidth=4)
15. plt.plot( 'x', 'zz', data=df, marker='h', color='green',
16.          linewidth=2, label="Hexagon")
17. plt.plot( 'x', 'ww', data=df, marker='8', color='red',
18.          linewidth=2, linestyle='dashdot', label="Octagon")
19. plt.plot( 'x', 'aa', data=df, marker='d', color='violet',
20.          linewidth=2, linestyle='dotted', label="Diamond")
21. plt.title('Linechart with Multiple Line Charts')
22. #Show the legend that displays colors and markers
23. plt.legend()
24. plt.show()
```

This produces the following output. This program takes the previous example by adding multiple elements of comparing the x-axis against various values for four different data arrays to compare with. This chart has a clear title definition and a legend for various lines used in the chart.

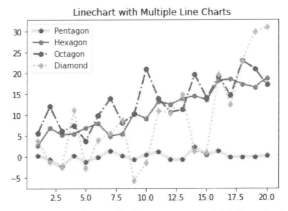

Figure 4.7: *Exercise 4-3 Python output – multiple line charts*

In the notebook covering examples and exercises for *Chapter 4*, we have included another code snippet (Exercise 4-4). This code showcases various style types. Let us see some examples using the Bar Chart.

Bar plots

Bar plots are one of the most popular charts used in any type of visualization as it shows the relative data points in an emphasized manner like a line chart. As explained in *Chapter 3*, a bar chart can be used to compare the progress of a particular element within an entity or across a set of entities to showcase a relative comparison of values.

Let us take a simple bar plot that displays the yearly revenues of a technology firm from 2008 onwards. We have used a simple parameter **color** to color the bar purple.

```
1.  #import the libraries
2.  import matplotlib.pyplot as plt
3.  #set style = default
4.  plt.style.use('default')
5.  #Let's put the years in an array for y axis
6.  year = [2008,2009,2010,2011,2012,2013,2014,2015,2016,2017,2018,20
    19,2020]
7.  #Let's define the revenue in an array for x axis
8.  #revenus of Technology firm in Billions - available in pub-
    lic sites
9.  revenue = [37.5,42.9,65.2,108.2,156.5,170.9,182.8,
```

```
      233.7,215.6,229.2,265.6,260.2,274.5]
10. #Let's build a bar chart with a purple color filling
11. plt.bar(year, revenue, color='purple')
12. #set title
13. plt.title('Technology revenues in billions of US $ dollar')
14. #set x and y axis labels
15. plt.xlabel('Year')
16. plt.ylabel('Revenue')
17. #show the plot
18. plt.show()
```

The output of the program will be as follows:

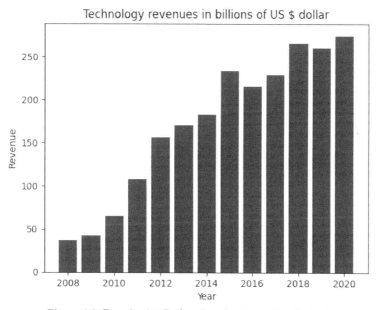

Figure 4.8: *Exercise 4-5 Python Bar chart example - Output*

Let us explore how to take the available features further with a bit more advanced features in a bar chart. This program covers subplots, setting figure size, xticks, xlabel/ylabel, title, and legend we used. It also uses various parameters of the bar function available in Matplotlib.

```
1.  import matplotlib.pyplot as plt
2.  import numpy as np
3.
4.  #Let's put the years in an array for y axis
```

```
5.  year = [2008,2009,2010,2011,2012,2013,2014,2015,2016,2017,2018,20
    19]
6.  #Let's define the revenue in an array for x axis
7.  #These are public data for big tech giants (anonymized)
8.  co1 = [37.5,42.9,65.2,108.2,156.5,170.9,182.8,233.7,215.6,229.2,2
    65.6,260.2]
9.  co2 = [60.42,58.44,62.48,69.94,73.72,77.85,86.83,93.58,85.32,89.9
    5,110.36,125.84]
10. co3 = [21.8,23.7,29.3,37.9,50.18,55.51,65.67,74.54,89.98,110.55,1
    36.36,160.74]
11. co4 = [19.17,24.51,34.2,48.08,61.09,74.45,88.99,107.01,135.99,177
    .87,232.89,280.52]
12. #Let's build a bar chart with a purple color filling
13. barWid = 0.18
14. #Define a subplot
15. fig = plt.subplots(figsize =(12, 10))
16. # Set position of bar on X axis for various bars
17. co1bar = np.arange(len(year))
18. co2bar = [x - barWid for x in co1bar]
19. co3bar = [x - 2* barWid for x in co2bar]
20. co4bar = [x + barWid for x in co3bar]
21.
22. # Make the plot
23. # Use different edge colors and bar colors
24. plt.bar(co1bar, co1, color ='purple', width = barWid,
25.         edgecolor ='skyblue', label ='Tech company-1')
26. plt.bar(co2bar, co2, color ='yellow', width = barWid,
27.         edgecolor ='green', label ='Tech company-2')
28. plt.bar(co3bar, co3, color ='violet', width = barWid,
29.         edgecolor ='black', label ='Tech company-3')
30. plt.bar(co4bar, co4, color ='blue', width = barWid,
31.         edgecolor ='yellow', label ='Tech company-4')
32.
33. # Add meaningful X and Y Labels and Ticks
34. plt.xlabel('Year of Reporting', fontweight ='bold')
```

35. ```
plt.ylabel('Annual Revenue (In Billions of US $)', font-
    weight ='bold')
```

36. ```
plt.xticks([r - barWid for r in range(len(year))],
```

37. ```
            year)
```

38. ```
#Add title
```

39. ```
plt.title('Revenues in Billions of US $Dollar')
```

40. ```
plt.legend()
```

41. ```
#Show Plot
```

42. ```
plt.show()
```

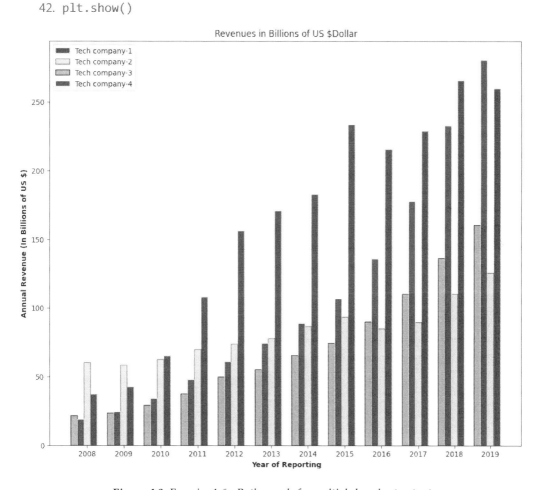

Figure 4.9: *Exercise 4-6 - Python code for multiple bar chart output*

If you want to create a bar chart horizontally, all you need to do is use **barh** instead of a **bar.** We shall be using patterns and the **edgecolor** parameters available in the library to dynamically generate the visualization.

```
1.  # Libraries
2.  import numpy as np
3.  import matplotlib.pyplot as plt
4.  import random
5.  # Make a dummy  dataset - Use Random number to create 4 heights
6.  height = np.random.randint(100, size=4)
7.  #define the names of the bars
8.  bars = ('One', 'Two', 'Three', 'Four')
9.  #Define the position in y-axis
10. pos = np.arange(len(bars))
11. #Let's define some patterns to fill the bar and col-
    ors to choose from
12. patterns = ('-', '+', 'x', '\\', '*', 'o', 'O', '.')
13. colorlist =('violet','indigo','blue','yellow','or-
    ange','red','green','purple','skyblue')
14. # Create horizontal bars
15. plt.barh(pos, height, hatch=random.choice(patterns),
16.          color=random.choice(colorlist),edgecolor=random.
    choice(colorlist))
17. # Create names on the y-axis
18. plt.yticks(pos, bars)
19. # Show graphic
20. plt.show()
```

This code produces the following output:

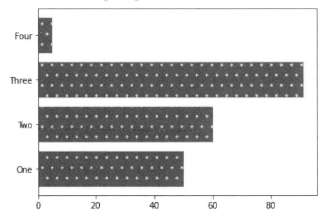

Figure 4.10: *Exercise 4-7 Python Code for horizontal bar chart- Output*

Scatter plots

Scatter plots are very widely used in some of the statistical and data science-oriented analyses and visualizations. In many cases, scatter plots are used in combination with other plots to show a visualization element in a very convincing manner.

The syntax of a Matplotlib scatter plot is as follows:

```
matplotlib.pyplot.scatter(x_axis_data, y_axis_data, s=None, c=None,
marker=None, cmap=None, vmin=None, vmax=None, alpha=None, linewidths=None,
edgecolors=None)
```

- **x_axis_data** ⇒ X-axis data in an array

- **y_axis_data** ⇒ Y-axis data in an array

- **s** - Marker size in a scalar value

- **c** - For color or sequence of colors for markers

- **marker** - Marker style to be used

- **cmap**- Colormap name

- **linewidths** - Marker's border width

- **edgecolor** - Border color of the marker

- **alpha** - Used for transparency of the scatter - 1 will be very opaque, and 0 will be transparent

Let us start with a simple example:

```
1.  import numpy as np
2.  import matplotlib.pyplot as plt
3.  #Set a Seed
4.  np.random.seed(1968)
5.  #Define Number of points
6.  number = 20
7.  #Assign the values to X & Y axis
8.  x = np.random.rand(number)
9.  y = np.random.rand(number)
10. #Choose a random color
11. colors = np.random.rand(number)
12. #choose a size for the scatter point
13. area = (40 * np.random.rand(number))**2.5
```

```
14.
15. #Show the first scatter plot
16. plt.scatter(x, y, c=colors, alpha=0.8)
17. plt.show()
18.
19. #Show the second scatter plot with the area
20. plt.scatter(x, y, s=area, c=colors, alpha=0.8)
21. plt.show()
```

This program produces two charts - one a simple scatter chart with randomized colors in a NumPy array and a second with area per scatter point getting displayed.

Output:

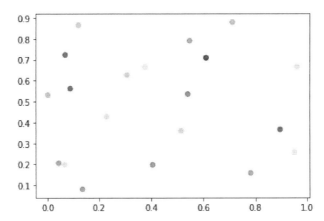

Figure 4.11: Exercise 4-8 Python code – scatter plot output-1

The second output produced is as follows:

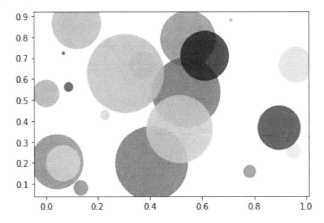

Figure 4.12: Exercise 4-8 Python code – scatter plot output-2

Let us see some additional examples of scatter plots.

Here's how to produce a scatter plot using rainbow colormap using a quadratic mapping:

```
1.  import numpy as np
2.  import matplotlib.pyplot as plt
3.  import matplotlib.cm as cm
4.  #define the formula
5.  x = np.arange(50)
6.  ys = [i+2*x+(i*x)**3.2
7.      for i in range(10)]
8.  colors = cm.rainbow(np.linspace(0, 1, len(ys)))
9.  for y, c in zip(ys, reversed(colors)):
10.   plt.scatter(x, y, color=c)
11. plt.title('scatter chart in a linear manner')
12. plt.show()
```

This program produces the following output:

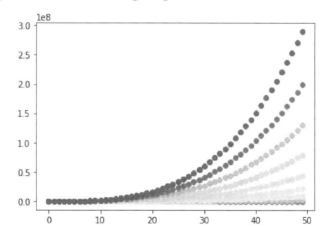

Figure 4.13: Exercise 4-9 Python code – scatter plot output

Let us see one of the most widely used statistical charts in Python.

Histogram plot

Histograms are one of the heavily used plots across functions as it gives a very good view of the distribution of data. The syntax for the histogram is as follows.

```
matplotlib.pyplot.hist(x, bins=None, range=None, density=False,
weights=None, cumulative=False, bottom=None, histtype='bar',
align='mid', orientation='vertical', rwidth=None, log=False,
color=None, label=None, stacked=False, *, data=None, **kwargs
```
The key parameters to consider are as follows:

- **x** - Input values - either a single array or a sequence of arrays with the same length.

- **bins** - A number (number of elements in each bin), a sequence (defining a sequence of edges), or a string defining a binning strategy that could be *auto, fd, doane, scott, stone, rice, sturges, or sqrt*.

- **range** - Is a tuple or none. If none it takes x.min() to x.max().

- **density** - Is a Boolean *True* or *False*. If *True*, it returns a probability density.

- **histtype** - A type of histogram from a *bar, barstacked, step, or stepfilled*.

- **orientation** - *vertical or horizontal*. If *'horizontal'* is specified, *barh* plot style histogram is used instead of a *bar* for the binned values.

- **color** - Self-explanatory.

- **label** - Label for the histogram.

Let us see some examples. Let us start with a simple histogram that uses some of the preceding parameters:

```
1.  import matplotlib
2.  import numpy as np
3.  import matplotlib.pyplot as plt
4.  np.random.seed(19681)
5.  x = np.random.randn(750)
6.  num_bins = 15
7.  fig, ax = plt.subplots()
8.  n, bins, patches = ax.hist(x, num_bins, density=False,col-
    or='skyblue',edgecolor='green',
9.                          histtype='bar',orientation='vertic
    al')
10. ax.set_xlabel('Distribution')
11. ax.set_title(r'Histogram')
12. fig.tight_layout()
13. plt.show()
```

This code produces the following output:

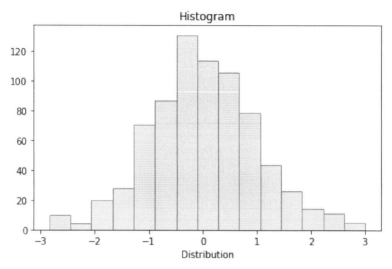

Figure 4.14: *Exercise 4-10 Python code – histogram plot output*

If you look at the parameters, it uses the number of elements instead of the probability of density and uses orientation and a histogram type of a bar. Suppose we change the parameters a little bit like the following code. If we change the *orientation* from *'vertical'* to *'horizontal'* and use set_ylabel instead of set_ylabel, we get the following output:

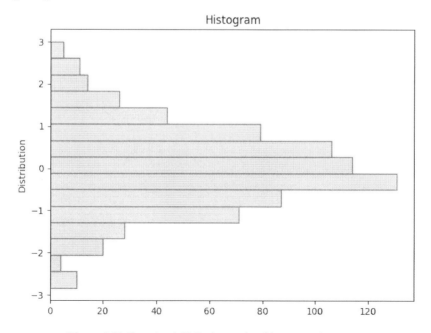

Figure 4.15: *Exercise 4-10 Python code – histogram plot output*

We can also use orientation, color, bintype options to visualize the histograms in different formats. Let us take a simple example to try some of the options.

Histogram example 1

```
1.  import matplotlib
2.  import numpy as np
3.  import matplotlib.pyplot as plt
4.
5.  np.random.seed(19681)
6.  x = np.random.randn(750)
7.  num_bins = 15
8.  fig, ax = plt.subplots()
9.  n, bins, patches = ax.hist(x,bins='doane', density=False,col-
    or='indigo',edgecolor='green',
10.                              histtype='step',orientation='vertic
    al')
11. ax.set_xlabel('Distribution')
12. ax.set_title(r'Histogram')
13. fig.tight_layout()
14. plt.show()
```

We can get the histograms as follows:

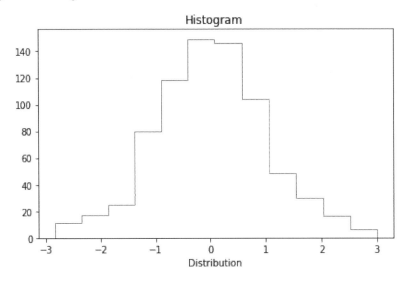

Figure 4.16: Exercise 4-10 Python code – histogram plot output

Histogram example 2

Let us try a histogram with the best fit line added to it based on standard deviation (sigma) and mean (mu). The data is generated using random numbers as well. The best fit line helps us form an outline like the Gaussian bell curve.

```
1.  import matplotlib
2.  import numpy as np
3.  import matplotlib.pyplot as plt
4.  np.random.seed(190007)
5.  mu = 120
6.  sigma = 11
7.  # example data
8.  x = mu + sigma * np.random.randn(1000)
9.  fig, ax = plt.subplots()
10. n, num_bins, patches = ax.hist(x, mu, density=1,color='gold')
11. y = ((1 / (np.sqrt(2 * np.pi) * sigma)) *
12.     np.exp(-0.5 * (1 / sigma * (num_bins - mu))**2))
13. ax.plot(num_bins,y, '.-',color='blue')
14. ax.set_xlabel('Distribution')
15. ax.set_ylabel('Probability density')
16. ax.set_title(r'Histogram with values of $\mu = $ '+ str(mu) + r' $\
    sigma = $'+ str(sigma))
17. fig.tight_layout()
18. plt.show()
```

This program produces the following output.

Output:

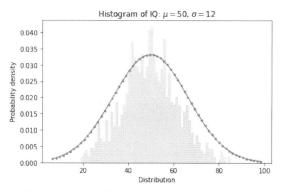

Figure 4.17: Exercise 4-11 Python Code – Histogram Plot Example-2 Output

As an exercise, can you try playing around with various options of histogram generation and how the bell curve is generated using the histogram?

Mid-chapter exercise

Exercise 1:

Let us take an example from the exercises undertaken so far. Let us show how data can be visualized uniquely. For this example, the same dataset was used for three different Matplotlib charts, and the result is three unique outputs. See the output for the scatter chart. What do you see? Can you think about the rationale for this outcome? We shall cover the reasons which we discussed briefly in earlier chapters a bit later in this book.

Data used - drawpython.csv	Code and graphs generated
x,y	**Code for the visualization**
25.641,68.2031	1. import pandas as pd
24.359,61.6647	2. import matplotlib.pyplot as plt
23.5897,52.4339	3. df = pd.read_csv('https://raw. githubusercontent.com/kalilurrahman/ datasets/main/drawpython.csv')
25.1282,46.6647	
27.4359,39.357	4. df.plot() *# plots all col-* *umns against index*
28.9744,35.8954	
33.3333,27.4339	5. df.plot(kind='scat-ter',x='x',y='y', col-or='green') *# scatter plot*
31.2821,32.4339	
28.9744,73.2031	
35.1282,76.28	6. df.plot(kind='density') *# esti-* *mate density function*
33.0769,76.28	
38.4615,77.0493	
42.3077,77.0493	
45.641,77.4339	
54.6154,76.28	
49.7436,77.4339	
52.0513,77.4339	
36.9231,25.5108	
50,22.8185	

44.1026,22.4339

40.5128,23.2031

60.2564,72.4339

56.9231,75.1262

61.0256,68.9724

61.2821,62.4339

61.0256,55.8954

60.7692,49.7416

60.5128,46.6647

58.7179,39.357

54.8718,32.4339

52.5641,28.9724

56.4103,36.28

33.5897,64.357

32.5641,60.1262

32.8205,55.8954

32.5641,53.2031

32.5641,48.2031

32.3077,44.7416

35.8974,65.1262

38.2051,64.7416

40.2564,62.4339

40.2564,57.8185

38.2051,55.1262

35.8974,54.357

44.1026,63.5877

45.641,58.5877

46.4103,56.6647

47.9487,59.7416

48.4615,62.0493

49.7436,66.6647

Output produced

1. Line chart

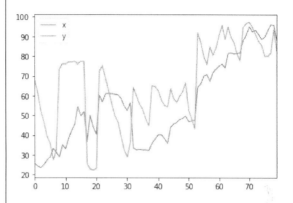

Figure 4.18: *Exercise 4-12 Python code – mid-chapter exercise – output-1*

2. Scatter chart

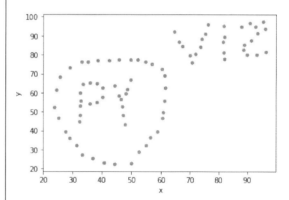

Figure 4.19: *Exercise 4-12 Python code – mid-chapter exercise – output-2*

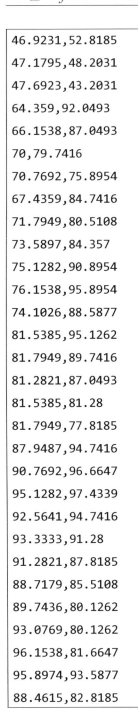

46.9231,52.8185

47.1795,48.2031

47.6923,43.2031

64.359,92.0493

66.1538,87.0493

70,79.7416

70.7692,75.8954

67.4359,84.7416

71.7949,80.5108

73.5897,84.357

75.1282,90.8954

76.1538,95.8954

74.1026,88.5877

81.5385,95.1262

81.7949,89.7416

81.2821,87.0493

81.5385,81.28

81.7949,77.8185

87.9487,94.7416

90.7692,96.6647

95.1282,97.4339

92.5641,94.7416

93.3333,91.28

91.2821,87.8185

88.7179,85.5108

89.7436,80.1262

93.0769,80.1262

96.1538,81.6647

95.8974,93.5877

88.4615,82.8185

3. Density plot

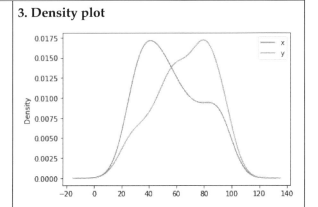

Figure 4.20: *Exercise 4-12 Python code – mid-chapter exercise – output-2*

Exercise 2:

Consider the following program and the output it produces. What do you think about the approach? How will you use it for your visualization? Where will you use it more frequently? (Clue: 3-dimensional plots are used for topographic representations when more than two types of data points are compared across three dimensions to show relevance).

```
1.  import matplotlib.pyplot as plt
2.  import numpy as np
3.  #Define the figure and axes
4.  fig = plt.figure(figsize=(10, 12))
5.  ax = fig.add_subplot(111, projection='3d')
6.  # Create the grid mesh with a polar coordinates type
7.  # use the values of RHO - r and PHI- p to determine  Theta - Z.
8.  r = np.linspace(0, 5/3.6, 100) # Define RHO
9.  p = np.linspace(0, 2.2*np.pi, 100) # Define PHI
10. R, P = np.mesh grid(r, p) # Generate a Mesh Grid
11. Z = ((R**2 - 0.989)**2) # Define Theta
12. # Express the mesh in the cartesian system.
13. X, Y = R*np.cos(P), R*np.sin(P)
14. # Plot the surface - Use a Spectral color map
15. ax.plot_surface(X, Y, Z, cmap=plt.cm.Spectral)
16. # Tweak the limits and add LaTeX based mathematical labels.
17. ax.set_zlim(0, 1.4) #Set Z-axis
18. ax.set_xlabel(r'$\phi_\mathrm{real}$', fontsize=18)
19. ax.set_ylabel(r'$\phi_\mathrm{imaginary}$', fontsize=18)
20. ax.set_zlabel(r'$V(\phi)-Phi$', fontsize=12)
21. plt.title('3D Surface Chart example')
22. #Show the visualization
23. plt.show()
```

We get the following output.

Output:

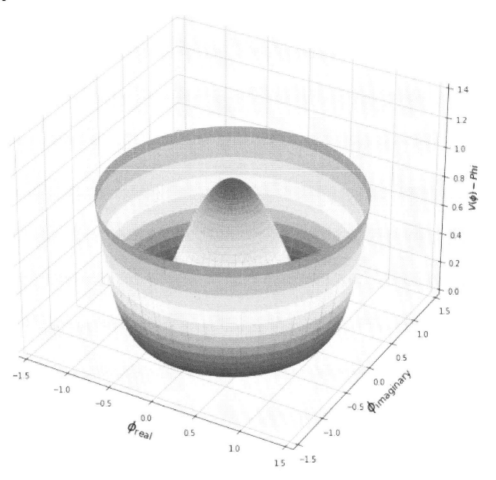

Figure 4.21: Exercise 4-23 Python code – mid-chapter exercise – 3D plots output

Tip: Python gives us a good number of libraries and functions to develop brilliant visualizations. One of the handy tools is having a standard colormap for various elements of visualization. We can leverage the pre-defined colormaps available or define our colormaps for the visualizations. Some of the cmap (Colormaps) combinations available for usage in charts are as follows:

'Accent', 'Accent_r', 'Blues', 'Blues_r', 'BrBG', 'BrBG_r', 'BuGn', 'BuGn_r', 'BuPu', 'BuPu_r', 'CMRmap', 'CMRmap_r', 'Dark2', 'Dark2_r', 'GnBu', 'GnBu_r', 'Greens', 'Greens_r', 'Greys', 'Greys_r', 'OrRd', 'OrRd_r', 'Oranges', 'Oranges_r', 'PRGn', 'PRGn_r', 'Paired', 'Paired_r', 'Pastel1', 'Pastel1_r', 'Pastel2', 'Pastel2_r', 'PiYG',

'PiYG_r', 'PuBu', 'PuBuGn', 'PuBuGn_r', 'PuBu_r', 'PuOr', 'PuOr_r', 'PuRd', 'PuRd_r', 'Purples', 'Purples_r', 'RdBu', 'RdBu_r', 'RdGy', 'RdGy_r', 'RdPu', 'RdPu_r', 'RdYlBu', 'RdYlBu_r', 'RdYlGn', 'RdYlGn_r', 'Reds', 'Reds_r', 'Set1', 'Set1_r', 'Set2', 'Set2_r', 'Set3', 'Set3_r', 'Spectral', 'Spectral_r', 'Wistia', 'Wistia_r', 'YlGn', 'YlGnBu', 'YlGnBu_r', 'YlGn_r', 'YlOrBr', 'YlOrBr_r', 'YlOrRd', 'YlOrRd_r', 'afmhot', 'afmhot_r', 'autumn', 'autumn_r', 'binary', 'binary_r', 'bone', 'bone_r', 'brg', 'brg_r', 'bwr', 'bwr_r', 'cividis', 'cividis_r', 'cool', 'cool_r', 'coolwarm', 'coolwarm_r', 'copper', 'copper_r', 'cubehelix', 'cubehelix_r', 'flag', 'flag_r', 'gist_earth', 'gist_earth_r', 'gist_gray', 'gist_gray_r', 'gist_heat', 'gist_heat_r', 'gist_ncar', 'gist_ncar_r', 'gist_rainbow', 'gist_rainbow_r', 'gist_stern', 'gist_stern_r', 'gist_yarg', 'gist_yarg_r', 'gnuplot', 'gnuplot2', 'gnuplot2_r', 'gnuplot_r', 'gray', 'gray_r', 'hot', 'hot_r', 'hsv', 'hsv_r', 'inferno', 'inferno_r', 'jet', 'jet_r', 'magma', 'magma_r', 'nipy_spectral', 'nipy_spectral_r', 'ocean', 'ocean_r', 'pink', 'pink_r', 'plasma', 'plasma_r', 'prism', 'prism_r', 'rainbow', 'rainbow', 'seismic', 'seismic', 'spring', 'springer', 'summer', 'summer_r', 'tab10', 'tab10_r', 'tab20', 'tab20_r', 'tab20b', 'tab20b_r', 'tab20c', 'tab20c_r', 'terrain', 'terrain_r', 'turbo', 'turbo_r', 'twilight', 'twilight_r', 'twilight_shifted', 'twilight_shifted_r', 'viridis', 'viridis_r', 'winter', 'winter_r'

Box plots

Let us check on another important plot that is widely used. **Box plots** are used for understanding the range in a visually representative manner. The basic syntax for Box plots is as follows.

```
matplotlib.pyplot.boxplot(x, notch=None, sym=None, vert=None, whis=None,
flierprops=None)
```

x is for data, the **notch** is used to give notched boxes, **vert** is used to set vertical or horizontal boxplots based on Boolean value, **whis** - is used to specify the whisker surrounding the box length, others are primarily used to show values, and **flierprops** is used for usage of a distinct prop (such as a square, diamond, or any marker shape available) for the outliers outside the box.

The simplest box plot command examples can be

```
boxplot(data)
```

or

```
boxplot(data, notch=True, showfliers=True).
```

Let us see how a box and whisker chart is built. It has the following key parts.

- min/max values show the highest or lowest value excluding the outliers

- an interquartile range covering the middle 50% of the values

- an upper-quartile showing values above 75%

- a median at 50%

  and

- lower-quartile showing the bottom 25% values.

This whisker shows the upper and lowers 25% of the quartile.

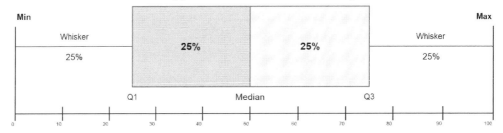

Figure 4.22: Anatomy of a Box Plot

Let us start with a comprehensive example using *Subplots:*

```
1.  import numpy as np
2.  import matplotlib.pyplot as plt
3.  np.random.seed(196998801)
4.  spread = np.random.rand(40) * 80
5.  center = np.ones(20) * 40
6.  flier_high = np.random.rand(8) * 80 + 80
7.  flier_low = np.random.rand(8) * -80
8.  blue_plus = dict(markerfacecolor='b', marker='+')
9.  data = np.concatenate((spread, center, flier_high, flier_low))
10. fig, axs = plt.subplots(2, 3, figsize=(16, 10))
11. axs[0, 0].boxplot(data)
12. axs[0, 0].set_title('Basic Plot')
13. axs[0, 1].boxplot(data, notch=True)
14. axs[0, 1].set_title('Notched Plot')
15. axs[0, 2].boxplot(data, flierprops=blue_plus)
16. axs[0, 2].set_title('Change outlier')
17. axs[1, 0].boxplot(data, showfliers=False)
18. axs[1, 0].set_title('Removed outliers')
19. axs[1, 1].boxplot(data, vert=False, flierprops=blue_plus)
```

```
20. axs[1, 1].set_title('Horizontal Plot')
21. axs[1, 2].boxplot(data, flierprops=blue_plus, whis=0.60)
22. axs[1, 2].set_title('Shorter Whisker size')
23. plt.show()
```

We get the following output:

Output:

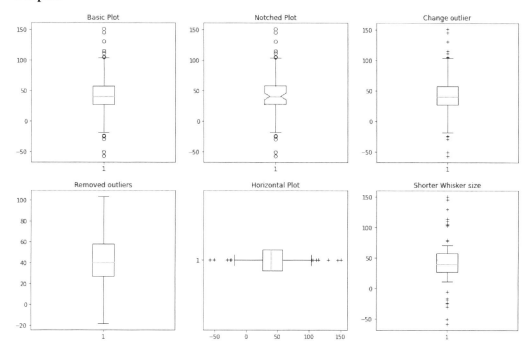

***Figure 4.23:** Exercise 4-14 Python code – box plot code output*

Let us see an example of multiple datasets in a box and whisker chart:

```
1.  import numpy as np
2.  import matplotlib.pyplot as plt
3.  np.random.seed(196998801)
4.  spread = np.random.rand(40) * 80
5.  center = np.ones(20) * 40
6.  flier_high = np.random.rand(8) * 80 + 80
7.  flier_low = np.random.rand(8) * -80
8.  indigo_triangle = dict(markerfacecolor='indigo', marker='v')
9.  data = np.concatenate((spread, center, flier_high, flier_low))
```

```
10. data2  =  np.concatenate((spread/2,  center/2,  flier_high/2,  flier_
    low/2))
11. data3  =  np.concatenate((spread*2,  center*2,  flier_high*2,  flier_
    low/2))
12. data=[data,data2,data3]
13. fig, ax = plt.subplots()
14. ax.set_title('Multiple Samples with Different sizes')
15. ax.boxplot(data)
16. plt.show()
```

We get the following output:

Output:

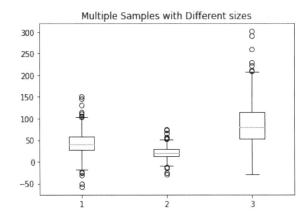

Figure 4.24: Exercise 4-15 Python code – box plot with whiskers – output

An exploratory question:

Where will you use Box and Whisker plot on a day-to-day basis? How will it help you?

Let us move to the exploration of some of the most common charts that we use regularly.

Pie charts

A **Pie chart** is one of the most widely used charts using any data visualization tool. It is the best way to represent part-of-a-whole by showing what percentage of a whole sum is represented by each of the pie represented.

The syntax of the Pie chart in Python is as follows:

```
matplotlib.pyplot.pie(data, explode, labels, colors, autopct, shadow)
```

Here are some of the key parameters to consider for pie chart definition:

- ***data*** ⇒ Data to be used for plotting
- ***explode*** ⇒ Used to show individual pies in an exploded or detached manner. Each of the wedges can be given a value greater than 0.0
- **labels** ⇒ Used for labels for the wedges in pie
- **colors** ⇒ Used for the color assignment for the wedges in the pie chart
- ***autopct*** ⇒ Used to specify a pie chart's pie percentage using a formatting string
- ***shadow*** ⇒ Used to add a shadow to the pie chart

Let us take an example to see how this chart can be programmed in Python:

```
1. from matplotlib import pyplot as plt
2. brands = ['Samsung', 'Apple', 'Huawei',
3.          'Xiaomi', 'Oppo', 'Others']
4. data = [30.25,26.53,10.44,9.67,4.83,18.28]
5. colors = ['green', 'yellowgreen', 'gold', 'lightskyblue', 'ol-
   ive','violet']
6. explode = (0.2, 0.0, 0.0, 0.0, 0.0, 0.1)
7. fig, axs = plt.subplots(2, 2, figsize=(16, 10))
8. axs[0, 0].pie(data, labels = brands)
9. axs[0, 0].set_title('Basic Pie Plot')
10.axs[0, 1].set_title('Basic Pie Plot with custom colors')
11.axs[0, 1].pie(data, labels = brands, colors=reversed(colors))
12.axs[1, 0].pie(data, labels = brands,colors=colors,
13.          autopct='%1.1f%%', shadow=True, startangle=90)
14.axs[1, 0].set_title('With percentage Pies and colors and shad-
   ows')
15.axs[1, 1].pie(data, labels = brands,colors=colors,ex-
   plode=(0.2,0.3,0.2,0.4,0.1,0.1),
16.          autopct='%1.0f%%', shadow=True, startangle=90)
17.axs[1, 1].set_title('Global Mobile Phone Market share')
18.plt.show()
```

We get the following output:

Output:

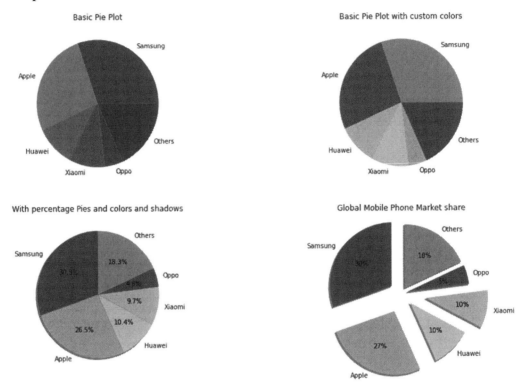

Figure 4.25: Exercise 4-16 Python code – pie charts - output

Donut/Doughnut charts

Donut charts use *matplotlib.pyplot.pie* as a base and build on top of it with a central circle added through the artist.

```
1.  # library
2.  import matplotlib.pyplot as plt
3.
4.  # create data
5.  brands = ['Samsung', 'Apple', 'Huawei',
6.           'Xiaomi', 'Oppo', 'Others']
7.  data = [30.25,26.53,10.44,9.67,4.83,18.28]
8.
9.  colors = ['green', 'yellowgreen', 'gold', 'lightskyblue', 'ol-
```

```
   ive','violet']
10.# Create a circle for the center of the plot
11.my_circle=plt.Circle( (0,0), 0.7, color='white')
12.plt.pie(data,    labels=brands,    wedgeprops    =    {    'line-
   width' : 7, 'edgecolor' : 'white' },colors=colors)
13.
14.p=plt.gcf()
15.p.gca().add_artist(my_circle)
16.plt.title('Global smartphone market share')
17.plt.show()
```

We get the following output:

Output:

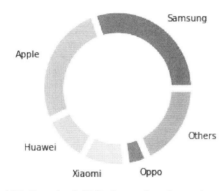

Figure 4.26: Exercise 4-17 Python code – donut charts - output

Let us take another example of a program to write a nested pie chart/donut chart. We can take different array values of a matrix (2x4) and flatten it draw the outer donut, and detail the internal donut.

```
1.  import numpy as np
2.  import matplotlib.pyplot as plt
3.  size = 0.25
4.  vals = np.array([[24., 68.], [22., 37.], [31., 10.], [22,11]])
5.  cmap = plt.get_cmap("prism")
6.  outer_colors = cmap(np.arange(4)*4)
7.  inner_colors = cmap(np.array([1, 2, 5, 6, 7, 8, 9, 10]))
8.  fig, ax = plt.subplots()
```

```
9.  ax.pie(vals.sum(axis = 1),radius = 1,
10.        colors = outer_colors,
11.          wedgeprops = dict(width = size, edgecolor = 'w'))
12. ax.pie(vals.flatten(), radius = 1 - size, colors = inner_colors,
13.          wedgeprops = dict(width = size-0.1, edgecolor = 'w'))
14. ax.set(aspect = "equal", title = 'Nested pie/donut chart example')
```

We get the following output:

Output:

Nested pie/donut chart example

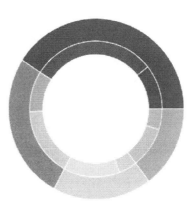

Figure 4.27: Exercise 4-18 Python code – multi-level nested pie/donut chart example output

Other examples (Shown with code and output)

Let us see some other chart examples using *Matplotlib.*

Area charts

For creating **Area charts** using *Matplotlib,* we use *Stackplot.* This program prints two charts one - a simple area chart and second - a wiggle area chart that is an option available in *matplotlib*

```
1.  import numpy as np
2.  import matplotlib.pyplot as plt
3.  plt.figure(figsize=(10,6))
4.  x=range(1,8)
5.  y=[ [1,4,6,8,9,11,14], [2,2,7,10,12,8,12], [2,8,5,10,6,10,12] ]
6.  plt.stackplot(x,y, labels=['Series 1','Series 2','Series 3'])
```

7. `plt.legend(loc='upper left')`

8. `plt.title('Basic Area Chart')`

9. `plt.show()`

10. `plt.stackplot(x,y,    labels=['Series    1','Series    2','Series 3'],baseline="wiggle")`

11. `plt.legend(loc='upper left')`

12. `plt.title('Basic Area Chart with Wiggle')`

13. `plt.show()`

We get the following output:

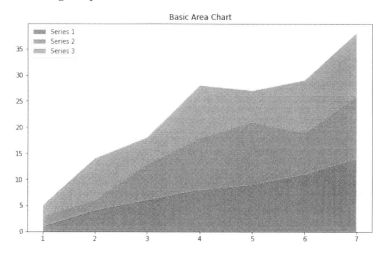

Figure 4.28: Exercise 4-19 Python code – area plot (stack plot) example – output-1

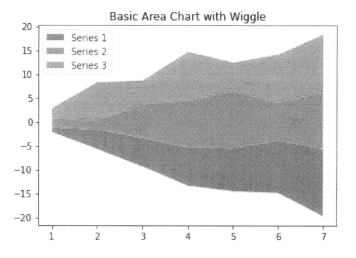

Figure 4.29: Exercise 4-19 Python code – area plot (stack plot) example – output-2

Let us see how we can plot a matrix plot or a type of heatmap using *Matplotlib*.

Matshow

For creating a matrix display, we leverage *matshow* that uses an array of elements to show a matrix. We can use colormap to colorize the columns and use text function to populate the values. *matshow* displays an array as a matrix in a new figure window. The first row of the matrix is displayed at the top and so on

```
1.  import matplotlib.pyplot as plot

2.  import numpy as np

3.  array = np.random.randint(10,40,(9,9))

4.  fig, ax = plt.subplots()

5.  ax.matshow(array , cmap='viridis')

6.  for (i, j), z in np.ndenumerate(array):

7.      ax.text(j, i, '{:0.0f}'.format(z), ha='center', va='cen-
        ter', color='w')

8.  plt.title('Matrix Show matshow() example')plot.show()
```

This code produces the following output:

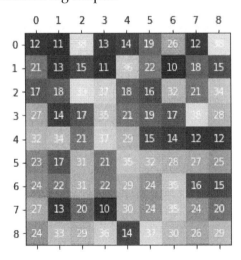

Figure 4.30: Exercise 4-20 Python code – matshow example output

Violin plot

A **violin plot** is a type of statistical plot – like a box plot. A violin plot shows additional information - a kernel density estimation – like a flipped histogram on either side of the violin. A violin plot is generated using *matplotlib.pyplot.violinplot(data)*.

Additional statistical choices such as *showmeans, showmedians,* and *showextrema* can be leveraged to distinguish statistical highlights.

```python
1.  import matplotlib.pyplot as plt
2.  import random
3.  import numpy as np
4.  ds1 = np.random.normal(0, 6, 100)
5.  ds2 = np.random.normal(0, 20, 200)
6.  ds3 = np.random.normal(0, 12, 400)
7.  data = list([ds1, ds2, ds3])
8.  fig, ax = plt.subplots()
9.  # build a violin plot
10. vio_part=ax.violinplot(data, showmeans=False, showmedians=True,-
    showextrema = True)
11. for pc in vio_part['bodies']:
12.     pc.set_facecolor('yellowgreen')
13.     pc.set_edgecolor('green')
14. ax.set_title('Sample Violin plot')
15. ax.set_xlabel('X-axis')
16. ax.set_ylabel('Y-axis')
17. xticklabels = ['Group 1', 'Group 2', 'Group 3']
18. ax.set_xticks([1,2,3])
19. ax.set_xticklabels(xticklabels)
20. ax.yaxis.grid(True)
21. plt.show()
```

This code produces the following output:

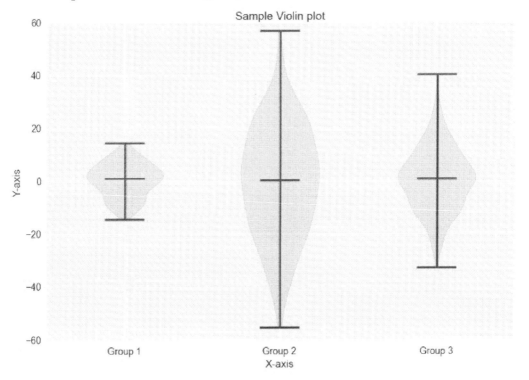

Figure 4.31: Exercise 4.21 – Violin Plot Output

Treemap charts

This chart uses the *squarify* library to build the plots. This implicitly uses *pyplot. plot* to render the diagram. The key is to ensure that the axis is removed. Formatting functions can be added to make sure the component details are displayed.

```
1.  #!pip install squarify
2.  import matplotlib.pyplot as plt
3.  import pandas as pd
4.  import squarify     # pip install squarify (algorithm for treemap)
5.  plt.figure(figsize=(6,4))
6.  squarify.plot(sizes=[33,22,15,45],
7.              label=["Area A", "Area B", "Area C", "Area D"],
8.              color=["yellowgreen","green","gold", "beige"],
9.              alpha=.91)
```

```
10. plt.axis('off')
11. plt.title('Sample Treemap - Matplotlib & Squarify')
12. plt.show()
```

This code produces the following output:

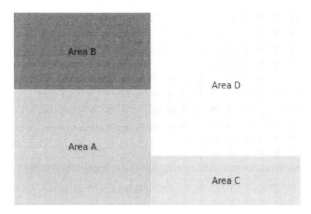

Figure 4.32: *Exercise 4.22 - Python code output*

Saving a file in Matplotlib

We can save a file in Matplotlib with a simple **savefig()** command. A Standard example is plt.savefig (*Filename, **dpi**=*number of pixels). For example, we can use the following command to save the plot from the previous exercise:

```
plt.savefig('DataVizUsingPythonEx4-22.png', dpi=300)
```

It is advisable to use **plt.savefig()** before calling **plt.show()** for rendering in the Jupyter notebook console to avoid any issues.

Annotating a plot

As discussed in an earlier chapter, a picture is worth a 1000 words, but having a picture without any explanation is useless. **Annotation** is a great way to add meaningful text inputs to ensure that the description befits the visualization to showcase a meaning. In *matplotlib,* we can use the ***annotate()*** function to take care of the annotations. Here's a standard syntax:

```
ax.annotate('text to display via annotation', xy=, xycoords=, xytext=,
arrowprops=,verticalalignment=, horizontalalignment=)
```

In the above example, the following is the purpose for some of the key parameters:

- Text to display via annotation ==> Self explanatory

- xy ==> x and y coordinate of where the text needs to be annotated

- xycoords ==> to specific annotation relative to "data," "axis fraction," or "figure pixels" in the plot

- arrowprops ==> If you are using arrows to annotate – you can define the properties with a dictionary

- horizontalaligment , verticalalignment ==> alignment for the annotation

Let us see the usage with a simple example:

```
1.  import numpy as np
2. import matplotlib.pyplot as plt
3.
4. n = 12
5. X = np.arange(n)
6. Y1 = (1-X/float(n)) * np.random.uniform(1.5,2.0,n)
7. Y2 = (1-X/float(n)) * np.random.uniform(1.5,2.0,n)
8.
9. plt.bar(X, +Y1, facecolor='#6666ff', edgecolor='white')
10. plt.bar(X, -Y2, facecolor='#ff4444', edgecolor='white')
11.
12. for x,y in zip(X,Y1):
13.     plt.text(x+0.2, y+0.05, '%.2f' % y, ha='center', va= 'bottom')
14. for x,y in zip(X,Y2):
15.     plt.text(x+0.05, -1*(y+0.2), '%.2f' % y, ha='center', va= 'bot-
    tom')
16.
17.
18. plt.annotate('Example of annotation in reference to data',
19.             xy=(8, 0),xycoords='data', xytext=(5, 1.5),
20.             arrowprops=
21.                 dict(facecolor='blue', shrink=0.10),
22.                 horizontalalignment='left',
23.                 verticalalignment='center')
24. plt.title('Example of bi-directional bar chart with annotations')
```

```
25. plt.ylim(-2.5,+2.5)
26. plt.show()
```

Output:

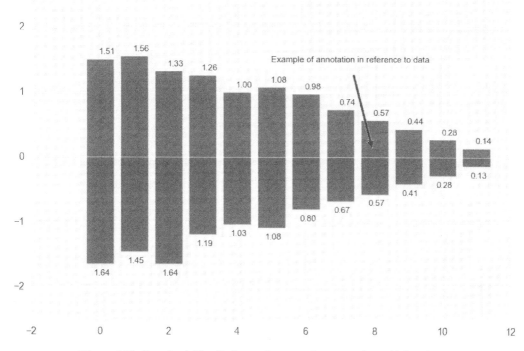

Figure 4.33: Exercise 4-23 – Python code output for annotation with bar charts

Exercises and Matplotlib resources

Let us cover this section in two parts. Some good exercises for topics not covered so far and some good resources to look at and leverage for further knowledge.

End of the chapter exercise covering key concepts

Take a look at the following code (*Exercise 4.24*) and the outputs produced. We shall have some exercises towards the end.

```
1. import numpy as np
2. import pandas as pd
3. import squarify
4. import matplotlib.pyplot as plt
5. import matplotlib as mpl
```

```
6.  #Read File
7.  titanic = pd.read_csv('https://raw.githubusercontent.com/
    kalilurrahman/datasets/main/Titanic.csv')
8.  #drop and create relevant columns
9.  titanic.drop(['Name', 'Ticket'], axis=1, inplace=True)
10.     titanic['Cabin_ind'] = np.where(titanic['Cabin'].isnull(),
    0, 1)
11.     gender_num = {'male': 0, 'female': 1}
12.     titanic['Sex'] = titanic['Sex'].map(gender_num)
13.     titanic.drop(['Cabin', 'Embarked'], axis=1, inplace=True)
14.     X_train_data = pd.DataFrame(titanic)
15.     bins= [10,20,30,40,50,60]
16.     labels = ['<20','21-30','31-40','41-50','>50']
17.     X_train_data['AgeGroup'] = pd.cut(X_train_data['Age'],
    bins=bins,
18.                                         labels=labels,
    right=False)
19.     # Try a Pie chart
20.     pie_data = (titanic.groupby('Pclass')['Fare'].sum()).to_
    frame()
21.     pie_data['Fare'] = round((pie_data.Fare/sum(pie_data.
    Fare))*100)
22.     plt.pie(pie_data.Fare, labels=pie_data.index,
23.             startangle=90, autopct='%.1f%%')
24.     plt.title("Chart-1 A pie chart of Fare Class",
25.             fontsize=16,fontweight="bold")
26.     plt.show()
27.     # Try a Doughnut chart
28.     donut_data = (titanic.groupby('Pclass')['Fare'].sum()).
    to_frame()
29.     donut_data['Fare']    =    (donut_data.Fare/sum(donut_data.
    Fare))*100
30.     my_circle=plt.Circle( (0,0), 0.6, color='white')
31.     plt.pie(donut_data.Fare,            labels=donut_data.index,
    autopct='%1.1f%%',
32.             colors=['red','green','blue'])
```

```
33.        p=plt.gcf()
34.        p.gca().add_artist(my_circle)
35.        plt.title("Chart-2 Titanic Fare Groups in a Donut chart",
36.                   fontsize=16,fontweight="bold")
37.        plt.show()
38.        # Try a Tree Map chart
39.        lbl = donut_data.index.join(map(str, donut_data['Fare']))
40.        lbl = lbl.join(map(str,'%'))
41.        norm = mpl.colors.Normalize(vmin=min(donut_data.Fare),
42.                              vmax=max(donut_data.Fare))
43.        colors = [plt.cm.Spectral(norm(value)) for value in donut_
    data.Fare]
44.        squarify.plot(label=lbl,sizes=donut_data.Fare,
45.                   color = colors, alpha=.6)
46.        plt.title("Chart-3 Titanic Classes in a Tree Map",
47.                   fontsize=16,fontweight="bold")
48.        plt.axis('off');
49.        plt.show()
50.        #Try a chart of the fare by age group
51.        pie_data = (titanic.groupby('AgeGroup')['Fare'].count()).
    to_frame()
52.        pie_data['AgeGroup'] = round((pie_data.Fare/sum(pie_data.
    Fare))*100, 2)
53.        plt.pie(pie_data.Fare, labels=pie_data.index,
54.                startangle=90, autopct='%.1f%%');
55.        plt.title("Chart-4 Titanic Age Groups in a pie chart",
56.                   fontsize=16,fontweight="bold")
57.        plt.show()
58.        # Doughnut chart
59.        donut_data = (titanic.groupby('AgeGroup')['Fare'].count()).
    to_frame()
60.        donut_data['AgeGroup'] = (donut_data.Fare/sum(donut_data.
    Fare))*100
61.        my_circle=plt.Circle( (0,0), 0.6, color='white')
62.        plt.pie(donut_data.Fare, labels=donut_data.index,
```

```
       autopct='%1.1f%%')
63.       p=plt.gcf()
64.       p.gca().add_artist(my_circle)
65.       plt.title("Chart-5 Titanic Age Groups in a Donut chart",
66.               fontsize=16,fontweight="bold")
67.       plt.show()
68.       # Change color
69.       norm = mpl.colors.Normalize(
70.           vmin=min(donut_data.AgeGroup),
71.           vmax=max(donut_data.AgeGroup)
72.       )
73.       colors = [plt.cm.Spectral(norm(value)) for value in donut_
   data.AgeGroup]
74.       colors[1] = "#FBFCFE"
75.       plt.figure(figsize=(10, 6))
76.       plt.rc('font', size=13)
77.       plt.title("Chart-6 Titanic Agewise Travel Group - In a
   Treemap",
78.               fontsize=16,fontweight="bold")
79.       plt.axis('off');
80.       perc    =    [str('{:5.2f}'.format(i/donut_data.AgeGroup.
   sum()*100))
81.               + "%"for i in donut_data['AgeGroup']]
82.       lbl = [el[0] + " = " + el[1] for el in zip(donut_data.index,
   perc)]
83.       squarify.plot(sizes=donut_data['AgeGroup'],     label=lbl,
   alpha=.8,
84.               edgecolor="white", linewidth=2)#, color=colors)
85.       plt.axis('off')
86.       plt.show()
87.       # Make data: I have 3 groups and 7 subgroups
88.       group_names=['First Class', 'Second Class', 'Third Class']
89.       group_size=[63.3,13.2,24.4]
90.       subgroup_names = labels
91.       subgroup_size = []
```

```
92.        for agegroup in pie_data.AgeGroup:
93.            subgroup_size.append(agegroup)
94.        # Create colors
95.        a, b, c=[plt.cm.Blues, plt.cm.Reds, plt.cm.Greens]
96.        perc2 = [str('{:5.2f}'.format(i/donut_data.Fare.sum()*100))
97.                + "%"for i in donut_data['Fare']]
98.        lbl2 = [el[0] + " = " + el[1] for el in zip(donut_data.index,
      perc2)]
99.        # First Ring (outside)
100.       fig, ax = plt.subplots()
101.       ax.axis('equal')
102.       mypie, _ = ax.pie(group_size,
103.                        radius=1.3,
104.                        labels=group_names,
105.                        colors=[a(0.6),b(0.7),c(0.8)]
106.                        )
107.       plt.setp( mypie, width=0.3, edgecolor='white')
108.       perc     =    [str('{:5.2f}'.format(i/donut_data.AgeGroup.
      sum()*100))
109.                + "%"for i in donut_data['AgeGroup']]
110.       lbl = [el[0] + " = " + el[1] for el in zip(donut_data.index,
      perc)]
111.       # Second Ring (Inside)
112.       mypie2, _ = ax.pie(subgroup_size,
113.                         radius=1.3-0.3,
114.                         labels=lbl, #subgroup_names,
115.                         labeldistance=0.7,
116.                         colors=[c(0.5), c(0.4), c(0.3), b(0.5),
      b(0.4),
117.                              a(0.6), a(0.5), a(0.4), a(0.3),
      a(0.2)])
118.       plt.setp( mypie2, width=0.4, edgecolor='white')
119.       plt.margins(0,0)
120.       plt.title("Chart-7 Titanic Agewise Travel Group \n In a
      multi donut chart\n",
```

```
121.                fontsize=16,fontweight="bold")
122.     # show it
123.     plt.show()
```

Output:

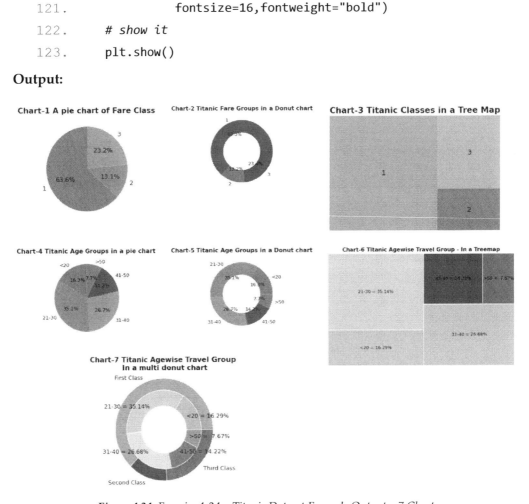

Figure 4.34: *Exercise 4-24 – Titanic Dataset Example Output – 7 Charts*

Example: Use of subplots and different charts in a single visualization

Let us see an example that covers subplots and different charts in a single visualization:

```
1. import matplotlib.pyplot as plt
2. import numpy as np
3.
4. np.random.seed(1961)
5. data = np.random.randn(5, 16)
6. fig, axs = plt.subplots(2, 3, figsize=(20, 10))
```

```
7.  axs[0, 0].hist(data[0],color='green')
8.  axs[0, 2].plot(data[0],color='green')
9.  axs[0, 1].plot(data[0], data[1],color='blue')
10.      axs[1, 0].scatter(data[0], data[1], color='purple')
11.      axs[1, 1].hist2d(data[0], data[1])
12.      axs[1, 2].bar(data[0],data[1],color='skyblue')
13.      plt.suptitle('Different Plots example',fontsize=24)
14.      plt.show()
```

We get the following output:

Output:

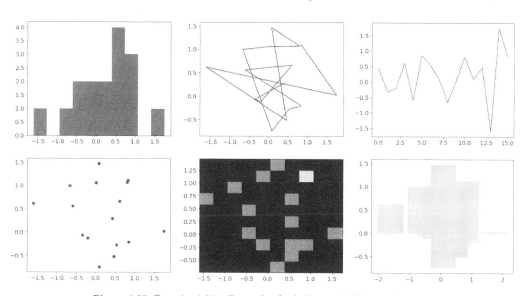

Figure 4.35: Exercise 4-25 – Example of subplots and different plot types

Example: Simple use of Error Bars – Using a horizontal bar chart and a standard error bar

Let us see an example that covers the use of error bars in a single visualization:

```
1.  import numpy as np
2.  import matplotlib.pyplot as plt
3.  import random
```

```
4.  val = 2 + 20*np.random.randn(4)

5.  pos = np.arange(4) + .75

6.  fig=plt.figure(figsize=(6,4))

7.  plt.barh(pos,val, align='center')

8.  plt.
    yticks(pos, ('Company-1', 'Company-2', 'Company-3', 'Company-4'))

9.  plt.xlabel('Performance')

10. plt.title('Stock performance for the day')

11. plt.barh(pos,val, xerr=np.random.randn(4), ecolor='g',

12.           align='center', color='blue')

13. plt.
    yticks(pos, ('Company-1', 'Company-2', 'Company-3', 'Company-4'))

14. plt.xlabel('Performance')

15.

16. plt.show()
```

Output:

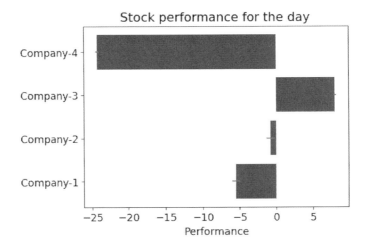

Figure 4.36: Exercise 4-26 – The use of error bars on horizontal bar chart

Example 4-27: Code to use error bars as a standalone feature

The following example uses the error bar function directly using the y axis error parameter specified:

```
1. import numpy as np
2. import matplotlib.pyplot as plt
3. fig = plt.figure()
4. x = np.arange(4)
5. y = 2.5 * np.tan(x / 200 * np.pi)
6. yerr = np.linspace(0.1, 0.4, 4)
7. plt.errorbar(x, y + 3, yerr=yerr, color='g')
8. plt.title('Sample Error bar chart')
```

Output:

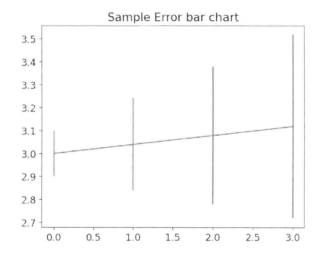

Figure 4.37: Exercise 4-27 – Standalone error bar charts

Example 4-28: Use of log charts in Matplotlib

Log charts or log plots are typically used to show a two-dimensional plot of numeric values using logarithmic scales. Logarithmic scales give a compressed view of big values, and the charts look compact.

Let us explore the use of log charts in Matplotlib with a simple exercise. For this, we shall use a simple exponential formula () on a data set. We shall produce charts for a linear, linear vs. logarithmic, and logarithmic vs. logarithmic of a base value for the dataset created.

```
1. import numpy as np
2. import warnings
3. warnings.filterwarnings("ignore")
```

```
4.
5.  data = np.arange(0.01, 40.0, 0.01)
6.  fig, ax = plt.subplots(2, 2)
7.  ax[0,0].plot(data, np.exp(data/3),color='green')
8.  ax[0,0].set_title('linear x , y plot')
9.  ax[0,0].grid()
10. ax[0,1].semilogy(data, np.exp(data/3),color='gold')
11. ax[0,1].set_title('linear x, log y')
12. ax[0,1].grid()
13. ax[1,0].semilogx(data, np.exp(data/3),color='skyblue')
14. ax[1,0].set_title('log x, linear y')
15. ax[1,0].grid()
16. ax[1,1].loglog(data, 40 * np.exp(data/3), basex=8,color='blue')
17. ax[1,1].set_title('Log x, Log Y on base 8')
18. ax[1,1].grid()
19. fig.tight_layout()
20. plt.show()
```

Output:

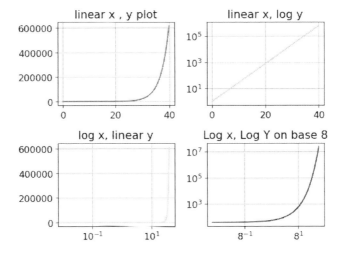

Figure 4.38: Exercise 4-28 – Use of logarithmic charts - output

Exercise 4-29: Contour plots on various mathematical equations

Contour plots are typically used to leverage lines to show the height or altitude of geographical indicators. They are also used to show the density of data, brightness, or engineering value such as electric potential.

Let us see the use of contour plots using various mathematical equations. This program uses a random creation of a formula to build a contour plot – an outline contour and a filled contour for the formula passed. It uses one of the formulas

$$((2*\sin(x) + \cos(y),(x^2 + y^2),$$

$$\sqrt{x^3 + 2y^2 + 4x}, \sqrt{x^2 + y^2},(x^2 - y^2),\sin(x)\cos(y),\ sin^2x - cos^2y \text{ or } \cos\left(\sqrt{x^2 + y^2}\right)$$

```
1.  import random
2.
3.  #Define a simple function to return different functions
4.  def funct(x, y):
5.      numbers = [11,22,33,44,55,66,77,88]
6.      randomchoice = random.choice(numbers)
7.      print(randomchoice)
8.      if randomchoice == 11:
9.          return np.sin(x) ** 2 + np.cos(y)
10.     elif randomchoice == 22:
11.         return x ** 2 + y ** 2
12.     elif randomchoice == 33:
13.         return (x ** 3 + 3 * y ** 2 + 4* x) ** 0.5
14.     elif randomchoice == 44:
15.         return (x ** 2 + y ** 2) ** 0.5
16.     elif randomchoice == 55:
17.         return (x ** 2 - y ** 2)
18.     elif randomchoice == 66:
19.         return np.sin(x) * np.cos(y)
20.     elif randomchoice == 77:
21.         return np.sin(x) ** 2 - np.cos(y) **2
22.     elif randomchoice == 88:
```

```
23.          return np.cos((x ** 2 + y **2) ** 0.5)
24.     else:
25.          return np.sin(x) * np.cos(y)
26.
27. x = np.linspace(0, 5, 50)
28. y = np.linspace(0, 5, 40)
29. X, Y = np.meshgrid(x, y)
30. Z = funct(X, Y)
31. plt.contour(X, Y, Z, 30, cmap=plt.cm.tab20b)
32. plt.colorbar()
33. plt.show()
34. plt.contourf(X,Y,Z, cmap=plt.cm.gnuplot2_r)
35. plt.colorbar()
36. plt.show()
```

Output:

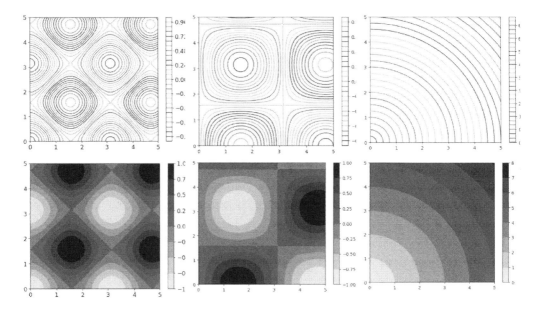

Figure 4.39: Exercise 4-29 – Use of contour charts - output

Exercise 4-30: An example of a comparison of pseudocolor, contour, and filled contour chart for a common dataset

Let us see a simple example of pseudocolor, contour, and filled contour example in Matplotlib:

```
1. matplotlib.style.use('default')
2. data = 2 * np.random.random((8, 8))
3. data2 = 3 * np.random.random((8, 8))
4. fig, axes = plt.subplots(1,3, figsize = (12,4))
5. axes[0].pcolor(data2,cmap='viridis')
6. axes[0].set_title('# Pseudocolor plot of 2D array')
7. axes[1].contour(data,cmap='plasma')
8. axes[1].set_title('# Contour plot')
9. axes[2].contourf(data,cmap='magma')
10. axes[2].set_title('# Filled contour plot')
11. fig.tight_layout()
```

Output:

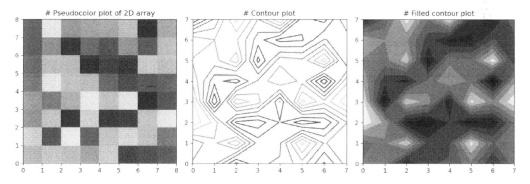

Figure 4.40: *Exercise 4-30 – Use of pseudocolor, contour, and filled contour charts - output*

Exercise 4-31: An example of a quiver plot using arrows

A **quiver plot** is used to plot vector lines as arrows in a 2-dimensional space. An example is to show electric potentials, such as infield theory for the flow of an electron or a charge. It could be showcased for an optical flow in a video as well.

It could also be used to show a stress gradient for mechanical engineering-related visualization.

Let us see a simple example of a simple quiver plot using a mathematical equation using a multi-dimensional mesh grid for a randomly generated x and y coordinate and an exponential formula of applied to the quiver plot with the flow shown in the form of coloured arrows.

```
1.  matplotlib.style.use('default')
2.  x = np.arange(-2,1.2,0.25)
3.  y = np.arange(-2,1.2,0.25)
4.  X, Y = np.meshgrid(x, y)
5.  z = X*np.exp(-X**2 -Y**2)
6.  dx, dy = np.gradient(z)
7.  n = -4
8.  color_array = np.sqrt((((dx-n)/2)**2 + ((dy-n)/2)**2)
9.  fig, ax = plt.subplots(figsize=(7,7))
10. ax.quiver(X,Y,dx,dy,color_array,cmap=plt.cm.Spectral)
11. ax.xaxis.set_ticks([])
12. ax.yaxis.set_ticks([])
13. ax.set_aspect('equal')
14. plt.title('Quiver Plot example')
15. plt.show()
```

Output:

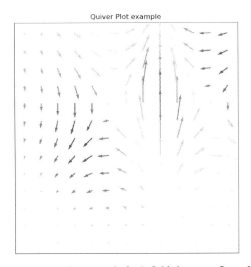

Figure 4.41: Exercise 4-31 – Quiver plot example for infield theory or flow of electron/charges-output

Exercise 4-32: An example of a lollipop plot

Lollipop plots are useful to compare categorical data like a bar chart. Typically, it shows the start and end values of the data value and combines bars and circles to show the data value range. It can also be used to showcase discrete signals used in digital signal processing.

To build a lollipop plot, we shall be using the plt.stem() function referred to earlier in the chapter. The stem and leaf plot can highlight the baseline, stem lines, and markers to showcase a lollipop-like chart. The same chart can be extended to show the value comparisons in one quadrant or multiple quadrants, to show either positive or negative comparison values between various parameters such as companies or functions or over the years.

```
1.  import matplotlib.pyplot as plt
2.  import numpy as np
3.  import numpy as np
4.  values=np.random.uniform(size=20)
5.  fig = plt.figure(figsize=(12,6))
6.  plt.title('A lollipop chart')
7.  plt.stem(values, markerfmt='.')
8.  # change color and shape and size and edges
9.  (markers, stemlines, baseline) = plt.stem(values)
10. plt.setp(markers, marker='h', markersize=14, markeredgecol-
    or="green", markeredgewidth=2)
```

Output:

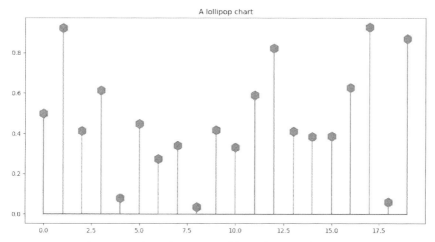

Figure 4.42: Exercise 4-32 – Lollipop plot example - output

Exercise 4-33: An example of 3D surface plots

One of the good visualization elements we can check is a 3-dimensional surface plot. It has three key elements – predictor values on x and y axes and the response values shown in a continuous surface in the z-axes. It can be used to showcase a dataset having 2-dimensional inputs and a 1-dimensional output. Combining both as predictors and response values gives us a 3-dimensional view.

We shall try different surface plots for the Laplacian of Gauss formulation for surface contouring and plotting. We shall be using a very well-proven formula, . This example covers a surface plot, a contour plot, a scatter plot, and a wireframe plot of the function outlined and plots it in a 3D-mesh grid developed.

```
1.  from matplotlib import cm
2.  import matplotlib.gridspec as gridspec
3.  def define3DFunc(x, y, sigma):
4.      #Define Laplacian Gauss Filter function
5.      exwhysig = (x ** 2 + y ** 2) / (2 * sigma ** 2)
6.      return -1 / 2 * (np.pi * sigma ** 4) * ((y **2 / sigma ** 2)
    - 1) * np.exp(-exwhysig )
7.  N = 64
8.  # Define a Mesh Grid
9.  X2, Y2 = np.meshgrid(range(N), range(N))
10. Z2 = define3DFunc(X2 - N/2, Y2 - N/2, sigma=(N**0.5))
11. X1 = np.reshape(X2, -1)
12. Y1 = np.reshape(Y2, -1)
13. Z1 = np.reshape(Z2, -1)
14. ax1 = plt.axes(projection='3d')
15. ax1.plot_wireframe(X2, Y2, Z2, cmap='viridis')
16. ax1.set_title("3D Wireframe Chart")
17. plt.axis('off')
18. plt.show()
19. ax2 = plt.axes(projection='3d')
20. ax2.plot_surface(X2, Y2, Z2, cmap='magma')
21. ax2.set_title("3D Surface Chart")
22. plt.axis('off')
23. plt.show()
```

```
24. norm = plt.Normalize(Z2.min(), Z2.max())
25. colors = cm.jet(norm(Z2))
26. ax3 = plt.axes(projection='3d')
27. surf = ax3.plot_surface(X2, Y2, Z2, facecolors=colors, shade=-
    False)
28. surf.set_facecolor((0,0,0,0))
29. ax3.set_title("3D Surface Chart 2")
30. plt.show()
31. ax4 = plt.axes(projection='3d')
32. ax4.scatter(X1, Y1, Z1, c=Z1, cmap='Spectral', linewidth=1)
33. ax4.set_title("3D Scatter Chart")
34. plt.axis('off')
35. plt.show()
36. ax5 = plt.axes(projection='3d')
37. ax5.contour3D(X2, Y2, Z2, 33, cmap='prism')
38. ax5.set_title("3D Contour Chart")
39. plt.show()
```

Output:

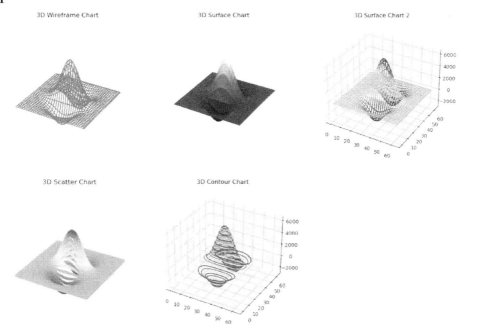

Figure 4.43: Exercise 4-33 – 3D surface plots example -output

Now that we have looked at multiple examples let us try an exercise. All the code along with the solutions are given in the notebook for *Chapter 4.*

End of the chapter exercise

Exercise 4-34: A stock market example

For this example, let us access stock market data of 3 leading technology firms and see their performance and do simple charting based on what we carried out in this chapter:

```
1. import numpy as np
2. import matplotlib.pyplot as plt
3. import pandas as pd
4. import math
5. import warnings
6. warnings.filterwarnings("ignore")
7. from pandas_datareader import data as pdr
8. #!pip install yfinance
9. import yfinance as yf
10. yf.pdr_override()
11. stocks = ['Apple', 'Amazon', 'Google']
12. symbols = ['AAPL','AMZN','GOOG']
13. x_pos = np.arange(len(stocks))
14. start = '2005-11-21'
15. end = '2020-11-20'
16. data = pdr.get_data_yahoo(symbols, start, end)['Adj Close']
17. normalize_stocks = data.apply(lambda x: x / x[0])
18. normalize_stocks.plot(figsize=(12,6)).axhline(1, lw=1,
    color='black')
19. plt.xlabel("Date")
20. plt.ylabel("Adj Close")
21. plt.grid()
22. plt.title("Stocks Adj Close Price")
23. plt.show()
24. for symbol in symbols:
```

```
25.    returns = data.pct_change()
26. ret_std=data.std()
27. ret_mean=data.mean()
28. Stocks = [ret_mean['AAPL'], ret_mean['AMZN'], ret_mean['GOOG']]
29. error = [ret_std['AAPL'], ret_std['AMZN'], ret_std['GOOG']]
30. # Build the plot
31. fig, ax = plt.subplots()
32. ax.bar(x_pos, Stocks, yerr=error, align='center',
       alpha=0.5, ecolor='black', capsize=10)
33. ax.set_ylabel('Stock Performance')
34. ax.set_xticks(x_pos)
35. ax.set_xticklabels(stocks)
36. ax.set_title('Example of Stock values with an error chart')
37. ax.yaxis.grid(True)
38. ret_std=returns.std()
39. ret_mean=returns.mean()
40. Stocks = [ret_mean['AAPL'], ret_mean['AMZN'], ret_mean['GOOG']]
41. error = [ret_std['AAPL'], ret_std['AMZN'], ret_std['GOOG']]
42. # Build the plot
43. fig, ax = plt.subplots()
44. ax.bar(x_pos, Stocks, yerr=error, align='center',
       alpha=0.5, ecolor='black', capsize=10)
45. ax.set_ylabel('Stock Performance')
46. ax.set_xticks(x_pos)
47. ax.set_xticklabels(stocks)
48. ax.set_title('Example of Stock returns with an error chart')
49. ax.yaxis.grid(True)
50. # Save the figure and show
51. plt.tight_layout()
52. plt.show()
```

Output:

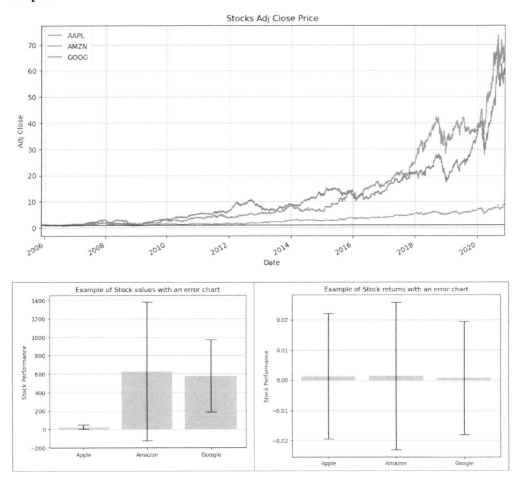

Figure 4.44: *Exercise 4-34 – Stock market charts example -output*

There are numerous ways to leverage the full potential of Matplotlib, and we can write a book on a particular plot itself if we want to dwell on the details of each function. The key to success is practice and relentlessly trying various permutations.

Matplotlib resources

In this chapter, we covered a good amount of introduction to data visualization. There are plenty of excellent resources on Matplotlib to refer to. Some of the resources to consider and leverage are as follows:

Resource	Purpose
Matplotlib Portal – Contains all the latest information about the library	**https://matplotlib.org/**
Matplotlib overview	**https://matplotlib.org/contents.html**
Matplotlib examples gallery	**Link-1 ->https://matplotlib.org/gallery/index.html** **Link-2 ->https://matplotlib.org/gallery.html**
Matplotlib tutorial	**https://matplotlib.org/tutorials/index.html**
Anatomy of Matplotlib – contains good tutorials to refer to with examples	**https://github.com/matplotlib/ AnatomyOfMatplotlib**
Matplotlib tutorial by Nicolas Rougier	**https://github.com/rougier/matplotlib-tutorial**
A Matplotlib chapter in a book by the creator of Matplotlib – John D Hunter	**http://www.aosabook.org/en/matplotlib.html**
A video on the Anatomy of matplotlib	**https://conference.scipy.org/scipy2013/tutorial_detail.php?id=103**
Real Python – Matplotlib guide	**https://realpython.com/python-matplotlib-guide/**
Matplotlib video tutorials	**https://youtu.be/UO98lJQ3QGI**
Free training program on edX on Python for Data Science covering Matplotlib	**https://www.edx.org/course/python-for-data-science-2**
Good professional training program on Matplotlib from Datacamp academy	**https://www.datacamp.com/courses/introduction-to-data-visualization-with-matplotlib**
Matplotlib cheat sheet from Datacamp	Matplotlib Cheat Sheet from Datacamp

Conclusion

In this chapter, we covered a good amount of introduction to data visualization elements using Matplotlib. We got introduced to various functions within Matplotlib and how to leverage them effectively. We covered a lot of programs to see how we can emulate various visualizations using Matplotlib. From the next chapter onwards, we shall explore other visualization libraries available for usage with Python to see and compare the features to understand the best approach for the visualization tasks.

In the upcoming chapters, we shall be covering Pandas, Seaborn, Plotly, and other libraries available to do extensive visualization.

Questions

1. What will you use to change the styling of the charts?

2. How will you use error bars as a graphical representation of the variability in data?

3. How will you design a dashboard using subplots?

4. What is the difference between a GridSpec and subplots in Python?

5. How will you create a gauge chart or a speedometer chart using a pie or donut chart?

6. What is the difference between a heatmap and a matrix showing – matshow plots?

7. Where will you use the lollipop charts?

8. What is the difference between a box chart and a stock market candlestick chart?

9. How do you take care of the scattered numbers all over the place?

10. How 3D charts help us in data visualization?

CHAPTER 5

Using Pandas for Plotting

> "The art and practice of visualizing data is becoming ever more important in bridging the human-computer gap to mediate analytical insight in a meaningful way."
>
> *-Edd Dumbill*

So far, we have covered good ground on how to use Python and matplotlib for visualization. We dwelled on hands-on coding after covering a high-level introduction to data visualization, key elements, and design perspectives for data visualization. This chapter will give an introduction to using two powerful tools that are becoming a tour-de-force for data visualization among data scientists. *NumPy* and *Pandas*-driven data visualization is leaping ahead of all the other tools for queries about usage over the last few years. *Pandas* queries for visualization are the most sought-after topic in forums such as *StackOverflow* and *quora* compared to other Python libraries. In this chapter, we shall cover how to unleash the power of *Pandas*, primarily to do wonderful visualization.

Structure

In this chapter, we will cover the following topics:

- Introduction to Pandas plotting

- Pandas plotting functions

- Pandas modules and toolkits

- Examples and case studies for various types of charts using Pandas

- Pandas resources

Objective

This chapter aims to give a basic introduction to Pandas to experiment with various data visualization elements such as charts and graphs. We will also touch upon details of how to use *Pandas* elements for effective visualization. We shall start with simple *Pandas* and explore the libraries and toolkits available before trying out some of the important charts and graphs covered in earlier chapters. We shall conclude the chapter with some examples to try out and resources to consume.

Introduction to Pandas plotting

Pandas is a leading Python library used extensively for various data analysis, data exploration, data cleansing, data transformation, and data visualization activities needed to work with data in Python. Pandas, *NumPy,* and *SciPy* give all the key functions needed for various algorithmic operations as they give a lot of functions in data structures, algorithms, and scientific calculations. For data science, artificial intelligence, and machine learning needs, Pandas is one of the preferred tools for data operations with large datasets.

Figure 5.1: *The Pandas logo*

Wes McKinney is the originator of *Pandas*. He started building a tool for high-performance financial data analysis in 2008. A decision was made to make Pandas open source, and it has moved from strength to strength. The origin of the name is supposed to have emerged from **Panel Data.**

Pandas features and benefits

Pandas library uses a key concept known as *dataframes.* Diverse data formats such as a flat-file, comma-separated-values, excel, or a database is loaded into a dataframe, and various data exploration and manipulation tasks are done. Pandas is a powerful tool for data exploration, data manipulation, and data creation. We can do this using very simple commands. The operations include append, insert, drop, group by, join, merge, cut, factorize, melt, and concatenate, to name a few. For data, wrangling functions exist for filling, imputing, or replacing null or other types of data elements. Some of the key benefits we can leverage with *Pandas* are as follows:

- We can use extensive indexing options available in a dataframe
- We can leverage rapid read and write choices of various file formats by leveraging high-performance in-memory Pandas data structures
- We can leverage the power of data management and easy handling of missing data for efficient data handling
- We can shape and reshape the datasets and pivot the data for various purposes
- We can use labels for slicing, indexing, and subsetting of data and datasets
- We can perform efficient data structure management through insertion and deletion
- We can benefit from easy management between datasets with a function such as a group by and by merging and joining datasets
- We can leverage hierarchical axis indexing to perform quicker data analytics
- We can build various statistical functions easily, such as date range, frequency, linear regression, lagging, and other functions.
- We can perform a very good data filtering

For plotting, the pandas' library uses *matplotlib* to build upon it. *Pandas* have simple plotting functions for data management and data visualization. The functions are very useful for exploratory data analysis and good visualization. However, the library is not very extensive like some other libraries with beautiful visualization features. *Pandas* is a very good tool for exploratory data analysis leveraging the real power of *Pandas,* which is for data analysis aspects using *Python.*

Let us see some of the basics of *Pandas* from a plotting aspect. This chapter shall not cover data analysis and management aspects of *Pandas*. This can be seen through the information available at the landing site for *Pandas* at **https://pandas.pydata.org/.**

> **Note:** We shall be referring to dataframe extensively in this chapter and throughout this book. A dataframe is a two-dimensional labeled data structure of potentially different data types. It can be a Structured Query Language (SQL) table, a spreadsheet, a structured file such as a comma-separated value file, or a dictionary of objects. Data is arranged in a two-dimensional structure in a tabular fashion like SQL – rows and columns.

Pandas plotting functions

We can group the plotting functions available in *Pandas* into two groups, **pandas. plotting** and **DataFrame.plot**. **DataFrame.plot** is used mainly for plotting the dataframe data associated with the plot function **Pandas.plotting** for some unique plotting functions.

Let us see the key functions available in each of these groups.

Dataframe.plot

DataFrame.plot is used extensively for quick exploratory data analysis in Python. Let us see the key functions available in **DataFrame.plot**:

Function	Purpose
DataFrame. boxplot([column, by, ax, …])	Used for plotting a standard box plot from dataframe columns. Parameters are passed to configure the plot. There is a subtle difference between *DataFrame.plot.box* and *DataFrame.boxplot*.
DataFrame.hist([column, by, grid, …])	Used for plotting a histogram of the dataframes. There is a subtle difference between *DataFrame.plot.hist* and *DataFrame .hist*.
DataFrame.plot([x, y, kind, ax, ….])	This is the main *dataframe* plotting function/access method. We can pass the type of plot we want to leverage by passing it to the kind parameter.
DataFrame.plot.area([x, y])	Used to draw an area plot. For a stacked area plot, we need to pass the relevant parameter.
DataFrame.plot.bar([x, y])	Used for plotting a standard vertical bar plot. Parameters are passed to configure the plot.
DataFrame.plot.barh([x, y])	Used for plotting a standard horizontal bar plot. Parameters are passed to configure the plot.
DataFrame.plot. box([by])	Used for plotting a standard box plot. Parameters are passed to configure the plot.
DataFrame.plot. density([bw_method, ind])	Used for plotting a standard Gaussian Kernel-based Density Plot.
DataFrame.plot. hexbin(x, y[, C, …])	Used for plotting a standard hexagonal binning plot. This is a type of histogram chart shown in a hexagonal bin.
DataFrame.plot. hist([by, bins])	Used for plotting a standard histogram plot. The bins parameter is used for the number of elements to be grouped in a bin.
DataFrame.plot.kde([bw_ method, ind])	Used for plotting a standard Gaussian Kernel-based Kernel Density Estimate Plot.

`DataFrame.plot.line([x, y])`	Used for plotting a standard Line Chart/Plot of a dataframe or a series in Pandas. Parameters are passed to configure the plot.
`DataFrame.plot.pie(**kwargs)`	Used for plotting a standard pie chart of a dataframe. Parameters are passed to configure the plot.
`DataFrame.plot.scatter(x, y[, s, c])`	Used for plotting a scatter plot. Parameters are passed to configure varying marker point sizes and colors.

Table 5.1: Pandas library – key functions for plotting

Pandas.plotting functions

Pandas.plotting functions are used for specific statistical and quantitative analysis related to plotting in Python. Let us see the key functions available in **Pandas. plotting**.

Function	Purpose
pandas.plotting. andrews_curves	This function is used to create the plot of *Andrews curves*. This plot is useful in multivariate data cluster visualization. Andrews curve is built on a mathematical function using trigonometric functions.
pandas.plotting. autocorrelation_plot	This function is used for the autocorrelation of data passed as a parameter. This plot renders a correlation plot with confidence bands between 95 and 99 percent. This gives an inference about the time series data being analyzed.
pandas.plotting. bootstrap_plot	We can use Bootstrap plot to render mean, median, and mid-range statistics summary. It uses random sampling with replacement and generates the plots for mean/median and midrange for any sized sample.
pandas.plotting. boxplot	This function is used to make a box-and-whisker plot from dataframe columns. This plot can be optionally grouped with other columns as well.
pandas.plotting. lag_plot	This function is used for creating lag plots. Lag plots are used to look for patterns in time series data. If there is a pattern seen in a lag plot, it can be inferred as not having any randomness but having a cyclical nature or other aspects.
pandas.plotting. parallel_coordinates	Used largely in time series visualizations, *parallel coordinates* are useful to visualize multi-dimensional data. Vertical and equally spaced parallel lines are drawn to show points in an n-dimensional space. In a way, it's a 2-dimensional perspective of a multi-dimensional dataset.

pandas.plotting. plot_params	This is a function for storing pandas plotting options in a canonical format.
pandas.plotting. radviz	*RadViz* is another way to render multi-dimensional data in a 2-dimensional view. Each data series is represented as a 2-dimensional format using space and dimension. Closely correlated data appear closely as a cluster.
pandas.plotting. scatter_matrix	It is a statistical comparison plot. A scatter matrix displays a matrix of scatter plots of two elements being compared. Based on the number of correlated columns in a *dataframe* (a.k.a, elements in a matrix), the size of the scatter matrix is shown in an NxN matrix. The diagonal comparison of the same elements is shown as the histogram of the data. Rest is shown as scatter plots.
pandas.plotting.table	It is a helper function to show the *dataframe* or a *series* as a *Matplotlib.table* for legends and graphical rendering.

Table 5.2: Pandas plotting library – key functions for plotting

Pandas modules and extensions

Pandas library has become very popular over the past decade. Due to its open-source nature and ease of extension, many tools and libraries have been developed over the past decade. Let us see the important module evolving or inspired by *Pandas*.

Pandas library has hundreds of utility functions, and all of them are available as a reference at **https://pandas.pydata.org/docs/reference/index.html**. They are categorized under the following categories:

Pandas standard modules and functions		
Panel	Index objects	Date offsets
Window	Group by	Resampling
Style	**Plotting**	General utility
Extensions	*Series*	*dataframe*
Input/output	Pandas arrays	General functions

Table 5.3: Pandas standard modules and functions

For this chapter, we shall be focusing primarily on the functions related to plotting and key functions in the *dataframe*.

Pandas extensions

Pandas extensions are available in multiple disciplines and capabilities, given their popularity. Pandas library is extended in visualization, data science, statistics, financial data analysis, and high-performance computing. Let us see some of the most popular extensions or libraries.

Library/ Extension	Purpose
Altair	A friendly, statistically inclined declarative visualization library. This tool has some visualization functions available to use with Pandas in Python. We shall cover some of the elements in a future chapter.
bokeh	Bokeh is an elegant and efficient, interactive visualization library for large datasets. It is useful for native apps using advanced web features. We shall cover some of the elements in a future chapter in detail.
seaborn	Seaborn is the favorite among data visualization enthusiasts using Python. It is used for creating very impactful, visual, and attractive visualization. It uses statistical models and performs aggregation and visualization to make the visualization very impactful. We shall be covering this in the next chapter in detail.
plotnine	Based on the Grammar of Graphics plot or ggplot2, it gives a generic way to render any plot simply.
Plotly	Plotly is an interactive library that can be leveraged to build interactive, animated visualization that is impactful and attractive in either a 2-dimensional or 3-dimensional manner.
pandas-datareader	It's a great helper function to read various types of open source and unstructured data to be read into a pandas dataframe. Most of the data reader functions are available for the financial services industry.
geopandas	Geopandas extends pandas to use geographic information along with support for geometric operations. This library is useful for working with maps and generate visualizations with maps.
Statsmodels	It is the most widely used and prominent library for statistics and econometric modeling in Python. Statsmodel uses Pandas for underlying computational capabilities.
sklearn-pandas	This is used for leveraging pandas dataframes in the machine learning pipelines for data science needs.

Table 5.4: Pandas extensions and other libraries

Now let us get on with practical examples of how to use Pandas for plotting purposes.

Examples for various types of charts using Pandas

We had an introduction to full Python programs that could be executed independently when we used Matplotlib. We have the overall solution notebook to refer to as well.

For this chapter, we shall be taking a Jupyter Notebook-centric approach. Before we start execution, we need to have the following installed.

> **Note:** The installation commands and approach may vary per operating system and version of Python we may be using. Please refer to the standard sites hosting the latest versions of the packages, such as https://www.python.org/, https://pypi.org/, or http://www.anaconda.com.

Library	Installation command

NumPy	*We can add NumPy to a requirements.txt file and execute*
	
	 `pip install -r requirements.txt`
	
	 or use
	
	 `pip install numpy`

Pandas	*We can add Pandas to a requirements.txt file and execute*
	
	 `pip install -r requirements.txt`
	
	 or use
	
	 `pip install pandas`

Matplotlib	*We can add matplotlib and its dependencies (Python, NumPy, setuptools, cycler, dateutil, kiwisolver, pillow, pyparsing) to a requirements.txt file and execute*
	
	 `pip install -r requirements.txt`
	
	 or use
	
	 `pip install matplotlib`

Jupyter Notebook	*We can install Jupyter Notebook by the installation of Jupyter Lab through Anaconda or PIP*
	
	 `conda install -c conda-forge jupyterlab`
	
	 or use
	
	 `pip install jupyterlab`
	
	 Once installed, we can start Jupyter Notebook by clicking the icon in Windows or MacOS or running the `jupyterlab` *command in the command prompt from the folder containing the executable or batch file.*

Table 5.5: Pandas Installation Steps

Let us start with the basics and simplest chart – line chart. For this, we shall be loading a simple CSV file that contains the global mobile phone market share for 2020 every month.

Exercise 5-1: Line Chart Example of a Mobile Marketshare Dataset

```
In [1]: ▶ import numpy as np
          import pandas as pd
          import matplotlib.pyplot as plt
          import warnings
          warnings.filterwarnings("ignore")
```

```
In [2]: ▶ mobile = pd.read_csv('mobilephonemktshare2020.csv')
          print(mobile.head(2))
```

```
        Date  Samsung  Apple  Huawei  Xiaomi   Oppo  Mobicel  Motorola   LG \
0    2019-10    31.49  22.09   10.02    7.79   4.10     3.15      2.41  2.4
1    2019-11    31.36  22.90   10.18    8.16   4.42     3.41      2.40  2.4

     Others  Realme  Google  Nokia  Lenovo  OnePlus  Sony   Asus
0      9.51    0.54    2.35   0.95    0.96     0.70  0.84   0.74
1      9.10    0.78    0.66   0.97    0.97     0.73  0.83   0.75
```

```
In [3]: ▶ mobile.plot(y='Samsung', x='Date')
          plt.show()
```

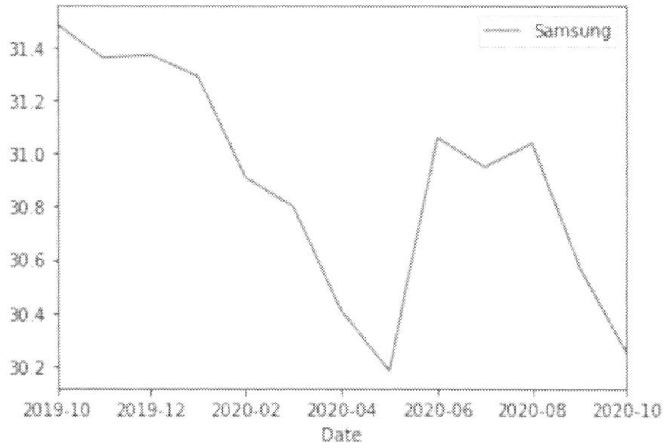

Figure 5.2: A Pandas sample Jupyter Notebook output – exercise 5-1

As we can see, we are loading the data to a dataframe named mobile, and we are plotting the values of 'Samsung' against the date/month value loaded in the dataframe.

Let us take it a bit further and try other options. Let us add an index for the X-axis by giving month names instead of the dates and add more line charts for other brands.

Exercise 5-2: Line Chart Example - Multiple values of a Mobile Marketshare Dataset

```
mobile.index=['Oct','Nov','Dec','Jan','Feb','Mar','Apr','May','Jun','Jul','Aug','Sep','Oct']
mobile.plot(y=['Samsung','Apple','Huawei','Others','Xiaomi'], x='Date',figsize=(12,8))
plt.show()
```

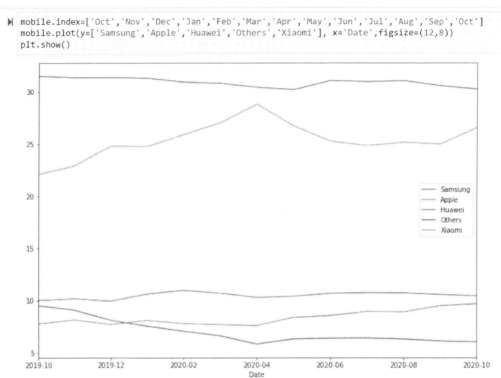

Figure 5.3: Pandas line charts Jupyter Notebook output – exercise 5-2

Let us explore some subplots options. This is achieved using the following command:

```
mobile.plot(subplots=True, layout=(4,4), figsize=(20,10))
```

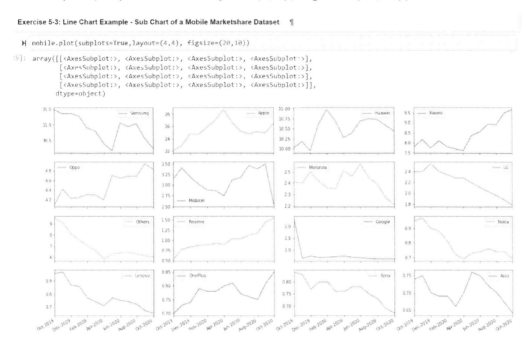

Figure 5.4: *Pandas subplots Jupyter Notebook output – exercise 5-3*

Bar charts

Let us explore how to create a bar chart in *Pandas*. This is achieved using the following command. We need to pass the chart as **'bar'** as the default plot option is a *line* chart in *pandas*. In addition to the kind parameter, we need to pass the values for the x-axis and y-axis. We are passing the value of one of the mobile brands and are passing the same data fields.

mobile.plot(kind='bar', y='OnePlus', x='Date')

plt.show()

We get the following output for the program rendered:

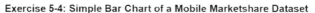

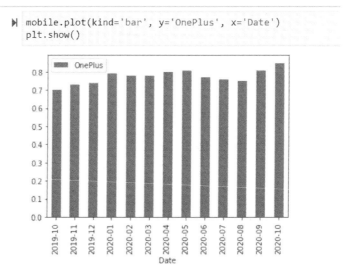

Figure 5.5: *Pandas bar charts Jupyter Notebook output – exercise 5-4*

If we want to get multiple bars in a bar chart, we can choose to send the parameters or use the entire dataset to generate the bar chart.

We can leverage the following command:

```
mobile.plot(kind='bar', y=['Samsung','Apple','Xiaomi','Others'],
x='Date', width=0.9,figsize=(20,10))

plt.show()
```

This will give us the following output:

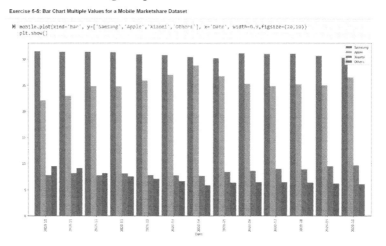

Figure 5.6: *Pandas multiple bar charts Jupyter Notebook output – exercise 5-5*

Horizontal bar chart

All we need to do is to change the parameter **kind='bar'to kind='barh'** for getting the output desired. We can execute the following code:

```
mobile.plot(kind='barh', y=['Samsung','Apple','Xiaomi','Others'],
x='Date', width=0.9,figsize=(20,10))

plt.show()
```

This will give us the following output:

Exercise 5-6: Horizontal Bar Chart of a Mobile Marketshare Dataset

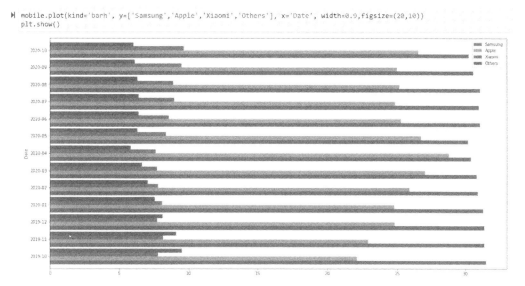

Figure 5.7: *Pandas horizontal bar charts Jupyter Notebook output – exercise 5-6*

Pie chart

All we need to do is update the parameter *kind='pie'* for getting the output desired. Let us execute the following code:

mobile.plot(kind='pie',y='Samsung')

We will get the following output. For better pie chart renditions, it is advised to leverage the advanced features available in *matplotlib,* as seen in the previous chapter. The pie chart in Pandas does not have advanced features.

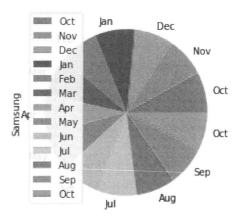

Figure 5.8: *Pandas pie chart output – exercise 5-7*

Let us combine the three charts by seeing the relevance of the dataset we are exploring:

```
01.   mobile.index=['Oct-2019','Nov-2019','Dec-2019','Jan-2020','Feb-2020','Mar-2020','Apr-2020',
02.         'May-2020','Jun-2020','Jul-2020','Aug-2020','Sep-2020','Oct-2020']
03.   mobile.plot(y=['Samsung','Apple','Xiaomi','Oppo','LG','Motorola'], subplots=True, layout=(2,3), figsize=(20,5))
04.   mobile.plot(kind='bar',y=['Samsung','Apple','Xiaomi','Oppo','LG','Motorola'], subplots=True, layout=(2,3), figsize=(20,5))
05.   mobile.plot(kind='pie',y=['Samsung','Apple','Xiaomi','Oppo','Others','Motorola'],
06.         subplots=True, layout=(2,3), figsize=(20,15))
07.   plt.legend(loc='lower right')
```

Figure 5.9: *Pandas combination of line, bar, and pie charts code – exercise 5-8*

We get the following output for this code:

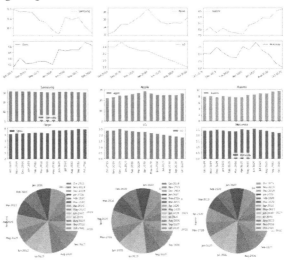

Figure 5.10: *Pandas combination of line, bar, and pie charts output – exercise 5-8*

Scatter plot

As covered earlier, the scatter plot is very useful for statistical visualization. We need to pass the dataframe with styling features such as markers, size, and Pandas automatically render the rest. If we take the following code, we create three columns in a pandas dataframe for scatter, and we render it with a marker type of a '+' sign.

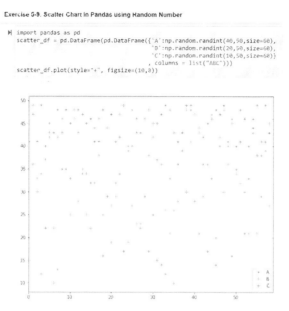

```
Exercise 5-9. Scatter Chart in Pandas using Random Number

N import pandas as pd
  scatter_df = pd.DataFrame(pd.DataFrame({'A':np.random.randint(40,50,size=60),
                                          'B':np.random.randint(20,50,size=60),
                                          'C':np.random.randint(10,50,size=60)}
                                          , columns = list("ABC")))
  scatter_df.plot(style="+", figsize=(10,8))
```

Figure 5.11: *Pandas scatter plot Jupyter Notebook example – exercise 5-9*

Exercises 5-10 to 5-40 – An exploration of the stock market using Pandas charts

In this exercise, we shall be covering all the charts in Pandas using a real-life example – of stock market data. We shall be using the *Yahoo! Finance* dataset for some of the key performer stocks for various visualization purposes. We use the *Yfinance* Python library provided by *Yahoo!* for this. In future case studies in this chapter, we shall be using similar datasets for our visualization.

Let us begin with a simple data collection task. We will use *Yahoo!* APIs to collect daily stock market-adjusted price data for a set of stocks. We shall be storing the data in a Pandas dataframe for our analysis and visualization needs.

1. As a first step, we shall load the libraries.
2. We shall specify a list of stock symbols we would like to load data for.
3. Specify the start and end date.

4. Use the *pandas_datareader* library to load the data into a dataset.

5. The output shows records for 2012 days of the past 8 years for processing.

Exercise 5-10: Loading stock market data from Yahoo Charts

First - Let us download the libaries

Use Pandas Data Reader for reading Data from Yahoo! Finance Specify start and end date for the stock charts and download the charts

```
import pandas as pd
import numpy as np
import matplotlib.pyplot as plt
import math
import warnings
warnings.filterwarnings("ignore")
from pandas_datareader import data as pdr
import yfinance as yf
yf.pdr_override()
```

```
symbols = ['AMZN','AAPL', 'GOOG', 'FB', 'MSFT', 'NFLX', 'NVDA','TSLA','DPZ','FICO','AVGO','URI','TDG']
start = '2012-09-01'
end = '2020-09-01'
data = pdr.get_data_yahoo(symbols, start, end)['Adj Close']
data.describe()
```

```
[*********************100%***********************]  13 of 13 completed
```

	AAPL	AMZN	AVGO	DPZ	FB	FICO	GOOG	MSFT	NFLX	NVDA	TDG
count	2012.000000	2012.000000	2012.000000	2012.000000	2012.000000	2012.000000	2012.000000	2012.000000	2012.000000	2012.000000	2012.000000
mean	35.069616	988.804121	153.908910	165.002496	121.431764	150.834026	827.506713	72.711162	172.873977	110.336733	233.617882
std	19.601968	718.837569	90.686348	96.296146	61.032603	107.671361	322.673844	47.179502	135.006095	107.302137	133.812497
min	12.116260	220.600006	25.191299	31.235662	17.730000	40.410217	322.361622	22.131687	7.685714	10.466008	70.786834
25%	21.750662	351.412498	64.175934	72.542252	74.415001	60.809282	542.719849	37.727328	60.736786	18.160028	136.113750
50%	28.342918	780.369995	145.615372	144.228447	120.530000	118.798046	768.950012	53.483440	117.105000	61.466919	199.315681
75%	44.013577	1656.309967	227.053902	244.101964	174.219897	197.799995	1102.467468	102.246502	302.814987	187.785053	306.336260
max	128.817749	3450.959961	344.013641	418.670544	303.910004	441.720001	1652.380005	228.312271	548.729980	534.819846	657.929993

Figure 5.12: Pandas Jupyter Notebook example for loading Yahoo! finance data

Now, we shall process the data loaded onto the dataset for exploratory data analysis and visualization purposes. We can start with a simple line chart using the plot function:

Exercise 5-11: Let us display the line chart of data downloaded from Yahoo Charts

```
data.plot(figsize=(16,10))
```

```
<AxesSubplot:xlabel='Date'>
```

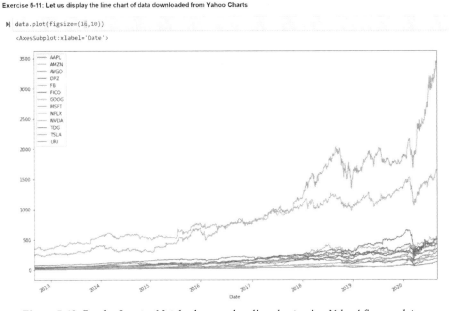

Figure 5.13: Pandas Jupyter Notebook example – line chart using Yahoo! finance data

Let us generate an overall correlation of stocks for the data downloaded. We use the **corr()** function that can be saved in a new dataframe **corr_rest**. Pairwise correlation of the stocks can be done using the following code snippet:

```
1. pair_value = corr_rest.abs().unstack()
2. pair_value.sort_values(ascending = True)
```

Exercise 5-12 - Data processing

Let us correlate the data using DataFrame.corr() function and assign to a new DataFrame

```
M corr_rest = data.corr()
  corr_rest
```

	AAPL	AMZN	AVGO	DPZ	FB	FICO	GOOG	MSFT	NFLX	NVDA	TDG	TSLA	URI
AAPL	1.000000	0.941825	0.869874	0.925664	0.874702	0.941934	0.912561	0.968345	0.903379	0.928474	0.878745	0.846840	0.722582
AMZN	0.941825	1.000000	0.914785	0.975635	0.913897	0.948003	0.960181	0.972461	0.980871	0.951397	0.890527	0.737193	0.740341
AVGO	0.869874	0.914785	1.000000	0.941411	0.971977	0.906982	0.965572	0.902762	0.911912	0.881328	0.915194	0.611212	0.796444
DPZ	0.925664	0.975635	0.941411	1.000000	0.937309	0.929845	0.966668	0.955451	0.970824	0.941431	0.886040	0.712032	0.760845
FB	0.874702	0.913897	0.971977	0.937309	1.000000	0.882064	0.969550	0.890021	0.910766	0.906536	0.877610	0.668413	0.826285
FICO	0.941934	0.948003	0.906982	0.929845	0.882064	1.000000	0.933964	0.983702	0.917907	0.868417	0.963365	0.694184	0.673288
GOOG	0.912561	0.960181	0.965572	0.966668	0.969550	0.933964	1.000000	0.946714	0.953789	0.932810	0.925310	0.678593	0.808889
MSFT	0.968345	0.972461	0.902762	0.955451	0.890021	0.983702	0.946714	1.000000	0.943997	0.916948	0.929121	0.760238	0.706073
NFLX	0.903379	0.980871	0.911912	0.970824	0.910766	0.917907	0.953789	0.943997	1.000000	0.934359	0.879105	0.674657	0.774872
NVDA	0.928474	0.951397	0.881328	0.941431	0.906536	0.868417	0.932810	0.916948	0.934359	1.000000	0.804529	0.768915	0.816514
TDG	0.878745	0.890527	0.915194	0.886040	0.877610	0.963365	0.925310	0.929121	0.879105	0.804529	1.000000	0.573872	0.703383
TSLA	0.846840	0.737193	0.611212	0.712032	0.668413	0.694184	0.678593	0.760238	0.674657	0.768915	0.573872	1.000000	0.535212
URI	0.722582	0.740341	0.796444	0.760845	0.826285	0.673288	0.808889	0.706073	0.774872	0.816514	0.703383	0.535212	1.000000

***Figure 5.14:** Pandas Jupyter Notebook example – data correlation*

Exercise 5-13: Building a scatter matrix from the dataset

Let us generate a scatter matrix based on the correlation data we produced and see how the data points are correlated and scattered. We can do this with the following simple lines of code:

```
1. from pandas.plotting import scatter_matrix
2. # Let us plot the Scatter Matrix for the Correlation
Dataframe created
3. scatter_matrix(corr_rest, figsize=(16,12), alpha=0.3)
```

A scatter matrix produces a correlation scatter matrix for all elements compared and a histogram, where the comparison is between the same variables. This can be seen in the following plot produced as a result. As we can see, the stocks are high performing and are zoned near the higher end of the spectrum with a right leaned skewness.

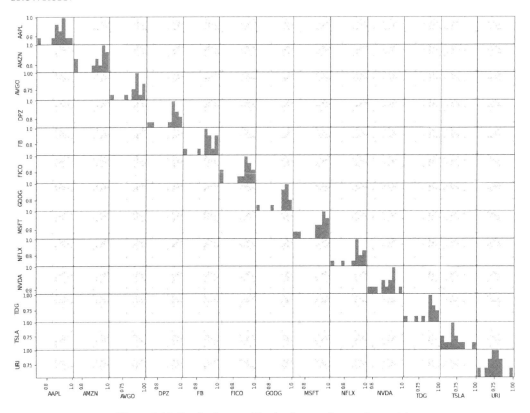

Figure 5.15: *Pandas Jupyter Notebook example – scatter matrix*

Let us analyze the returns made by the stocks. This can be seen using a simple dataframe function *pct_change()* as it uses the daily data collected per stock to create a daily percentage in the stock values. We shall be using this for further analysis and visualization in the next few exercises.

```
1. # Let us calculate the daily percent-
   age change for each of the stock
2. # Use pct_change() function available in Pandas
3. for  symbol in symbols:
4.     returns = data.pct_change()
5. returns.head()
```

As we can see, we have some NaN (Not a Number) values for some of the rows. To ignore this data (especially for weekend days when no trading took place), we can use the **dropna()** function available in *Pandas*. If we need to fill data, we can use other functions such as **fillna()** with various methods and value-based filling options.

```
#Let us drop the NA values from the Dataframe
returns_na =returns.dropna()
returns_na.head()
```

	AAPL	AMZN	AVGO	DPZ	FB	FICO	GOOG	MSFT	NFLX	NVDA	TDG	TSLA	URI
Date													
2012-09-04	0.014627	-0.001571	-0.018594	0.008465	-0.018272	0.039803	-0.005912	-0.013952	-0.063463	-0.053457	0.000361	-0.013324	0.065305
2012-09-05	-0.007022	-0.006697	-0.019783	-0.011471	0.047941	-0.009007	-0.000470	0.000000	-0.017343	0.003012	-0.011827	-0.007107	-0.001453
2012-09-06	0.009012	0.020957	0.040648	0.017549	0.020452	0.027052	0.027442	0.031589	0.030750	0.030781	0.024666	0.021833	0.073611
2012-09-07	0.006166	0.030870	-0.011199	0.005842	0.001055	-0.009296	0.009651	-0.012759	0.000177	-0.024035	0.022221	0.028021	0.025203
2012-09-10	-0.026013	-0.007911	-0.033149	-0.001936	-0.008957	0.001564	-0.007619	-0.007431	-0.013060	-0.008955	-0.014352	-0.067462	0.002379

Figure 5.16: Pandas Jupyter Notebook example – dropping null values

Exercise 5-14: Generating a stock returns graph

We can create a simple stock returns graph using a plot function applied on the dataset we just created – **returns_na.plot()**. We can use the legend to specify the color coding, font size, and other parameters as we deem necessary.

```
1.  #Let us plot the Returns Plot
2.  returns_na.plot(legend=True,fontsize=16,figsize=(20,12))
```

We get the following output on executing the code:

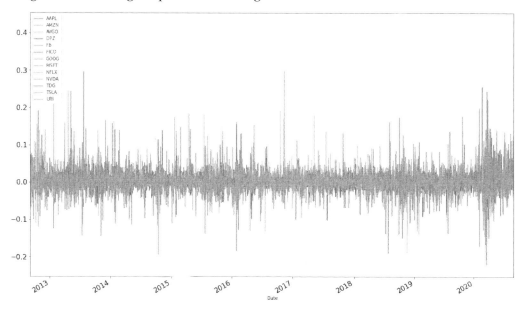

Figure 5.17: Pandas Jupyter Notebook example – stock returns graph

Exercise 5-15

Let us generate a histogram plot for all the stock returns. This can be done using the following piece of code in our Jupyter Notebook:

```
1. #Let us plot a histo-
   gram plot with a bin size of 30 for each stock (subplots=True)
```

```
2. returns_na.plot(kind="hist",bins=30, alpha=0.6, subplots=True,ti-
   tle="Returns of Stock",layout=(5, 3),legend=True, fontsize=24,fig-
   size=(30,32))
```

We get the following histogram output for the code in Jupyter Notebook:

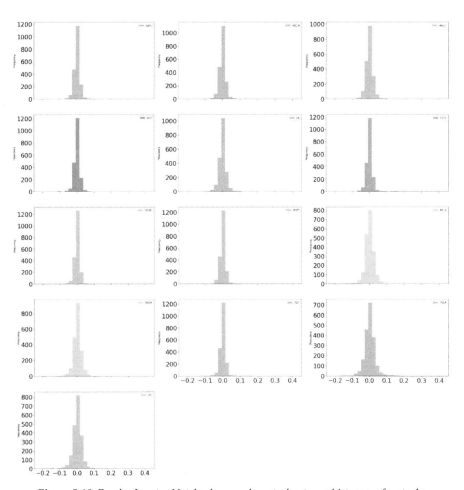

Figure 5.18: *Pandas Jupyter Notebook example – stock returns histogram for stocks*

Exercise 5-16: Histogram of all stocks

Let us combine all histograms in a single master histogram by disabling the subplots option in the previous exercise:

```
1.  #Increase the bin size and prepare a big Histogram
    (subplots=False)
2.  returns_na.plot(kind="hist", bins=360, alpha=0.4,
    subplots=False, title="Returns of Stock",layout=(5, 3),
    legend=True, figsize=(20,16))
```

We get the following histogram output for the code in Jupyter Notebook:

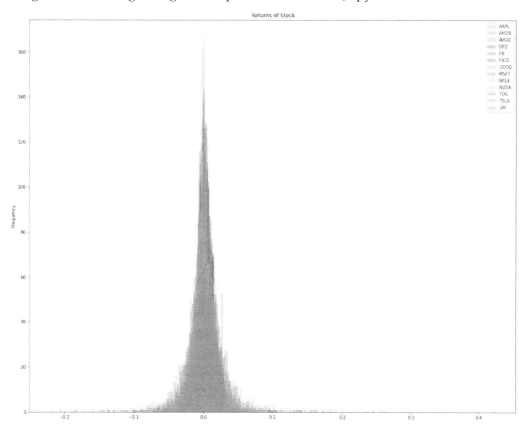

Figure 5.19: *Pandas Jupyter Notebook example – master histogram for all stock returns*

Exercise 5-17: Individual line plot of all stocks

Let us generate an individual plot for all the stock prices. This can be done using the following piece of code in our Jupyter Notebook:

```
1.  # Let us plot a line chart of all returns
2.  data.plot(kind="line",      subplots=True,      grid=True,      ti-
    tle="Stock   Performance",layout=(8,   2),   sharex=True,   sharey=-
    False, legend=True, figsize=(20,32))
```

We get the following output for the code in Jupyter Notebook:

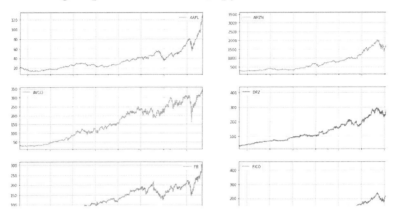

Figure 5.20: Pandas Jupyter Notebook example – line chart for all stock returns

Exercise 5-18 - Generating a simple HexBin chart comparing two stocks

Let us generate a simple *HexBin* chart comparing two stocks – *Amazon* and *Microsoft:*

```
1.  #Let us build a HexBin Chart comparing Amazon and Microsoft
2.  ax = data.plot.hexbin(x='AMZN', y='MSFT', gridsize=20,sharex=-
    False)
```

We get the following output for the code in Jupyter Notebook:

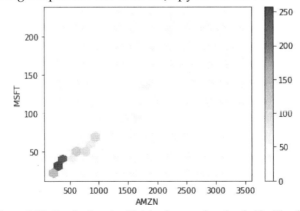

Figure 5.21: Pandas Jupyter Notebook example –simple HexBin chart

Exercise 5-19: Subplots of HexBin charts comparing stocks

Let us generate a matrix of *HexBin* charts comparing two stocks using random stock combination and colormaps.

The following code has two functions: generating a random colormap and choosing three stocks from the stocklist. These stocks are used for generating *HexBin* chart comparisons.

```
1.  import random
2.  fig, axes = plt.subplots(nrows=3, ncols=4)
3.  #Let us build a random HexBin Chart using unique Color maps
4.  def randomCmap():
5.      cmap=np.random.choice(plt.colormaps())
6.      return cmap
7.  def retcombo():
8.      sampled_list = random.sample(symbols, 3)
9.      return sampled_list
10.
11. for i, ax in enumerate(axes.reshape(-1)):
12.     sampled_list=retcombo()
13.         ax = returns_na.plot.hexbin(x=sampled_list[0], y=sampled_
    list[1],C=sampled_list[2],ax=axes.flat[i],figsize=(20,12),reduce_C_
    function=np.sum,gridsize=20,cmap=randomCmap(),sharex=False)
14. fig.tight_layout()
```

We get the following output for the code in Jupyter Notebook:

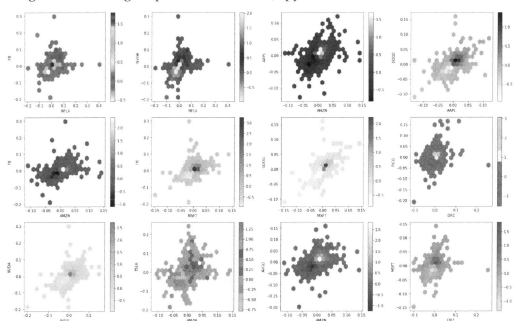

Figure 5.22: Pandas Jupyter Notebook example –
HexBin chart of various stocks using random colormaps

Exercise 5-20: Generating a density chart for stock values

Let us generate a matrix of *kernel density estimate* charts analyzing the stock data value and stock returns dataframes created earlier.

Following code has three functions – one for generating a standard kernel density estimate plot for stock values, one for stock returns, and third for a density plotting method by giving a value **(bw_method=3)**.

```
1. import random
2. data.plot.kde(figsize=(10,30),sharex=False)
3. returns_na.plot.kde(figsize=(10,30),sharex=False)
4. returns_na.plot.kde(bw_method=3,figsize=(20,10),sharex=False)
5. fig.tight_layout()
```

We get the following output for line-4 of the code in Jupyter Notebook. Can we guess how the first two density plots look? The solution is given in the Jupyter Notebook that will be shared as a link with the book.

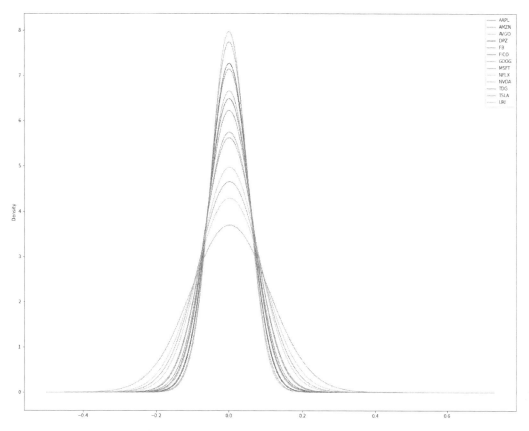

Figure 5.23: *Pandas Jupyter Notebook example – KDEPlot (Kernel Density Estimate)*

Exercise 5-21: Bootstrap plot for stocks

Let us generate a matrix of *Bootstrap Plots* for analyzing the stock data value and stock returns dataframes created earlier. We shall intersperse the bootstrap plots with a unique colormap bar.

```
1.  import pandas.plotting
2.  import matplotlib as mplt
3.  import matplotlib.pyplot as plt
4.
5.  #Let us get a colormap perspective by passing a parameter
6.  def plot_colorMaps(cmap):
7.      fig, axes = plt.subplots(figsize=(4,0.4))
```

```
8.      color_map = plt.get_cmap(cmap)
9.      mplt.colorbar.ColorbarBase(axes, cmap=color_map, orientation
   = ‹horizontal›)
10.     plt.show()
11.
12. # Get all Colormaps and set the index to zero
13. cmaps=plt.colormaps()
14. count=0
15. # Generate a bootstrap plot for the stock and re-
    turns for all symbols
16. for symbol in symbols:
17.     print(‹Bootstrap Plot for›,symbol)
18.     pd.plotting.bootstrap_plot(data[symbol])
19.     pd.plotting.bootstrap_plot(returns_na[symbol])
20.     cmap_id = cmaps[count]
21.     count = count + 1
22.     plot_colorMaps(cmap_id)
```

We get the following output for one of the iterations in for loop in Jupyter Notebook. Can we guess how the full output looks? The solution is given in the notebook link with the book.

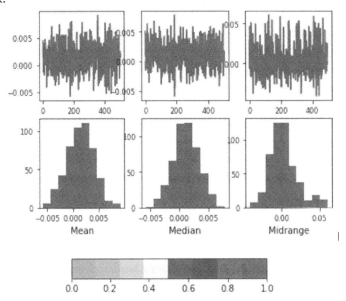

Figure 5.24: *Pandas Jupyter Notebook example – bootstrap plot*

Exercise 5-22: Autocorrelation plot for a stock

Let us generate an *autocorrelation plot* for analyzing the stock data value and stock returns dataframes created earlier. We shall use the *Apple* dataset captured through *Yfinance* call for this. The following lines of code help us do the same:

```
1. # Let us generate an autocorrelation chart for AAPL Stock
2. pd.plotting.autocorrelation_plot(data.AAPL)
```

We get the following output for one of the iterations in for loop in Jupyter Notebook:

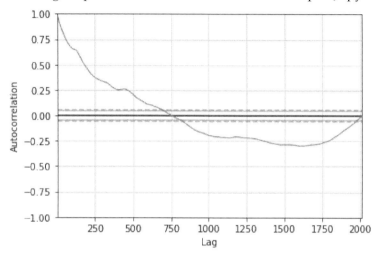

Figure 5.25: *Pandas Jupyter Notebook example – autocorrelation chart for Apple stock*

Exercise 5-23: Question – What will be the outcome?

Take the following piece of code for stock returns. How will the output look? The solution is given in the Jupyter Notebook link shared with this book.

```
1. # Let us generate  a histogram chart for all stocks
2. returns_na.hist(bins=15, figsize=(16,12))
```

Think about the output before we take a look at the solution.

Exercise 5-24: Box plots for stocks

Take the following piece of code for creating a box plot for stock performance. We pass the stock data and set the visualization figure size.

```
1.  # Let us generate a box plot for all stocks
2.  pd.plotting.boxplot(data,figsize=(15,10))
```

We get the following output in Jupyter Notebook:

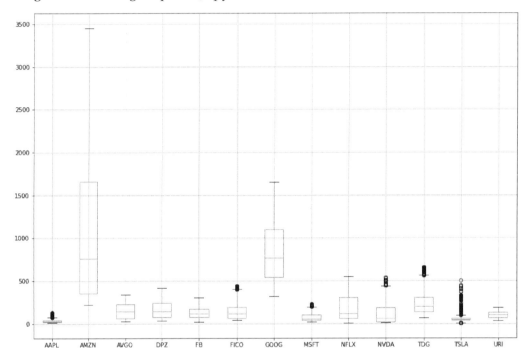

Figure 5.26: *Pandas Jupyter Notebook example – box plot for stock performance*

Exercise 5-25: Box plots for stock returns

Take the following piece of code for creating a box plot for stock returns. We pass the stock data and set the visualization figure size.

```
1.  # Let us generate a box plot for all stocks
2.  returns_na.boxplot(data,figsize=(15,10))
```

We get the following output in Jupyter Notebook:

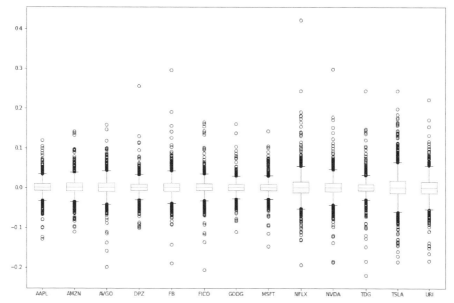

Figure 5.27: *Pandas Jupyter Notebook example – box plot for stock returns*

Exercise 5-26: Lag plot for stocks

Take the following piece of code for creating a lag plot for stock performance. We pass the stock data and the lag parameter.

```
1.  # Let us generate a lag plot for all stocks
2.  pd.plotting.lag_plot(data, lag=1)
```

We get the following output in Jupyter Notebook:

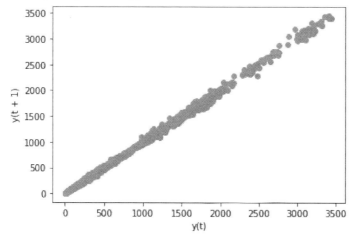

Figure 5.28: *Pandas Jupyter Notebook example – lagplot*

Exercise 5-27: Lag plot for stock returns

Take the following piece of code for creating a lag plot for stock returns. We pass the stock data and the lag parameter.

```
1.  # Let us generate a lag plot for all stocks
2.  pd.plotting.lag_plot(returns_na, lag=1)
```

Exercise 5-28: Lag plot for stock returns

Take the following piece of code for creating a lag plot for stock returns. We pass the stock data and the lag parameter.

```
1.  # Let us generate a lag plot for all stocks
2.  pd.plotting.lag_plot(returns_na.TSLA, lag=1)
```

We get the following output in Jupyter Notebook for exercises 5-27 and 5-28:

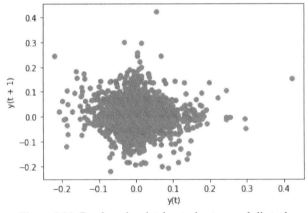

Figure 5.29: Pandas – lagplot for stock returns of all stocks

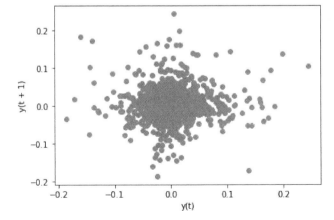

Figure 5.30: Pandas – lagplot for stock returns of Tesla

What we see is a staring similarity in terms of the lag plot in both the charts

Exercise 5-29: Calculating the total returns of the stocks

Now, let us draw some analytical insight into the performance of stocks. Let us start by calculating the high and low values of the stocks, highest and lowest returns, and the total return range.

For the total return range, we use a simple calculation:

$$Total\ Returns_{stock} = \frac{(Maximum\ Stock\ Value_{stock} - Mininum\ Stock\ Value_{stock})}{Mininum\ Stock\ Value_{stock}}$$

Note that this is one measure to see the range of the performance, and it does not showcase the number of times the stocks have multiplied from a particular point in time.

Once we create the dataframe with the analysed data, we can progress with the rest of the charts to analyse.

```
1.  import pandas as pd

2.  import os

3.  import numpy as np

4.  import matplotlib.pyplot as plt

5.  numRows = len(symbols)

6.  index =symbols

7.  bar_data=pd.DataFrame(index=np.arange(0,numRows),col-
    umns=('Stock','High','Low','MaxRet','LowRet','TotReturns'))

8.  x = 0

9.  for symbol in symbols:

10.     TotRet = ((data[symbol].max()- data[symbol].
    min()) / data[symbol].min())

11.     bar_data.loc[x] = [symbol, data[symbol].max(), data[symbol].
    min(),

12.                             returns_na[symbol].max(),returns_
    na[symbol].min(), TotRet]

13.     x = x + 1

14. bar_data.set_axis(symbols,  axis='index', inplace=True)

15. ax=bar_data['TotReturns'].plot.bar(figsize=(15,10),rot=0,sub-
    plots=True)
```

We get the following output in the Jupyter Notebook:

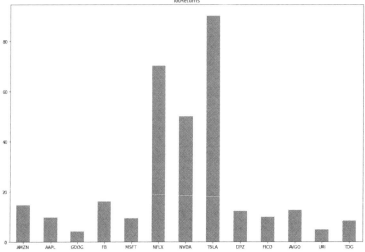

Figure 5.31: *Pandas – bar chart depicting all stock returns*

Exercise 5-30: Visualizing some area charts

Let us visualize these elements created in **bar_data** with three distinct area charts. First one is a standard chart with **stacked=True**, second a non-stacked area chart, and third one is an area plot for each of the stocks we are analysing.

1. `ax = bar_data.plot.area(figsize=(15,10),rot=0)`

2. `ax = bar_data.plot.area(figsize=(15,10),rot=0, stacked=False)`

3. `ax = bar_data.plot.area(figsize=(15,10),rot=0, subplots=True)`

We get the following output for the first two area charts:

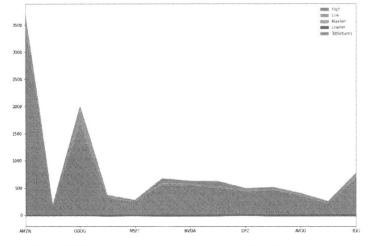

Figure 5.32: *Pandas – stacked area chart depicting all stock returns*

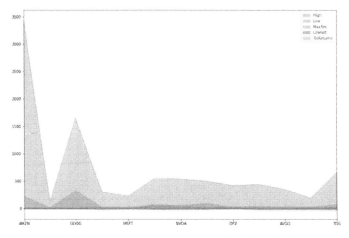

Figure 5.33: Pandas – non-stacked area chart depicting all stock returns

We get the following for the third command of subplots for each analyzed variable in the dataframe.

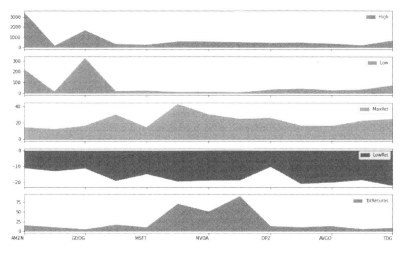

Figure 5.34: Pandas – subplots of area charts depicting all stock returns

Exercise 5-31: Visualizing some bar charts

Let us visualize these elements created in **bar_data** with two distinct bar charts. The first one is a stacked bar chart using **stacked=True**, and the second is a non-stacked bar chart for each of the stocks we are analyzing.

The following is the line of code to use for this:

```
1. bar_data_ind = pd.DataFrame(index=symbols, col-
   umns=('Stock','High','Low','MaxRet','LowRet','TotReturns'))
2. bar_data_ind = bar_data.copy()
```

```
3. bar_data_ind.set_axis(symbols, axis='index', inplace=True)

4. ax=bar_data_ind.plot.bar(figsize=(15,10),rot=0, subplots=True)

5. ax=bar_data_ind.plot.bar(figsize=(15,10),rot=0, subplots=-
   False, stacked=True) #df.plot(table=True, ax=ax)
```

We get the following output for the exercise in the Jupyter Notebook:

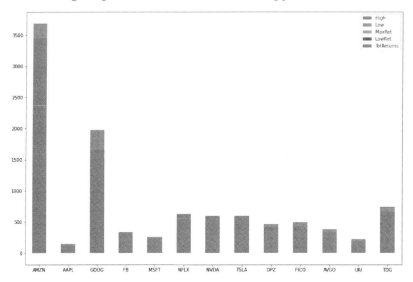

Figure 5.35: *Pandas – stacked bar chart depicting all stock returns*

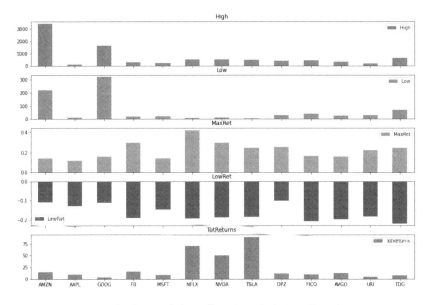

Figure 5.36: *Pandas – subplots of bar chart depicting all stock returns*

Exercise 5-32: Using a table as a legend

Now let us use the legend in the form of a table. Let us use a simple line chart for the analysis dataframe **bar_ind** and pass the legend in a table. Before we do that, let us first round the decimals to two digits, confirm the results, and then set the y-axis locations to make the graphs look better. We do this with the following piece of code. The Jupyter Notebook shows the code in two distinct cells.

```
1. bar_data.describe()
2. bar_data['Low']=bar_data['Low'].apply(lambda x:round(x,2))
3. bar_data['High']=bar_data['High'].apply(lambda x:round(x,2))
4. bar_data['MaxRet']=bar_data['MaxRet'].apply(lambda x:round(x,2))
5. bar_data['LowRet']=bar_data['LowRet'].apply(lambda x:round(x,2))
6. bar_data['TotReturns']=bar_data['TotReturns'].apply(lamb-
   da x:round(x,2))
7. bar_data.head()
8. fig, ax = plt.subplots(1, 1, figsize=(10, 8))
9. ax.xaxis.tick_top()
10. bar_data.plot(table=np.round(bar_data.T, 1), ax=ax)
11. ax.set_ylim(0, 800) #set the limits for the y-axis for bet-
    ter display
12. plt.show()
```

We get the following output for the exercise in Jupyter Notebook:

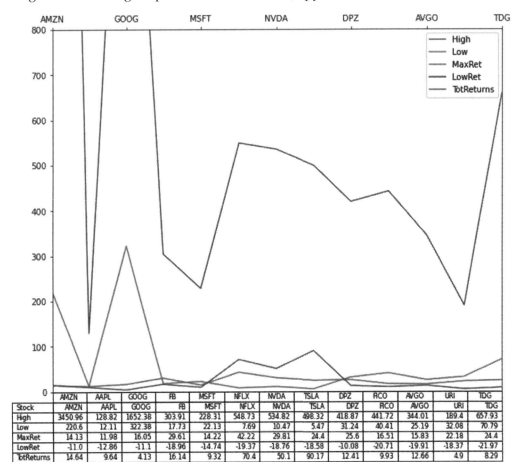

	AMZN	AAPL	GOOG	FB	MSFT	NFLX	NVDA	TSLA	DPZ	RCO	AVGO	URI	TDG
Stock	AMZN	AAPL	GOOG	FB	MSFT	NFLX	NVDA	TSLA	DPZ	RCO	AVGO	URI	TDG
High	3450.96	128.82	1652.38	303.91	228.31	548.73	534.82	498.32	418.87	441.72	344.01	189.4	657.93
Low	220.6	12.11	322.38	17.73	22.13	7.69	10.47	5.47	31.24	40.41	25.19	32.08	70.79
MaxRet	14.13	11.98	16.05	29.61	14.22	42.22	29.81	24.4	25.6	16.51	15.83	22.18	24.4
LowRet	-11.0	-12.86	-11.1	-18.96	-14.74	-19.37	-18.76	-18.58	-10.08	-20.71	-19.91	-18.37	-21.97
TotReturns	14.64	9.64	4.13	16.14	9.32	70.4	50.1	90.17	12.41	9.93	12.66	4.9	8.29

Figure 5.37: Pandas – use of tables as a legend in a chart

Exercise 5-33: Using horizontal bar charts

Now let us use the horizontal bar charts for the data analysis. We shall use **barh** and pass the data for rendering. The code produces two horizontal bar charts: each for the high/low values and maximum/lowest returns. The second chart produces a bi-directional horizontal chart displaying the actual performance of the stocks. These charts can be further beautified using various parameters available. Let us see the code:

```
1. bar_data.reset_index().set_index(bar_data['Stock'])

2. bar_data_stock = bar_data[['Stock','High','Low']]

3. bar_data_returns = bar_data[['Stock','MaxRet','LowRet']]
```

```
4.  bar_data_stock.set_index('Stock')
5.  bar_data_stock.set_axis(symbols,  axis='index', inplace=True)
6.  bar_data_returns.set_axis(symbols,  axis='index', inplace=True)
7.  ax = bar_data_stock.plot.barh(figsize=(15,10),rot=0, subplots=-
    False, width=0.8)
8.  ax = bar_data_returns.plot.barh(figsize=(15,10),rot=0, subplots=-
    False, width=0.8)
```

We get the following output for the exercise in the Jupyter Notebook:

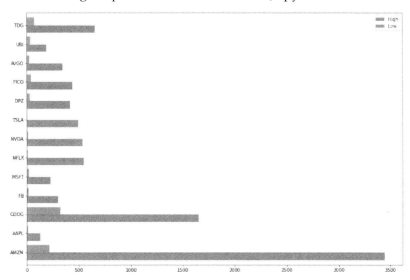

Figure 5.38: *Pandas – use horizontal bar charts for stock analysis*

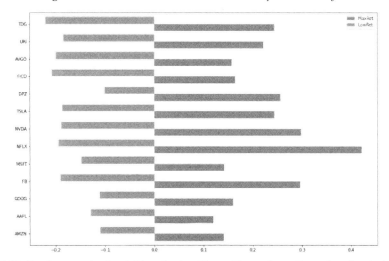

Figure 5.39: *Pandas – use horizontal bar charts with positive and negative values for stock analysis*

Exercise 5-34: Using parallel coordinates charts

Now let us use the parallel coordinates charts for the data we are analysing. The following code passes the dataframe, reference column for the analysis for which we share the *Stock* column. Other columns passed are used for the creation of the parallel coordinate charts.

```
1.  pd.plotting.parallel_coordinates(bar_data,class_column='Sto
    ck',cols=['High','Low','MaxRet','LowRet','TotReturns'],col-
    or=('#556270','#4ECDC4','#C7F464','#99FFCC','#CC22EE'))
```

Exercise 5-35: Using RadViz charts

Now let us use the *RadViz* charts for the data we are analyzing. We need to pass the dataframe and **class_column** we want to use for the analysis. The recommendation is that we pass a dataframe containing numbers and use the string-based column for the class column.

The following code is used for the creation of a RadViz Chart for our analysis:

```
1.  pd.plotting.radviz(bar_data,class_column='Stock')
```

We get the following output for the exercises 5-34 and 5-35 in the Jupyter Notebook:

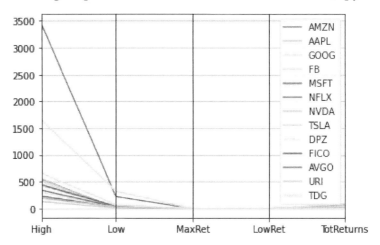

Figure 5.40: Pandas – use of a parallel coordinates chart

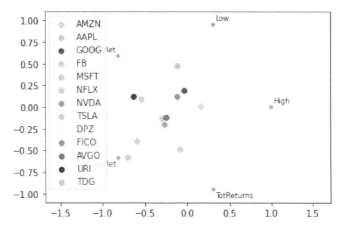

Figure 5.41: *Pandas – use of a RadViz chart*

Exercise 5-36: Question – scatter matrix

In *Exercise 5-13*, we created a scatter matrix for the correlated stocks and saw the output. What would the scatter matrix visualization look like for the standard dataset without correlation? Visualize the outcome of the following code:

```
1. pd.plotting.scatter_matrix(data,alpha=0.2,figsize=(30,20))
```

The solution for this is available in the Jupyter Notebook for the chapter included in the resources link.

Exercise 5-37: Using secondary axis in a line chart

So far, we have been using only the primary axes for our plotting. What will happen if we use the secondary axes to plot the output? This exercise aims at addressing this question. In order to do this, we share the parameters we want to plot against the secondary axes through **secondary_y** parameter.

```
1. bar_data.LowRet=bar_data.LowRet*100
2. bar_data.MaxRet=bar_data.MaxRet*100
3. bar_data['TotReturns']=bar_data['TotReturns'].
   apply(lambda x:round(x,2))
4. bar_data['Low']=bar_data['Low'].apply(lambda x:round(x,2))
5. bar_data['MaxRet']=bar_data['MaxRet'].apply(lambda x:round(x,5))
6. bar_data['LowRet']=bar_data['LowRet'].apply(lambda x:round(x,5))
7. bar_data.plot(secondary_y=['MaxRet', 'LowRet','TotRe-
   turns'], mark_right=False)
```

We get the following output for the exercise in Jupyter Notebook:

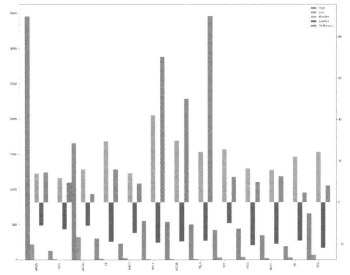

Figure 5.42: Pandas – use of secondary y-axis for plotting

Exercise 5-38: Using secondary axis in a bar chart

The case is simple for a bar chart, just like what we saw in the preceding example. We share the parameters we want to plot against the secondary axes through the **secondary_y** parameter.

```
1. bar_data.plot.bar(secondary_y=['MaxRet', 'LowRet','TotRe-
   turns'], mark_right=False,figsize=(20,16), width=1.0)
```

We get the following output for the exercise in Jupyter Notebook:

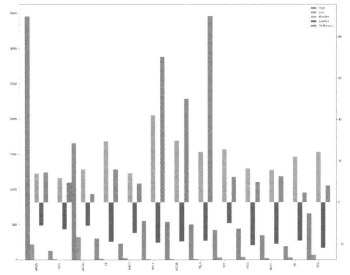

Figure 5.43: Pandas – use of secondary y-axis for plotting in a bar chart

Exercise 5-39: Andrews curves using subplots

We can generate Andrews curves by passing the first 100 rows of the dataframe for analysis and by passing the stock as a **class_column** parameter. The full code for the creation of Andrews curves is as follows.

```
1. from pandas.plotting import andrews_curves
2. # Andrews> curves
3. returns_na_new=returns_na.apply(lambda x:round(x,2))
4. fig, axes = plt.subplots(nrows=6, ncols=2,figsize=(30, 40))
5. for i, ax in enumerate(axes.reshape(-1)):
6.     ax=andrews_curves(returns_na_new[:100], class_column=symbol-
       s[i],samples=50,ax=axes.flat[i])
```

We get the following output for the exercise in the Jupyter Notebook. The image showcased is only a part of the full image, and the full output is available in the solution notebook shared with this book.

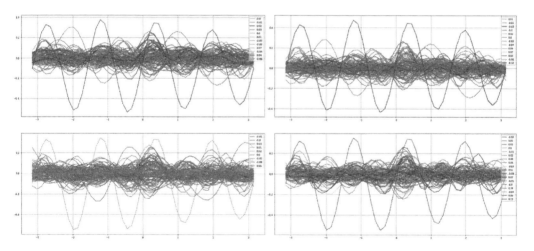

Figure 5.44: Pandas – use of Andrews curves for AMZN, APPL, GOOG, FB Stocks

Exercise 5-40 to 5-48: Chapter exercises

Let us start with some questions to test the understanding so far in this chapter.

Exercise 5-40: Question – Random HexBin chart exercise

How will we generate the following HexBin chart based on the examples shared earlier? The clues are given in the graph very clearly.

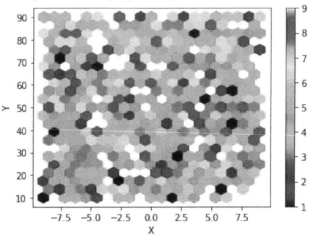

Figure 5.45: Pandas – a random HexBin chart

Exercise 5-41 to 5-48: Question on multiple charts

Let us change gears and try some standard and simple plots-related questions to test our understanding. We shall try the following charts using Pandas:

- Box chart
- Area chart
- Bar chart
- Density charts
- Histogram charts
- Line chart
- Pie chart
- Usage of subplots

To test this, we shall be referring to the output (remember that many of them use random numbers) shared to write programs that will generate similar outputs.

Let us see the output images in a simple table.

What code would we use `df.plot.kde()`/`df.plot.kde(bw_method=4)`/`df.plot.kde(bw_method=0.25)` to produce the following?

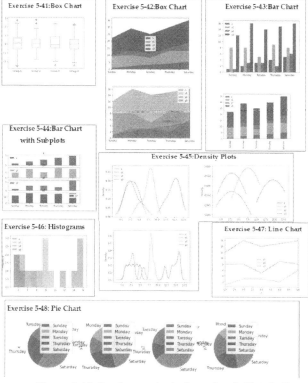

Figure 5.46: *Pandas – output of exercises 5-41 to 5-48*

The exercise is to produce the lines of code that will produce charts similar to the charts displayed in the table.

Please note that all the solutions and code are available in the Jupyter Notebook solutions shared with this book.

Case study 3: Analyzing the Titanic passenger dataset

Let us now take a new dataset, analyze it, and produce visualizations like what we did above for the mobile sales data and the real-time stock data. Now we shall analyze the *Titanic* passenger dataset.

Exercise 5-49: Data exploration and a histogram

Let us start with loading the dataset into a dataframe and perform some *Pandas* operations. A simple histogram of age wise passenger list. The following program does all the tasks mentioned above:

```
1.  import numpy as np
2.  import pandas as pd
3.  import squarify
4.  import matplotlib.pyplot as plt
5.  import matplotlib as mpl
6.  #Read File
7.  titanic = pd.read_csv('https://raw.githubusercontent.com/kalilur-
    rahman/datasets/main/Titanic.csv')
8.  #drop and create relevant columns
9.  titanic.drop(['Name', 'Ticket'], axis=1, inplace=True)
10. titanic['Cabin_ind'] = np.where(titanic['Cabin'].isnull(), 0, 1)
11. titanic.drop(['Cabin', 'Embarked'], axis=1, inplace=True)
12. X_train_data = pd.DataFrame(titanic)
13. bins= [10,20,30,40,50,60]
14. labels = ['Be-
    low 20','21 to 30','31 to 40','41 to 50',' Above 50']
15. X_train_data['AgeGroup'] = pd.cut(X_train_data['Age'], bins=bins,
16.                                   labels=labels, right=False)
17. # Try a Histogram chart
18. ax1 = titanic['Age'].hist(bins=25)
19. ax1.set_xlabel('Age')
20. ax1.set_ylabel('Count')
21. ax1.set_title('Distribution by Age')
22. plt.show()
```

We get the following output, and it gives a clear view that most of the passengers were below 40 years of age:

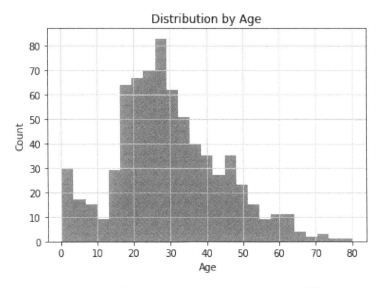

Figure 5.47: Pandas – histogram of ages of passengers of Titanic

Exercise 5-50: Histogram of two parameters

If we want to expand the histogram parameters, we can achieve the same with two histogram functions. In the following code, we can see that we extract the male and female passenger list in two statements and use the age parameter to do the histogram with a bin size of 25 each. We refer to the same axis of the first histogram to overlay the second histogram on top of the first.

```
1. ax2 = titanic['Age'][titanic['Sex']=='male'].hist(bins=25, la-
   bel='Male')
2. titanic['Age'][titanic['Sex']=='female'].
   hist(bins=25, ax = ax2, label='Female')
3. ax2.set_xlabel('Age')
4. ax2.set_ylabel('Count')
5. ax2.set_title('Distribution by Age')
6. ax2.legend()
7. plt.show()
```

Exercise 5-51: Histogram of two parameters

We can take the same dataset and make a simple change to include *fare* instead of *age:*

```
1. ax2 = titanic['Fare'][titanic['Sex']=='male'].
   hist(bins=25, label='Male')

2. titanic['Fare'][titanic['Sex']=='female'].
   hist(bins=25, ax = ax2, label='Female')

3. ax2.set_xlabel('Fare')

4. ax2.set_ylabel('Count')

5. ax2.set_title('Distribution by Fare')

6. ax2.legend()

7. plt.show()
```

We get the following output for the exercises 5-50 and 5-51 in Jupyter Notebook:

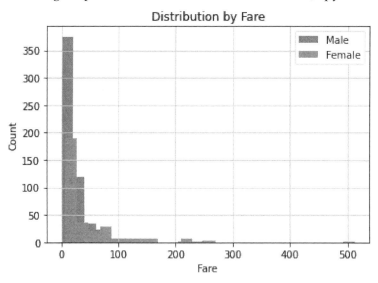

Figure 5.48: *Pandas – histogram of two parameters – fare and gender of passengers in Titanic*

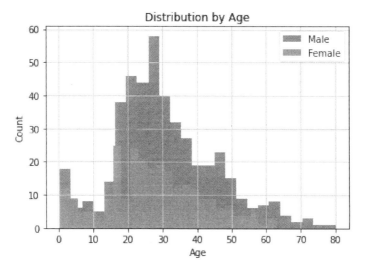

Figure 5.49: Pandas – histogram of two parameters – age and gender of passengers in Titanic

Exercise 5-52 to 5-68: Further analysis and visualization of the Titanic dataset

Let us see the code and the visualization in a tabularized manner:

Exercise & Code	Output / Visualization

Exercise 5:52 : A density chart
 	
1. `ax = titanic['Age']`
`[titanic['Sex']=='male'].plot.`
`kde( label='Male')`
 	
2. `titanic['Age']`
`[titanic['Sex']=='female'].plot.`
`kde(ax = ax, label='Female')`
 	
3. `ax.set_xlabel('Age')`
 	
4. `ax.set_ylabel('Density')`
 	
5. `ax.set_title('Distribution by Age')`
 	
6. `ax.legend()`
	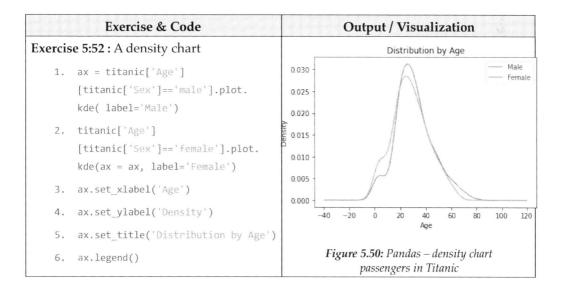
	
	Figure 5.50: Pandas – density chart passengers in Titanic

Exercise 5-53: A bar plot grouped by gender and survival status

1. ```
   titanic['Survived']=titanic
   ['Survived'].map({0: 'Dead', 1:
   'Survived'})
   ```

2. ```
   titanic.groupby(['Sex',
   'Survived']).size().unstack().
   plot(kind='bar', stacked=True)
   ```

3. ```
   ax.set_xlabel('Gender')
   ```

4. ```
   plt.ylabel('Count')
   ```

5. ```
   plt.title('Survival rate by
   Gender')
   ```

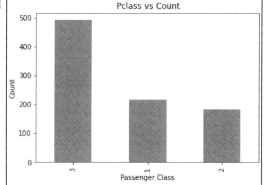

Figure 5.51: Pandas – survival rate by gender – bar chart Titanic

Exercise 5-54: A bar plot grouped by travel class

1. ```
   pclass_count =titanic['Pclass'].
   value_counts()
   ```

2. ```
   ax = pclass_count.plot.bar()
   ```

3. ```
   pclass_count.re-
   name({1: 'First Class', 2:'Sec-
   ond Class', 3:'Third Class'}, in-
   place=True)
   ```

4. ```
   ax.set_ylabel('Count', rotation=90)
   ```

5. ```
   ax.set_xlabel('Passenger Class')
   ```

6. ```
   ax.set_title('Pclass vs Count')
   ```

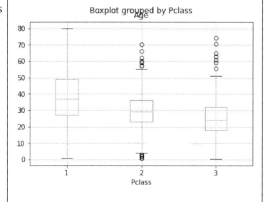

Figure 5.52: Pandas – a bar plot of passenger class - Titanic

Exercise 5-55: A box plot grouped by class with age

1. ```
   titanic.boxplot(by='Pclass',
   column=['Age'])
   ```

Figure 5-53: Pandas – a box plot of passenger class – Titanic

Exercise 5-56: Density plots with sub plots and no sharing axis

```
1.  titanic.plot(kind='density',
    subplots=True,layout=(3,3),ls='--',
    lw=5,sharex=False,figsize=(12,10))
```

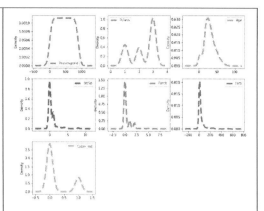

Figure 5-54: Pandas – density plot with subplots of various parameters - Titanic

Exercise 5-57: Box plots with sub plots and no sharing axis

```
1.  titanic.plot(kind='box',
    subplots=True, lay-
    out=(3,3), sharex=False,sharey=-
    False,figsize=(10,10))
```

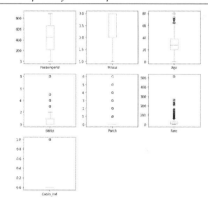

Figure 5.55: Pandas – a box plot with various parameters with no sharing axes - Titanic

Exercise 5-58: Density plots for fare

```
1.  titanic['Fare'].plot.kde(l-
    w=5,ls='-.')

2.  ax.set_xlabel('Fare')

3.  ax.set_ylabel('Density')

4.  ax.set_title('Distribu-
    tion by Fare')

5.  ax.legend()
```

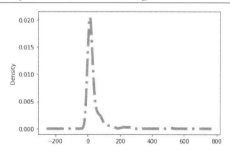

Figure 5.56: Pandas – a density plot for fares - Titanic

Exercise 5-59: Histogram by age 1. `titanic['Age'].hist(bins=100,l-w=5,ls='-.')`	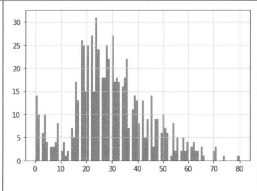 ***Figure 5.57:** Pandas – histogram for the age of passengers - Titanic*
Exercise 5-60: Histogram by fare 1. `titanic['Fare'].hist(bins=100,l-w=5,ls='-.')`	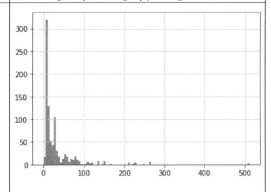 ***Figure 5.58:** Pandas – histogram for the fare paid by passengers – Titanic*

Exercise 5-61: Pie chart by age group

1.   colors = ["#FFCA00", "#15FF58",
       "#E70488", "#66CA00",
       "#150458","#E70FF8" ,"#880458", "#
       88CA00", "#870488"]

2.   pie_data = (titanic.groupby('Age-
       Group')
       ['Fare'].count()).to_frame()

3.   pie_data['AgeGroup'] = round((pie_
       data.Fare/sum(pie_data.
       Fare))*100, 2)

4.   pie_data['AgeGroup'].plot.pie(la-
       bels=pie_data.index, subplots=True,

5.   startangle=90, au-
       topct='%.1f%%',colors=colors)

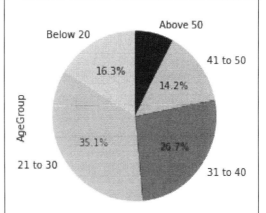

Figure 5.59: *Pandas – pie chart by age group of passengers - Titanic*

Exercise 5-62: Create a new column with fare group

1.   X_train_data = pd.DataFrame(titanic)

2.   bins= [50,100,150,200,250,300]

3.   labels = ['Below 51','51 to 100','101 to 150','151 to 200','Above 250']

4.   X_train_data['FareGroup'] = pd.cut(X_train_data['Fare'], bins=bins,

5.   labels=labels, right=False)

Exercise 5-63: Pie chart by fare group

1. ```
   pie_data = (titanic.groupby('Fare-
   Group')['Fare'].count()).to_frame()
   ```

2. ```
   pie_data['FareGroup'] = round((pie_
   data.Fare/sum(pie_data.
   Fare))*100, 2)
   ```

3. ```
   pie_data['FareGroup'].plot.
   pie(labels=pie_data.index, sub-
   plots=True,startangle=90, au-
   topct='%.1f%%',colors=colors)
   ```

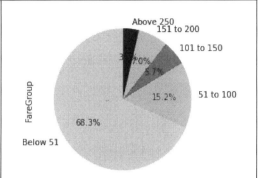

Figure 5.60: *Pandas – pie chart by fare group of passengers – Titanic*

Exercise 5-64: Pie chart by gender

1. ```
   colors = ["#FFCA00", "#15FF58",
   "#E70488",
   "#66CA00", "#150458","#E70FF8","#88
   0458", "#88CA00", "#870488"]
   ```

2. ```
   pie_data = (titanic.groupby('Sex')
   ['Fare'].count()).to_frame()
   ```

3. ```
   pie_data['Gender'] = round((pie_
   data.Fare/sum(pie_data.
   Fare))*100, 2)
   ```

4. ```
   pie_data['Gender'].plot.pie
   (labels=pie_data.index,
   subplots=True,startangle=90,
   autopct='%.1f%%',colors=colors)
   ```

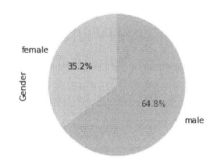

Figure 5.61: *Pandas – pie chart by gender of passengers - Titanic*
   ```

Exercise 5-65: Pie chart by survival

1.  ```
    pie_data = (titanic.groupby('Sur-
    vived')['Fare'].count()).to_frame()
    ```

2.  ```
    pie_data['Surv'] =
    round((pie_data.Fare/sum(pie_data.
    Fare))*100, 2)
    ```

3.  ```
    pie_data['Surv'].plot.pie(la-
    bels=pie_data.index, sub-
    plots=True,startangle=90, au-
    topct='%.1f%%',colors=colors[:2])
    ```

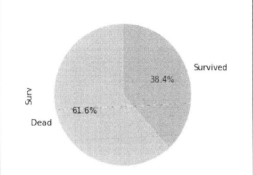

Figure 5.62: *Pandas – pie chart by the survival of passengers – Titanic*

Exercise 5-66: Auto correlation chart

1.  ```
    pd.plotting.autocorrelation_
    plot(titanic.Fare)
    ```

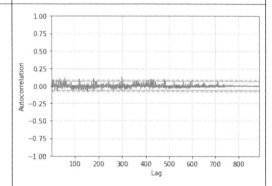

Figure 5.63: *Pandas – autocorrelation chart of Titanic*

Exercise 5-67: RadViz chart

1.  ```
    from pandas.plotting import radviz
    ```

2.  ```
    titanic_radviz=titanic.
    filter(['Age','Fare','Sur-
    vived','Pclass'],axis=1)
    ```

3.  ```
    titanic_radviz.head()
    ```

4.  ```
    titanic_radviz.ffill(axis=0,in-
    place=True, limit=None, downcast=-
    None)
    ```

5.  ```
    titanic_radviz.head(40)
    ```

6.  ```
    radviz(titanic_radviz, 'Survived')
    ```

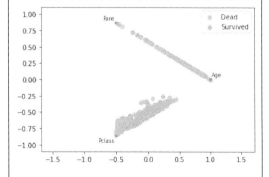

Figure 5.64: *Pandas – RadViz chart of Titanic*

Exercise 5-68: Parallel coordinates chart	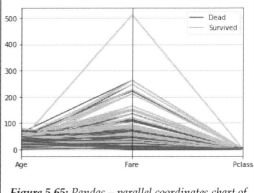

1. `pd.plotting.parallel_coordi-`
`nates(titanic_radviz, 'Sur-`
`vived', colormap='prism')`
	Figure 5.65: Pandas – parallel coordinates chart of Titanic

Exercise 5-69 to 5-71 Generating map outline using scatter plot using latitude/longitude and population data

Exercise 5-69: Creation of an approximate outline of India map using a scatter plot

Given we have done a good amount of coding exercise in *Chapter 4* and *Chapter 5* so far, let us put it into good use of an outline generation. To do this, we shall leverage a good dataset available in the **simplemaps.com** site (link is given in the Notebook) and use it to create the visualization.

We shall start with the outline creation of Indian cities. To do this, we will use the data provided in two datasets available on the site and merge it into a single dataset. The dataset contains *city, latitude, longitude, population, population_proper* columns. We shall be creating a population density bubble by dividing the *population_proper* by 1000.

The first program for creation of the output is as follows:

```
1. import pandas as pd
2. #Read the files
3. cities = pd.read_csv('https://raw.githubusercontent.com/kalilur-
   rahman/datasets/main/in2merged.csv')
4. cities.describe()
5. #Let us load the data from the file
6. latitude, longitude = cities['lat'], cities['lng']
```

7. #Let us load the Population and Proper Population (of metro area)

8. population, properpop = cities['population'], cities['population_proper']

9. #Let us Convert the Population into multiples of 1000s

10. properpop = properpop/1000

11. plt.figure(figsize=(25,20))

12. plt.scatter(longitude, latitude, label=None,c=np.log10(population), cmap='tab20c_r',s=properpop, linewidth=0, alpha=0.5)

13. plt.axis('equal')

14. plt.title('Creating an India Map outline through Population data',fontsize=24)

15. plt.xlabel('longitude of the City',fontsize=24)

16. plt.ylabel('latitude of the City',fontsize=24)

17. plt.colorbar(label='Logarithm$_{10}$ of population')

What this program produces is a visualization covering all the cities and towns available in the dataset. While this is not a true outline of the borders, what we can see is an outline using just scatter charts!

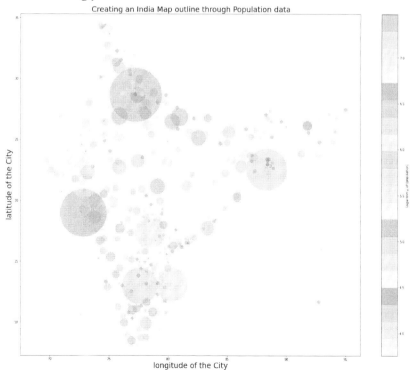

Figure 5.66: *Pandas – use of scatter plot to generate an India map chart*

Exercise 5-70 and 5-71: Creating an approximate outline of the world and US maps using a scatter plot

Let us extend this program to create two additional maps, one for the world map creation and another to create the continental United States map. Some features available in NumPy and Pandas are used for some improvements from Exercise 5-69.

Exercise & Code
Exercise 5:70 : World Map Creation – Code

```
1.  import pandas as pd

2.  worldcities = pd.read_csv('https://raw.githubusercontent.com/
    kalilurrahman/datasets/main/worldcities.csv')

3.  worldcities.describe()

4.  latitude, longitude = worldcities['lat'], worldcities['lng']

5.  population, city = worldcities['population'], worldci-
    ties['city_ascii']

6.  popbub = population/100

7.  plt.figure(figsize=(120,100))

8.  plt.scatter(longitude, latitude, label=None,

9.              c=np.log10(population), cmap='tab20c',

10.             s=popbub, linewidth=0, alpha=0.5)

11. plt.axis('equal')

12. plt.xlabel('longitude')

13. plt.ylabel('latitude')

14. plt.colorbar(label='log$_{10}$(population)')

15. plt.clim(3, 7)

16. plt.title('World Cities: Population')
```

Exercise 5:70: World map creation – output

Figure 5.67: *Pandas – use of scatter plot to generate a world map chart*

Exercise 5:71: US map creation – code

```
1.  import pandas as pd
2.  uscities = pd.read_csv('https://raw.githubusercontent.com/kali-
    lurrahman/datasets/main/uscities.csv')
3.  uscities = uscities[ uscities['lng'] > -154.00]#Filter for con-
    tinental USA
4.  uscities = uscities[ uscities['lat'] < 54.00]
5.  latitude =  uscities['lat']
6.  longitude =  uscities['lng']
7.  population, density = uscities['population'], uscities['densi-
    ty']
8.  density = density/50
9.  plt.figure(figsize=(10,8))
10. plt.scatter(longitude, latitude, label=None,c=np.log2(popula-
    tion), cmap='YlGnBu',s=density, linewidth=0.1, alpha=0.5)
11. plt.axis('equal')
12. plt.xlabel('longitude')
13. plt.ylabel('latitude')
14. plt.colorbar(label='log$_{2}$(population)')
15. plt.title('Continental US Cities:  Outline through Population')
```

Exercise 5:71: US map creation – output

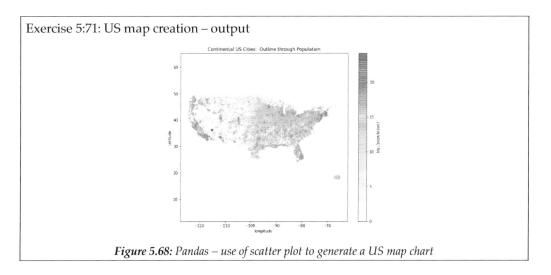

Figure 5.68: *Pandas – use of scatter plot to generate a US map chart*

Pandas resources

There are lots of resources available on the Internet to learn about Pandas. The following is a curated list of some of the best resources available for learning and understanding Pandas better for doing better Python coding and visualization:

Resource Name	Link
Pandas official site	https://pandas.pydata.org/
Pandas documentation	https://pandas.pydata.org/docs/
Pandas API reference	https://pandas.pydata.org/docs/reference/index.html
Pandas user guide	https://pandas.pydata.org/docs/user_guide/index.html
Data school Pandas Q&A – Notebook	https://nbviewer.jupyter.org/github/just-markham/pandas-videos/blob/master/pandas.ipynb
Chris Albon – data science and machine learning notes	https://chrisalbon.com/
Modern Pandas by Tom Augspurger -	http://tomaugspurger.github.io/modern-1-intro.html
Pandas dataframes cheatsheet by Mark Graph	https://drive.google.com/file/d/1oySbjLpT_PuDf3hN66-mzSjcPIThBOmC/view

Pandas resources by Chris Fonnesbeck of Vanderbilt University • Introduction to Pandas • Pandas fundamentals • Data wrangling with Pandas	1. https://nbviewer.jupyter.org/github/fonnesbeck/Bios8366/blob/master/notebooks/Section2_1-Introduction-to-Pandas.ipynb 2. https://nbviewer.jupyter.org/github/fonnesbeck/Bios8366/blob/mastcr/notebooks/Section2_2-Pandas-Fundamentals.ipynb 3. https://nbviewer.jupyter.org/github/fonnesbeck/Bios8366/blob/master/notebooks/Section2_3-Data-Wrangling-with-Pandas.ipynb
Greg Reda's Pandas data structures	http://www.gregreda.com/2013/10/26/intro-to-pandas-data-structures/
Udemy Course - Master Data Analysis with Python - Intro to Pandas by Ted Petrou	https://www.udemy.com/course/master-data-analysis-with-python-intro-to-pandas/
Coursera Guided Course – Pandas Python Library for beginners in Data Science Coursera Guided Course – Pandas Python Library for Intermediate in Data Science	https://www.coursera.org/projects/pandas-python-library-beginners-data-science https://www.coursera.org/projects/intermediate-pandas-python-library-data-science
Udemy Course on Learn Data Analysis using Pandas and Python	https://www.udemy.com/course/learn-data-analysis-using-pandas-and-python/
W3 Resource – Pandas Exercises, Practice, and Solution	https://www.w3resource.com/python-exercises/pandas/index.php
Kaggle - Pandas Collection	https://www.kaggle.com/learn/pandas
Udemy Course on Pandas with Python	https://www.udemy.com/course/pandas-with-python/
Pandas Cookbook	https://github.com/jvns/pandas-cookbook
Learn Pandas by Hernan Rojas	https://bitbucket.org/hrojas/learn-pandas/src/master/
Pandas from The Ground Up – Brandon Rhodes	https://www.youtube.com/watch?v=5JnMutdy-6Fw
Pandas Exercises for New Users	https://github.com/guipsamora/pandas_exercises

Conclusion

In *Chapters 4* and *5*, we have explored over 120 programs to understand in-depth how to use *Python* to generate complex visualization and charting. Visualization is an in-depth field with innate opportunities to explore, innovate, and avow the audience. It is like magic. In this chapter, we used the power of *Pandas*, which leverages *NumPy* and *Matplotlib* to create various types of charts needed for visualization. *Matplotlib* was developed with plotting and visualization as the main objective, taking a cue from the *Matlab* programming tool. However, *Pandas* was created with high-performance data analysis and operations in mind. Still, the plotting capabilities of *Pandas* are phenomenal. If we combine Chapters 4 and 5, we will see an element missing in these two tools: interaction and dynamic plotting. While the charts are beautiful and impactful, they miss out on the interaction. Over the next two chapters, we shall see some advanced features in some tools that extended the features of *Matplotlib* and *Pandas* to add capabilities to do interaction, dynamic data rendering, and user-driven animation to make the visualization more impactful. We shall be covering the capabilities of *Seaborn, Bokeh, and Plotly* in detail.

Questions

1. For what types of plotting will we choose the Pandas library over Matplotlib?

2. What are the benefits of Matplotlib when compared with Pandas?

3. Is interactive plotting possible with Pandas?

4. What are different types of visualization functions available in Pandas?

Using Seaborn for Visualization

> "Information graphics should be aesthetically pleasing, but many designers think about aesthetics before they think about structure, about the information itself, about the story the graphic should tell."
>
> *– Alberto Cairo*

After learning on *Pandas* and *Matplotlib* to perform major types of visualization, it is now time for using one of the most aesthetic tools available for great visualization – *Seaborn*. It takes statistical visualization to a whole new level. All the libraries and tools have a specific purpose, and their usefulness or relevance ends after a while, and we need other nice extensions or toolkits to take it to the next level. This is the story of *Python* and how it is leap-frogging as one of the preferred programming languages to be used by many across the globe. Visualization is no different, and Seaborn is a nice tool that helps us achieve the benefits of leveraging the power of beautiful and amazing visualizations and features to leverage the power of statistical functions.

Structure

In this chapter, we will cover the following topics:

- Introduction to Seaborn

- Seaborn plotting functions
- Examples and case studies for various types of visualizations using Seaborn
- Seaborn resources

Objective

This chapter aims to give a basic introduction to Seaborn for experimenting with various data visualization elements such as charts and graphs. We will also touch upon details of how to use Seaborn elements for effective visualization. We shall start with simple examples of Seaborn and explore the libraries and various functions available before trying out some of the important charts and graphs we covered in earlier chapters. We shall conclude the chapter with some examples to try out and resources to consume.

Introduction to *Seaborn* visualization

Figure 6.1: *The Seaborn logo*

Seaborn is a nice statistical visualization that has taken over the world by storm over the last few years. It is very easy to use and powerful when it comes to aesthetic and impactful visualizations. *Seaborn* was created by *Michael Waskom* and introduced in 2012. *Seaborn* is based on *Matplotlib* and gives the flexibility to perform statistical visualizations with as few as one line of code with the dataset. It's a combination of *Matplotlib* and *Pandas* with nice statistical functions to develop concise and nice statistical graphics that are highly informative and impactful.

The brilliance of *Seaborn* emerges from the fact that *Seaborn*

- Uses data as the core element for visualization
- Allows easy visualization of complex datasets by providing support to different types of data variables by providing high-level visual abstractions
- Uses nice themes for colors, palettes, and visualization element for taking matplotlib to the next level
- Encompasses various statistical functions to perform *univariate* and *bivariate* statistical distributions in an aesthetic manner
- Can perform linear regression and time series based statistical plotting with different types of plots
- Gives the flexibility to build various types of grids to plot comparative and abstract visualization to compare various data elements statistically in a beautiful manner

Seaborn features and benefits

Seaborn uses *Pandas* and *Matplotlib* as an underlying foundation and leverages *SciPy, NumPy, StatsModels,* and *FastCluster* for doing various statistical tasks. The key features include the following:

- Unlike the other libraries, *Seaborn* provides a very high level of *Library* or *API* abstraction across visualizations.

  o The designer needs to focus only on data, and *Seaborn* takes care of most aspects. In *Matplotlib,* it is important to remember many parameters to ensure visualization is done in an impactful manner.

- Automatic calculation of Statistical calculations and functions.

  o *Seaborn* automatically calculates many functions implicitly including, error bars, calculation of averages, linear regression certainty of estimates, etc.

- Very good information distribution summarization visually. *Seaborn* takes away the statistical analysis knowledge about the variable distribution in the datasets. *Seaborn* offers multiple options for the same type of plot with each of its functions. For example, a **displot()** or **catplot()** function provides multiple ways to visualize the same dataset.

- Availability of specialized plotting functions for categorical variables.

  o *Seaborn* offers multiple functions for categorical data visualization through **catplot()** such as *swarmplot* that avoids scattering data overlap for categories and violin plot.

- Complex data views in a composited manner with more than one visualization view.

  o **jointplot()** and **jointgrid()** functions offer a way to combine multiple plots into a summary view of a dataset. Similarly, **pairplot()** *and* **PairGrid()** gives a comprehensive summary of all elements in a dataset in a pairwise relationship format.

- Ability to build complex visualization with simple lines of code with the API.

- Nice default visualizations and the ability to customize easily.

- Ease of extension of the features of Matplotlib and other bases the tool is built upon.

- Great coloring themes, palettes, and maps for better visualization.

Seaborn is very powerful in multiple ways, like the statements mentioned above. Further features, API library, examples, and user guide, along with other useful information, is available at the landing site for *Seaborn* at **https://seaborn.pydata. org/index.html.**

Seaborn visualization functions

Seaborn has functions categorized under the following groups. This allows the selection of the functions easily depending on what we want to do with visualization. The key categories include:

1. Relational plot functions
2. Distribution plot functions
3. Regression plot functions
4. Matrix plot functions
5. Functions for grids displaying multiple plots
6. Aesthetic functions including
   a. Themes-related functions
   b. Colour palette functions
   c. Palette widget functions
   d. Utility functions

Let us see the categories in the form of a table. There are new terms specific to Seaborn referred to in this table, such as facet, grid, etc. The details will be clarified during the exercises explained on their purpose. This table intends to introduce the readers to the key concepts available in Seaborn:

Category	Function	Purpose
Relational plots for data	*relplot(*params[])*	Used to show the relationship between two variables which can be shown for different subsets of data. This plot leverages the relationship of two variables along the x and y-axis. The different data subsets get categorized using different parameters such as *hue, size,* and *style.*
	scatterplot(*params[])	Draws a scatter plot of the relationship between two variables plotted along the x and y-axis. The different subset is shown using hue, size, and style as in the case of *relplot.*
	relplot(*params[])	Used to show the relationship between two variables, which can be shown for different subsets of data. This plot leverages the relationship of two variables along the x and y-axis. The different data subsets get categorized using different parameters such as *hue, size,* and *style.*

Distribution plots for data		
	displot(*params[])	`displot()` function provides access to several approaches (`kdeplot()`, `ecdfplot()` or `histplot()`) for univariate or bivariate visualization of data distribution. Data subsetting can be done through mapping specified earlier into multiple subplots. `displot()` is normally used in conjunction with a FacetGrid with a figure-level interface.
	ecdfplot(*params[])	ecdfplot() is used for empirical cumulative distribution function for the data parameters passed.
	histplot(*params[])	histplot() is used for univariate or bivariate histograms to show distributions of datasets. Data and other parameters are passed for visualization.
	kdeplot(*params[])	kdeplot() is used for univariate or bivariate kernel density estimation of datasets. Data and other parameters are passed for visualization.
	rugplot(*params[])	rugplot() is normally used in combination with other plots and is used to plot marginal distributions for x and y axes as tick extensions along the x and y axes.
Regression plot for data	*lmplot(*params[])*	Used for plotting data and regression models across a FacetGrid.
	regplot(*params[])	Used for fitting data and linear regression model fit for the data under visualization.
	residplot(*params[])	Used for plotting residuals of linear regressions.
Categorical plotting of data	*barplot(*params[])*	*barplot()* is shows confidence intervals and point values in a bar plot.
	boxenplot(*params[])	*boxplot()* is basically a *boxplot()* for large datasets to show categorization in a better manner.
	boxplot(*params[])	*boxplot()* is a standard plot we've discussed earlier showing simple distributions by category.
	catplot(*params[])	*catplot()* like *displot()* function provides access to several category-based visualization approaches (*stripplot()*, *swarmplot()*, *boxplot()*, *violinplot()*, *boxenplot()*, *pointplot()*, *barplot()*, *countplot()*) for visualization of relationship between numerical and categorical variables. This is normally used with a FacetGrid with a figure level interface, just like *displot()*.
	countplot(*params[])	*countplot()* is a way to show counts in various categories using bars to show the value.
	stripplot(*params[])	*stripplot()* is a type of scatterplot where one variable is categorical (such as male/female, etc.).
	swarmplot(*params[])	*swarmplot()* is a type of scatterplot where categorical variables are shown in a scatter without overlaps.
	violinplot(*params[])	*violinplot()* is a combination of *boxplot()* and a kernel density estimate plot in one showing distributions by category.

Data in a matrix plot	*clustermap(*params[])*	*clustermap()* is an enhanced *heatmap()* as it showcases a hierarchically clustered heatmap of the dataset being visualized.
	heatmap(*params[])	*heatmap()* is used to plot rectangular data in a color-coded heat value based on the correlation. The numbers visually represent the level of correlation between the two elements of the matrix in comparison. This is a very useful tool for financial comparisons.
Multi plot grid-based representation of data	*Facet grids*	Facet grids are used for showing conditional relationships in multiple plots. Key Functions available in Facet Grids include, *Facetgrid.map(*params[])* and *Facetgrid.map_dataframe(*params[])*.
	Joint grids	Joint grids are used for showing Bivariate (two data variables) plots with marginal univariate plots on two axes. This uses *jointplot()* primarily to plot two variables with univariate and bivariate plots. *JointGrid()* is used for plotting the grid-like Facet or Pair Grids and *JointGrid.plot(), JointGrid.plot_joint(), JointGrid.plot_marginals()* functions are used to lot along joint axes and marginals to visualize.
	Pair grids	Pair Grids are used for showing pairwise relationships of a dataset in multiple plots. Pair Grid primarily uses pairplot() that uses a dataset to plot pairwise relationships. It also has functions such as PairGrid() to subplot grids for plotting pairwise comparisons. It also uses PairGrid.map(), .map_diag(), map_offdiag(), map_lower(), map_upper() to plot various plots in different grid positions.
Themes, color palette, and utility functions	Plenty of functions exist for extending the features and customize the visualization to suit the needs.	**Theme functions** • set_theme(), axes_style(), set_style(), plotting_context(), set_context(), set_color_codes(), reset_defaults(), reset_orig(), set() **Colour palette functions** • set_palette(), color_palette(), husl_palette(), hls_palette(), cubehelix_palette(), dark_palette(), light_palette(), diverging_palette(), blend_palette(), xkcd_palette(), crayon_palette(), mpl_palette() **Palette widget functions** • choose_color_brewer_palette(), choose_cubehelix_palette(), choose_light_palette(), choose_diverging_palette(), choose_cubehelix_palette(), choose_dark_palette()` **Utility functions** • load_dataset(), get_dataset_names(), get_data_home(), despine(), desaturate(), saturate(), set_hls_values()

Table 6.1: Seaborn functions

Concepts such as *FacetGrids, PairGrids, JointGrids, PairPlots,* and *JointPlots* are introduced to *Python* by the *Seaborn* library. They are a good way to visualize the relationships between various data elements in a dataset.

Given that we have a very high-level overview of Seaborn's various functions let us try some examples in the next section.

Examples and case studies for various types of visualizations using Seaborn

As covered in the section above, we shall be covering the key plots and shall use smaller plots for effective use of the pages. The Jupyter Notebook with the solution will have the full results for the reading and experimentation needs.

Before we start, one of the first checks we can do is to use the latest version of Seaborn to ensure we do not get errors for the plots we shall render. This can be done using the following code:

```
1. import seaborn as sns
2. print(sns.__version__)
3. if (sns.__version__ >= "0.11.0") :
4.     print("We are good")
5. else:
6.     print("Please Upgrade Seaborn Library")
```

Seaborn offers a good number of datasets to experiment with for various visualizations, and we shall leverage some of the datasets for this chapter. We can get the names through the following command:

```
1.   dsnames=sns.get_dataset_names()
```

For our first exercise, let us use a common dataset available to do some stock analysis. We shall be using the NIFTY-500 (National Stock Exchange of India's top 500 stocks) dataset for our analysis. This data is available in the public domain at the Kaggle site supported by Google (**https://www.kaggle.com/dhimananubhav/nifty-500-fundamental-statistics**). Let us see some code snippets and corresponding outputs.

Exercise 6-1: Plotting stock market analysis data

Let us see the code for analysis, including initial setup and data modifications to plot the top 20 performing stocks and the bottom-20 stocks of the NIFTY-500 index data:

```
01.  #Let us import all the key libaries
02.  import time
03.  import matplotlib.pyplot as plt
04.  import seaborn as sns
05.  import matplotlib as mpl
06.  import numpy as np
07.  import pandas as pd
08.  #Let us ignore the warnings posted in the Notebook
09.  import warnings
10.  warnings.filterwarnings('ignore')
11.  #Let us use Matplotlib Inline in the Notebook
12.  %matplotlib inline
13.  nifty_500_index = pd.read_csv("nifty_500_stats.csv",sep=';',encoding='utf-8',thousands=',', na_values='No Data')
14.  #nifty_500_index.head(50)
15.  nifty_500_index.columns
16.  # Let us deleted irrelevant colums
17.  del nifty_500_index['Unnamed: 0']
18.  # Let us calculate new ratios based on availability of the data
19.  nifty_500_index['price_to_book_value'] = np.round(nifty_500_index.current_value / nifty_500_index.book_value, 3)
20.  nifty_500_index['3_year_Price_earnings'] = np.round(nifty_500_index.price_earnings / nifty_500_index.sales_growth_3yr, 3)
21.  #Let us plot the top 20 and bottom 20 market cap in the chart
22.  sort_nifty=nifty_500_index.sort_values("market_cap", ascending=False).head(20)
23.  sort_nifty2=nifty_500_index.sort_values("market_cap", ascending=False).tail(20)
24.  # Set the themes
25.  sns.set_theme(style="dark")
26.  # Initialize the matplotlib figure
27.  fig, (ax1, ax2) = plt.subplots(figsize=(16, 8), ncols=2, sharex=False, sharey=False)
28.  # Let us plot
29.  sns.set_color_codes("bright")
30.  sns.barplot(y="symbol", x="market_cap", data=sort_nifty,
31.          label="Market Cap in Crores", color="b", ax=ax1)
32.  #sns.set_color_codes("pastel")
33.  sns.barplot(y="symbol", x="market_cap", data=sort_nifty2,
34.          label="Market Cap in Crores", color="m", ax=ax2)
35.  sns.despine(left=False, bottom=True)
```

Figure 6.2: Plotting stock market analysis data - code

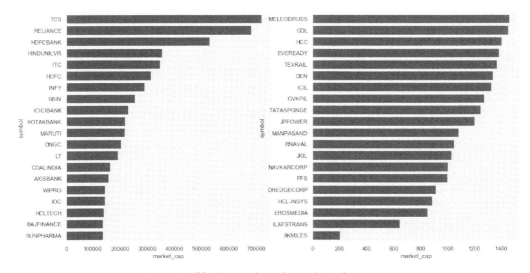

Figure 6.3: Plotting stock market analysis data - output

Exercise 6-2 : Trying Seaborn set_theme(), color_codes, despline(), and barplot()

Let us see try some of the key functions in Seaborn with the following example:

```
01.   #Let us see the high, low and current values of the stocks.
02.   sns.set_theme(style="ticks")
03.   sns.set_color_codes("bright")
04.   sort_nifty=nifty_500_index.sort_values("market_cap", ascending=False).head(10)
05.   sns.barplot(y="symbol", x="high_52week", data=sort_nifty,
06.               label="High Value", color="b")
07.   sns.set_color_codes("muted")
08.   sns.barplot(y="symbol", x="current_value", data=sort_nifty,
09.               label="Current Value", color="g")
10.   sns.set_color_codes("muted")
11.   sns.barplot(y="symbol", x="low_52week", data=sort_nifty,
12.               label="Low Value", color="y")
13.   sns.despine(left=True, bottom=True)
14.   #Where there are only 2 colors it means the stock is currently at it's top value
```

Figure 6.4: *Plotting stock market analysis data – exercise 6-2 code*

This code produces the following output:

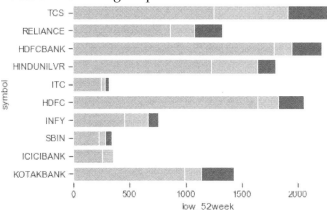

Figure 6.5: *Plotting stock market analysis data – exercise 6-2 output*

Exercise 6-3: Categorical data plotting – boxplot(), violinplot(), and boxenplot()

Let us see try some of the key functions in Seaborn with the following example. We shall leverage the same Nifty-500 stock summary.

```
1.   sns.set()
2.   sort_cat=sort_nifty.loc[:,['current_value','high_52week','low_52week']]
```

```
3. sort_nifty2=nifty_500_index.sort_values("market_cap", ascending=-
   False).head(10)

4. sort_cat=sort_nifty.loc[:,['current_value','high_52week','low_52w
   eek']]

5. sort_cat2=sort_nifty2.loc[:,['price_earnings','roce','sales_
   growth_3yr','3_year_Price_earnings','price_to_book_value']]

6. #Let us try to set some axes to avoid some overlapping text

7. g=sns.catplot(data=sort_cat2, kind="box")

8. g.set_xticklabels(rotation=30)

9. g=sns.catplot(data=sort_cat2, kind="violin")

10. g.set_xticklabels(rotation=30)

11. g=sns.catplot(data=sort_cat2, kind="boxen")

12. g.set_xticklabels(rotation=30)

13. sns.catplot(data=sort_cat, kind="box")

14. sns.catplot(data=sort_cat, kind="violin")

15. sns.catplot(data=sort_cat, kind="boxen")
```

We get the following output for the category plots executed:

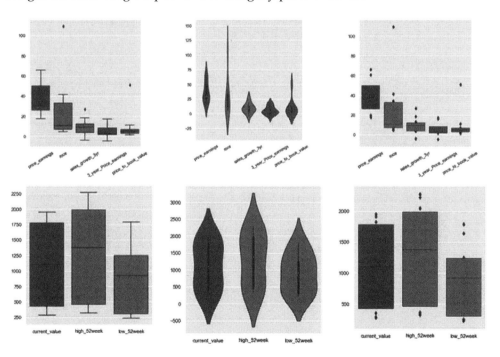

Figure 6.6: Plotting stock market analysis data – exercise 6-3 output

Exercise 6-4: Categorical data plotting – catplot() with the point, bar, strip, and swarm plot

Let us try some of the category plots by passing the parameters through *kind()*. *Seaborn* automatically plots the data as per categories with a single line of code. The line ax1.set_xticklabels(rotation=30) is used to tilt the axis variable ticks to avoid overlapping along the axes.

```
1.  ax1 = sns.catplot(data=sort_cat2, kind="point")
2.  ax1.set_xticklabels(rotation=30)
3.  sns.catplot(data=sort_cat, kind="point")
4.  ax1 = sns.catplot(data=sort_cat2, kind="bar")
5.  ax1.set_xticklabels(rotation=30)
6.  sns.catplot(data=sort_cat, kind="bar")
7.  ax1 = sns.catplot(data=sort_cat2, kind="strip")
8.  ax1.set_xticklabels(rotation=30)
9.  sns.catplot(data=sort_cat, kind="strip")
10. ax1 = sns.catplot(data=sort_cat2, kind="swarm")
11. ax1.set_xticklabels(rotation=30)
12. sns.catplot(data=sort_cat, kind="swarm")
```

We get the following output for the eight plots:

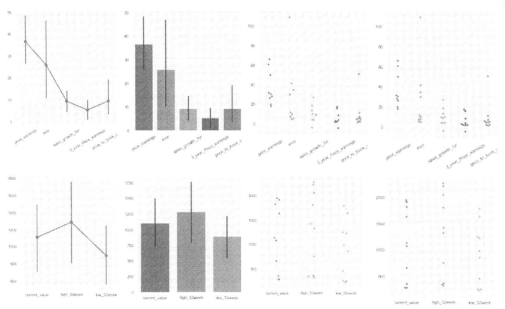

Figure 6.7: *Plotting stock market analysis data – exercise 6-4 output*

Exercise 6-5: Distribution of data plotting – distplot() kernel density estimate

Let us try some of the data distribution plots by passing the parameters through *kde* and *rug* parameters. The code leverages **distplot()** and *kernel density estimation* and rug plot options. We shall be covering this in detail in a short while.

```
1. import matplotlib.pyplot as plt
2. plt.style.use("seaborn-darkgrid")
3. fig = plt.figure(num=None, figsize=(24, 20), dpi=80, facecol-
   or='w', edgecolor='k')
4. sns.set_palette("Spectral")
5. plt.subplot(2, 3, 1)
6. ax1 = sns.distplot(sort_nifty2.book_value, rug=True, kde=True)
7. plt.subplot(2, 3, 2)
8. ax2        =        sns.distplot(sort_nifty2.price_earnings.drop-
   na(), rug=True, kde=True)
9. plt.subplot(2, 3, 3)
10. ax3 = sns.distplot(sort_nifty2.roce, rug=True, kde=True)
11. plt.subplot(2, 3, 4)
12. ax4 = sns.distplot(sort_nifty2.roe, rug=True, kde=True)
13. plt.subplot(2, 3, 5)
14. ax5 = sns.distplot(sort_nifty2.dividend_yield, rug=True, kde=True)
15. plt.subplot(2, 3, 6)
16. ax6 = sns.distplot(sort_nifty2.sales_growth_3yr, rug=True, kde=Tr
   ue)
17. plt.show()
```

The following is the output we get. As we can see, there is a display of the rugs in the form of ticks along the x-axis.

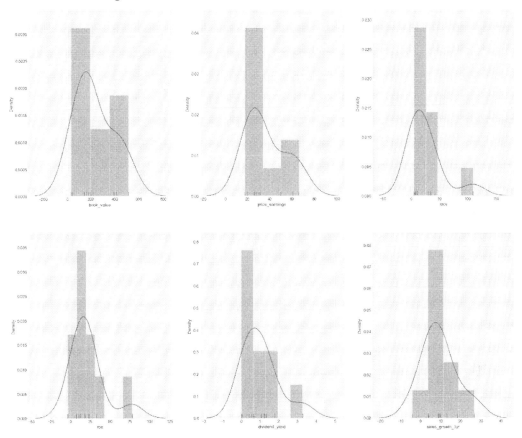

Figure 6.8: *Plotting stock market analysis data – exercise 6-5 output*

Exercise 6-6: Distribution of data plotting – barplot() with NumPy filter functions

In this exercise, we shall leverage the NumPy aggregate and filter choices to filter data for comparison. This relative comparison is one way to check the performance of various types under comparison.

```
01.   # Get various ratios across the industry spread given the Nifty Index
02.   ratio_type = 'median'
03.   ratios = nifty_500_index.groupby('industry').agg({'price_to_book_value':[ratio_type], 'price_earnings':[ratio_type],
04.                               '3_year_Price_earnings':[ratio_type], 'roce':[ratio_type],
05.                               'roe':[ratio_type], 'dividend_yield':[ratio_type]})
06.   ratios.columns = ratios.columns.get_level_values(0)
07.   ratios = ratios.reset_index()
08.   ratios = ratios.sort_values('price_earnings', ascending=False)
09.
10.   fig = plt.figure(num=None, figsize=(24, 16), dpi=80, facecolor='w', edgecolor='k')
11.
12.   # First chart needs Y axis so let us use matplot and Seaborn to plot this
13.   plt.subplot(1, 6, 1)
14.   ax1 = sns.barplot(x="price_to_book_value", y="industry", data=ratios, palette=("tab10"))
15.   ax1.set_xlabel('Price by Book Value', weight='bold')
16.   ax1.set_ylabel('Industry', weight = 'bold')
17.   ax1.set_title('Average across industries\n')
18.   # Let us define a function for repeat calls
19.   def plot_bar_chart(xval,yval,dataframe,xlabeltext,ylabeltext,axno,subplotno):
20.       plt.subplot(subplotno)
21.       axno = sns.barplot(x=xval, y=yval, data=dataframe, palette=("tab10"))
22.       axno.set_xlabel(xlabeltext, weight='bold')
23.       axno.set_ylabel(ylabeltext, weight = 'bold')
24.       axno.set_yticks([])
25.       sns.despine()
26.       plt.tight_layout();
27.   # Let us use the function to set the rest of the value comparison
28.   plot_bar_chart('price_earnings','industry',ratios,'Price By Earnings','',ax2,162)
29.   plot_bar_chart('3_year_Price_earnings','industry',ratios,'Price By Earnings 3 Yrs','',ax2,163)
30.   plot_bar_chart('roce','industry',ratios,'Return on Equity','',ax2,164)
31.   plot_bar_chart('roce','industry',ratios,'Return on Capital Employed','',ax2,165)
32.   plot_bar_chart('dividend_yield','industry',ratios,'Dividend Yield','',ax2,166)
```

Figure 6.9: *Plotting stock market analysis data – exercise 6-6 output*

We get the following output for the code executed. This is one way to decipher.

Figure 6.10: *Plotting stock market analysis data – exercise 6-6 output*

Exercise 6-7: Simple jointplot() with HexBin option

This exercise shall generate two sets of *Pandas* data series using the *NumPy* **random()** function. We shall make the second dataset with values bigger than the first to give a progressive trend in terms of random numbers and call the **Seaborn jointplot()** function with the **kind** parameter passed as *hex* to indicate a *HexBin* chart type.

The code to do this is as follows:

```
1. np.random.seed(1234)
2. sns.set_palette("prism")
3. datas1 = pd.Series(np.random.normal(0,30,125), name='dataset1')
4. datas2  =  pd.Series(2*datas1  +  np.random.normal(70,30,125),
   name='dataset2')
5. sns.jointplot(datas1, datas2, kind='hex')
```

The output is as follows:

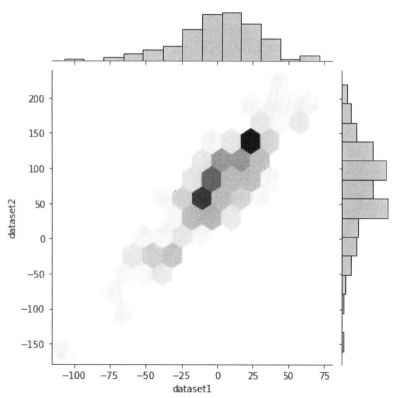

Figure 6.11: *Seaborn jointplot() – exercise 6-7 output*

Exercise 6-8: Simple pairplot()

In this exercise, let us try something with the Seaborn dataset of diamonds and use the **pairplot()** function and hue options on the subset. We shall try two pairplots - one each on the cut of the diamond and another on the carats.

The code is as follows:

```
1.  import seaborn as sns

2.  sns.set_theme(style="ticks")

3.  diamond = sns.load_dataset("diamonds")

4.  #Let  us  pickup  one  distinguishing  column  and  numer-
    ic data for pairplot

5.  diamond_subset=diamond.loc[:,['cut','carat','depth','ta-
    ble','price']]

6.  sns.pairplot(diamond_subset,    hue="cut")    #Let  us  pair-
    plot with a hue on cut type

7.  sns.pairplot(diamond_subset,    hue="carat")    #Let  us  pair-
    plot with a hue on carat type
```

The output of the program is as follows:

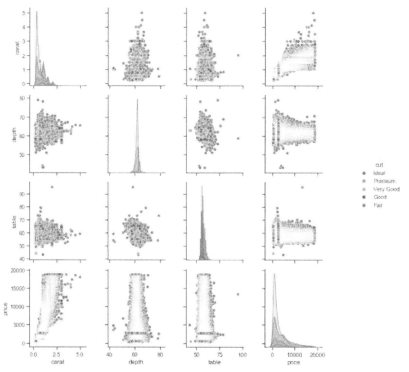

Figure 6.12: *Seaborn pairplot() – exercise 6-8 output – first plot*

It also produces the following output:

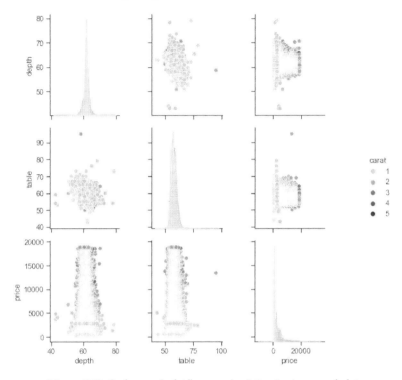

Figure 6.13: Seaborn pairplot() – exercise 6-8 output – second plot

Exercise 6-9: A pairplot with the Titanic dataset

Note: This exercise needs to be tried out. The solution is available in the Python Notebook given along with this book.

Question: Use the Titanic dataset available with the *Seaborn* library. Load the dataset and create a **pairplot()** output using the class of travel of the passenger. Try to use a unique *Seaborn* theme for the style.

Exercise 6-10: A pair grid with the Titanic dataset

In this exercise, let us try the **PairGrid()** function with the Titanic dataset. We use the grid diagonals and upper and lower sections of the grid with three distinct plots: a histogram - histplot, scatterplot, and a kdeplot and configure some color and colormap settings. We subset the data to include the columns with numerical values and the *Pandas* dataframe function **df.loc()**.

The code looks as follows:

```
1.  #Let us subset columns with numeric values
2.  titanic_subset=df.loc[:,['survived','age','pclass','sex','fare','
    class']]
3.  titapair = sns.PairGrid(titanic_subset)
4.  titapair.map_upper(sns.scatterplot,color='fuchsia',alpha=0.5)
5.  titapair.map_lower(sns.kdeplot,cmap='Spectral')
6.  titapair.map_diag(sns.histplot,bins=30, alpha=0.6)
```

The output of the program looks as follows:

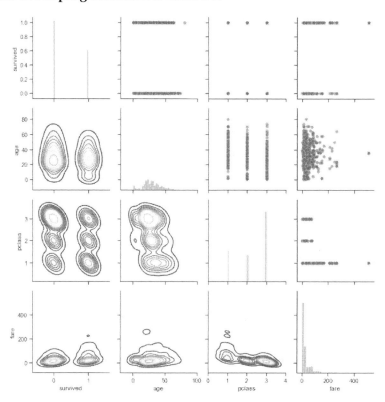

Figure 6.14: Seaborn PairGrid() – exercise 6-10 output

Exercise 6-11: A pair plot with the Titanic sub dataset

Note: This exercise needs to be tried out. The solution is available in the Python Notebook given along with this book.

Question: Use the Titanic Sub dataset available with the *Seaborn* library. Load the dataset and create a **pairplot()** output using the class column. What is your interpretation of the output?

Exercise 6-12: Application of various plots for real-time stock visualization

Let us try a visualization that could be very handy as an application. In this exercise, we leverage Yahoo! Finance APIs for fetching historical stock data for various firms. We shall use the data for plotting various trends and doing stocks analysis.

Let us first see the code for this exercise:

```
1.  import pandas as pd
2.  import numpy as np
3.  import matplotlib.pyplot as plt
4.  import math
5.  import seaborn as sns
6.  %matplotlib inline
7.  import warnings
8.  warnings.filterwarnings("ignore")
9.  from pandas_datareader import data as pdr
10. #!pip install fix_yahoo_finance --user
11. #import fix_yahoo_finance as yf
12. import yfinance as yf
13. yf.pdr_override()
14. symbols = ['TCS.NS','INFY.NS', 'WIPRO.NS', 'HCLTECH.NS', 'TECHM.
    NS', '^CNXIT', '^CRSMID','^NSEI']
15. symbols_2 = ['TCS.NS','INFY.NS', 'WIPRO.NS', 'HCLTECH.NS', 'TECHM.NS']
16. start = '2019-09-14'
17. end = '2020-11-30'
18. data = pdr.get_data_yahoo(symbols, start, end)['Adj Close']
19. data2= pdr.get_data_yahoo(symbols_2, start, end)['Adj Close']
20. normalize_stocks = data.apply(lambda x: x / x[0])
21. relate_industry = data2
22. relate_ind_summary=relate_industry.describe()
23. corr_rest = data.corr()
24. pair_value = corr_rest.abs().unstack()
```

```
25. # Returns
26. for symbol in symbols:
27.     returns = data.pct_change()
28. returns.head()
29. returns = returns.dropna()
30.
31. plt.style.use("seaborn-darkgrid")
32. fig = plt.figure(num=None, figsize=(24, 20), dpi=80,
    facecolor='w', edgecolor='k')
33. sns.set_palette("Spectral")
34. plt.subplot(3, 2, 1)
35. ax1 = sns.lineplot(data=normalize_stocks)
36. plt.subplot(3, 2, 2)
37. ax2 = sns.lineplot(data=data)
38. normalize_stocks = data2.apply(lambda x: x / x[0])
39. plt.subplot(3, 2, 3)
40. ax3 = sns.lineplot(data=normalize_stocks)
41. plt.subplot(3, 2, 4)
42. ax4 = sns.lineplot(data=data2)
43. plt.subplot(3, 2, 5)
44. ax5=sns.heatmap(returns.corr(),annot=True,fmt='g')
45. plt.subplot(3, 2, 6)
46. ax6=sns.heatmap(relate_ind_summary,annot=True, fmt='g')
47. plt.show()
48.
49. #Let us plot pair plots with a hue on symbol
50. sns.pairplot(returns[1:],hue=symbol)
51. sns.set_palette("bright")
52. #Let us plot pair plots without a hue
53. sns.pairplot(returns.dropna())
54. #Let us plot PairGrid with a scatter/kde and histogram
55. returns_fig = sns.PairGrid(returns.dropna())
56. returns_fig.map_upper(sns.scatterplot,color='dodgerblue',
```

```
      alpha=0.5)
57. returns_fig.map_lower(sns.kdeplot,cmap='prism')
58. returns_fig.map_diag(sns.histplot,bins=30, alpha=0.6)
59. rest_rets = returns.corr()
60. pair_value = rest_rets.abs().unstack()
61. # Normalized Returns Data
62. Normalized_Value = ((returns[:] - returns[:].min()) /(returns[:].
      max() - returns[:].min()))
63. Normalized_Value.corr()
64. normalized_rets = Normalized_Value.corr()
65. normalized_pair_value = normalized_rets.abs().unstack()
66. #Let us plot PairGrid with a scatter/kde and histogram
67. returns_fig = sns.PairGrid(normalized_rets.dropna())
68. returns_fig.map_upper(sns.scatterplot,color='fuchsia',alpha=0.5)
69. returns_fig.map_lower(sns.kdeplot,cmap='Spectral')
70. returns_fig.map_diag(sns.histplot,bins=30, alpha=0.6)
```

What does the code do?

- Import the libraries needed for visualization.
- Set the stock symbols we want to download. There are two stock sets – a longer one and a shorter one.
- Specify the dates for the stock details.
- Use Pandas Data Reader to download stock data between the dates specified from Yahoo! Finance.
- Normalize the stock returns to see the performance.
- Correlate the stock returns to understand the correlation between the symbols.
- Calculate the daily returns data for each stock.
- Plot line plots for stock trend and normalized returns for both longer and shorter stock symbols.
- Plot heatmaps of the stock performance with annotations.
- Plot a pairplot() on returns of the stocks.
- Plot a PairGrid() on returns data.

- Plot a PairGrid() on normalized returns data.

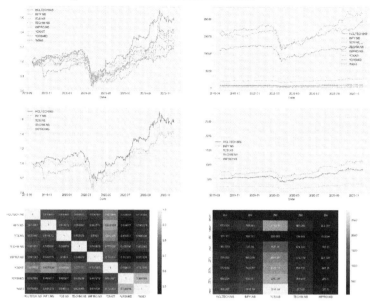

Figure 6.15: *Seaborn stock performance graphs of exercise 6-12 – part-1 line graphs and heatmap*

The following are the graphs produced for the **pairplot()** and **PairGrid()** code:

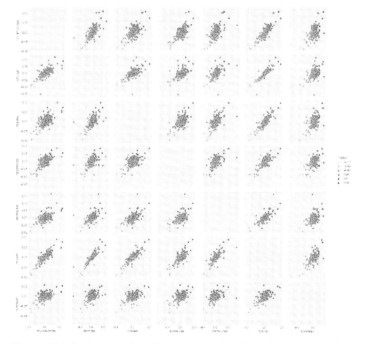

Figure 6.16: *Seaborn stock performance graphs of exercise 6-12: pairplot-1*

The second **`pairplot()`** looks as follows:

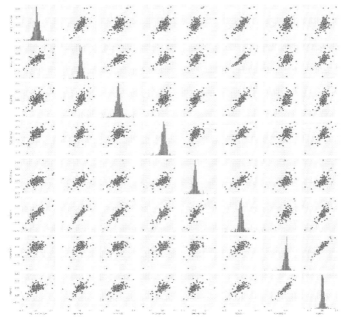

Figure 6.17: *Seaborn stock performance graphs of exercise 6-12: PairGrid-2*

The first **`PairGrid()`** looks as follows:

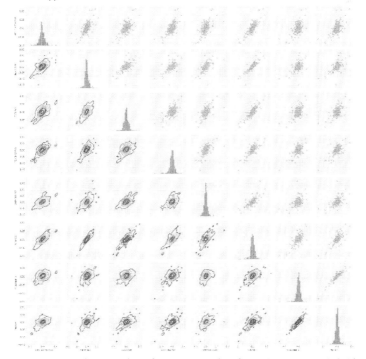

Figure 6.18: *Seaborn stock performance graphs of exercise 6-12 – PairGrid-1*

The second **PairGrid()** looks as follows:

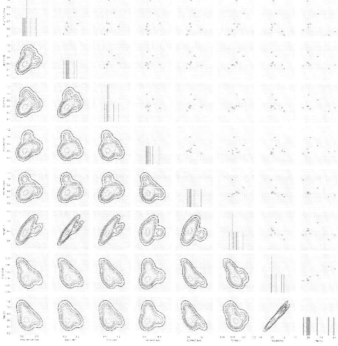

Figure 6.19: *Seaborn stock performance graphs of exercise 6-12: PairGrid-2*

Now that we have explored a fully relevant industry-specific visualization let us use other datasets and try category and distribution plots in the upcoming exercises.

Exercise 6-13 to 6-20: Application 2 - Data visualization of soccer team rankings using Seaborn

For this set of exercises, let us use a dataset on soccer team rankings provided by the FiveThirtyEight dot com site. This is available at **https://data.fivethirtyeight. com/**. For simplicity, we have downloaded the data **soccerleaguerankings538. csv**. This file contains current SPI ratings and rankings for men's soccer club teams.

Exercise 6-13: A simple pair plot with the soccer team rankings dataset

We load the relevant libraries, delete irrelevant columns, and plot a pairplot() with a hue on the leagues for this exercise.

Let us first see the code for this exercise:

```
1.  import pandas as pd

2.  import numpy as np

3.  import matplotlib.pyplot as plt

4.  import math

5.  import seaborn as sns

6.  %matplotlib inline

7.  import warnings

8.  warnings.filterwarnings("ignore")

9.  #Let us read the CSV file and Load the data

10. soccer = pd.read_csv("soccerleaguerankings538.csv",sep=',',encod-
    ing='utf-8',thousands=',', na_values='No Data')

11. soccer.head(2)

12. soccer_subset=soccer.loc[2:]

13. soccer_subset.head(2)

14. sns.pairplot(soccer_subset, hue="league")
```

We get the following output:

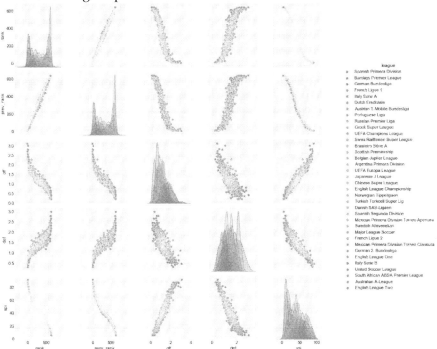

Figure 6.20: *Seaborn soccer team ranking of exercise 6-13: pairplot*

Let us try other types of plots on this dataset.

Exercise 6-14: Different types of jointplots() on the soccer rankings dataset

Let us try jointplots of various kinds in this exercise. To do this, let us cut down the number of divisions and focus on the top-5 leagues. We shall try a standard jointplot with a hue, a key density estimate, scatter, histogram, hexbin, regression, and residual plot. We would also use the **despine()** function.

The code looks as follows:

```
1. sns.set_style("white")

2. soccer_subset2=soccer_subset.loc[soccer_subset['league'].
   isin(['Barclays Premier League','Spanish Primera Division','
   German Bundesliga','French Ligue 1','Italy Serie A',])]

3. sns.jointplot(data=soccer_sub-
   set2, x="off", y="def", hue="league")

4. sns.jointplot(data=soccer_sub-
   set2, x="off", y="def", hue="league", kind='kde')

5. sns.jointplot(data=soccer_sub-
   set2, x="off", y="def", hue="league", kind='scatter')

6. sns.jointplot(data=soccer_sub-
   set2, x="off", y="def", hue="league", kind='hist')

7. sns.jointplot(data=soccer_subset2, x="off", y="def", kind='hex')

8. sns.jointplot(data=soccer_subset2, x="off", y="def", kind='reg')

9. sns.jointplot(data=soccer_sub-
   set2, x="off", y="def", kind='resid')

10. sns.despine(left=True)
```

The following is the output we see:

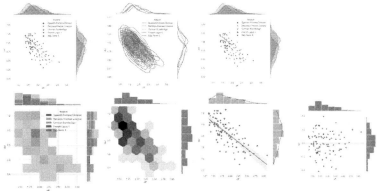

Figure 6.21: Seaborn soccer team ranking of exercise 6-14: different types of jointplot()

Exercise 6-15: Different types of relplots() with the soccer team rankings dataset

Let us try a simple **relplot()** option with the soccer team rankings dataset. We try two different replots – one, a standard **relplot()** with a hue on the league name and the second, one line plot across different leagues on offense and defense strength of various teams.

The code looks as follows:

```
1.  sns.relplot(data=soccer_subset2, x="off",
    y="def", hue="league")
2.  sns.relplot(data=soccer_subset2, x="off", y="def",hue="league",
    style="league", col="league",height=4, aspect=.7, kind="line")
```

We get the following output with the two lines of code above:

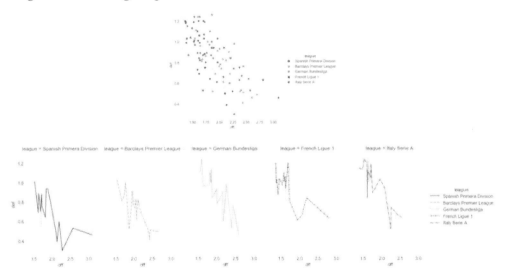

Figure 6.22: Seaborn soccer team ranking of exercise 6-15: relplot() outputs

Let us see a **clustermap()** in action in the next section.

Exercise 6-16: A clustermap() with the soccer team rankings dataset

We can create a **clustermap()** with the same dataset. To create a **clustermap()** that does not take certain types of columns, such as non-numeric data, we shall delete a few columns and create a **clustermap()** with a single line of code.

The code looks as follows:

```
1.  soccer2=soccer
2.  soccer2.head(2)
3.  del soccer2['league']
4.  del soccer2['name']
5.  g = sns.clustermap(soccer2, z_score=1,cmap="tab20c")
```

We get the output as follows:

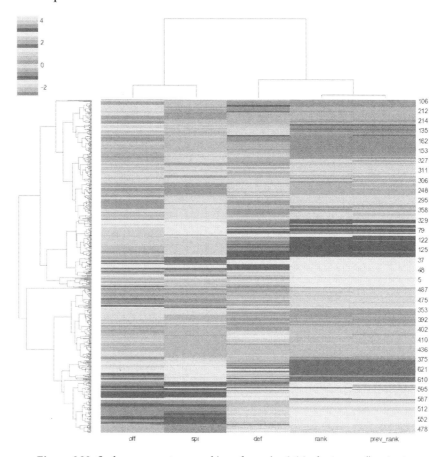

Figure 6.23: Seaborn soccer team ranking of exercise 6-16: clustermap() output

Exercise 6-17: Write code to create a PairGrid using Soccer team rankings dataset to create Scatter/KDE and histogram across the grid

Note: This exercise needs to be tried out. The solution is available in the Python Notebook given along with this book.

Question: Use the soccer subset dataset we used for the past few exercises. Build a **PairGrid()** with **scatterplot()** in the upper grid, **kdeplot()** in the lower grid, and **histplot()** in the diagonal portion of the grid. Try to use the *Spectral* colormap and a *Fuchsia* color to the plots we write code for.

Exercise 6-18: Write code for a simple pairplot() for one of the leagues with a hue on the team name

Note: This exercise needs to be tried out. The solution is available in the Python Notebook given along with this book.

Question: Use the soccer subset dataset we used for the past few exercises. Create a subset for one of the leagues, say *'Barclays Premier League.'* Use the dataset to create a **pairplot()** and use a hue on the team name.

Exercise 6-19: Write a program to create a PairGrid for English Premier League (Barclays Premier League)

Note: This exercise needs to be tried out. The solution is available in the Python Notebook given along with this book.

Question: Use the soccer subset dataset we used for Exercise 6-18. Create a **PairGrid()** with **swarmplot()** on the upper grid, **kdeplot()** on the lower grid, and a histogram on the diagonal portion. Use a colormap and color along with transparency parameter *alpha* for better visuals.

Exercise 6-20: Simple relationship plot between two variables on the soccer dataset

In this exercise, we can try a simple relationship plot of two variables - a simple **boxplot()** and **stripplot()** for various leagues in the dataset. The result will be a combination of both plots.

The code looks as follows:

```
1. import numpy as np
2. sns.set_style("white")
3. soccer_subset2=soccer_subset.loc[soccer_subset['league'].
   isin(['Barclays Premier League', 'Spanish Primera Division','Ger-
   man Bundesliga','French Ligue 1','Italy Serie A',])]
4. ax = sns.boxplot(x="rank", y="league", data=soccer_sub-
   set2, whis=np.inf)
```

```
5. ax = sns.stripplot(x="rank", y="league", data=soccer_subset2, col-
   or=".3")
```

We get the following output:

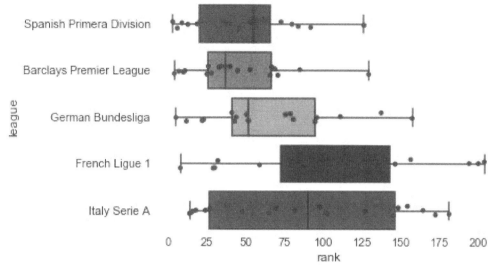

Figure 6.24: *Seaborn soccer team ranking of exercise 6-20: combination plot of boxplot() and stripplot()*

Exercise 6-21: Simple relationship plot between two variables on the Titanic dataset

In this exercise, we will use the Titanic dataset to try a few categorical plots such as **stripplot()**, **swarmplot()**, **catplot()**, **violinplot()**, **countplot()**, and **catplot()** with point, bar, and count types.

Each plot can be rendered with a single line of code. Each plot has certain parameters passed from the dataset to the Seaborn function, and it takes care of the statistical visualization automatically. Each line is executed in a unique Jupyter Notebook cell for better outcomes for this exercise of multiple plots.

The code looks as follows:

```
1. sns.set_style("white")

2. titanic = sns.load_dataset("titanic")

3. ax = sns.stripplot(x="class", y="age", hue="sex", data=titan-
   ic)   #stripplot with a hue on gender

4. ax = sns.stripplot(x="sex", y="fare", hue="class", data=titan-
   ic)  #stripplot with a hue on travel class
```

```
5.  ax = sns.swarmplot(x="class", y="age", hue="sex", data=titan-
    ic) #swarmplot with a hue on gender
6.  ax = sns.swarmplot(x="sex", y="fare", hue="class", data=titan-
    ic) #swarmplot with a hue on travel class
7.  #catplot with kind of stripplot with gender and class segregation
8.  g = sns.catplot(x="survived", y="fare",
9.                      hue="sex", col="class",
10.                     data=titanic, kind="strip",
11.                     height=4, aspect=.7)
12. ax = sns.violinplot(x="class", y="age", hue="sex", data=titan-
    ic) #violinplot with a hue on gender
13. ax = sns.stripplot(x="survived", y="age", hue="class", data=ti-
    tanic) #stripplot with a hue on class on survival
14. ax = sns.countplot(x="class", hue="who", data=titanic) #count-
    plot with a hue on passenger type
15. #catplot with kind of countplot with survival, passen-
    ger type and class segregation
16. g = sns.catplot(y="class", hue="who", col="survived",
17.                     data=titanic, kind="count",
18.                     height=4, aspect=1.5)
19. #catplot with kind of pointplot with gen-
    der, age, fare, and class segregation
20. g = sns.catplot(x="age", y="fare",
21.                     hue="sex", col="class",
22.                     data=titanic, kind="point",
23.                     dodge=True,
24.                     height=4, aspect=.7)
25. #catplot with kind of barplot with  age, passenger type, gen-
    der and class segregation
26. g = sns.catplot(x="class", y="age",
27.                     hue="who", col="sex",
28.                     data=titanic, kind="bar",
29.                     height=4, aspect=1.2)
```

The consolidated output is as follows:

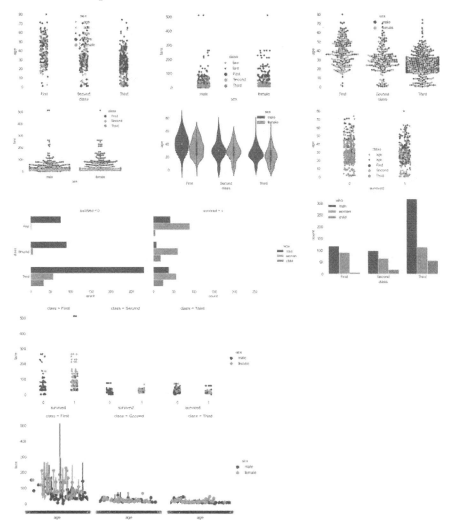

Figure 6.25: Seaborn Titanic dataset of exercise 6-21: consolidated categorical plots

Exercise 6-22: Use of distribution plots

In this exercise, we shall leverage the *Seaborn* library available to plot various distributions of data using the Titanic and soccer datasets we are using. We shall be using **scatterplot()**, **rugplot()**, **-kdeplot()** and **rugplot()**, **scatterplot()**, and **rugplot()** with a longer rug and different types of **ecdfplot()**.

Like Exercise 6-21, each plot can be rendered with a single line of code. Each plot has certain parameters passed from the dataset to the Seaborn function, and it takes care of the statistical visualization automatically.

Let us see the code:

```
1.  #Plot-1 Combination of Scatter and Rug Plot
2.  sns.scatterplot(data=soccer_subset2, x="rank", y="s-
    pi", hue="league")
3.  sns.rugplot(data=soccer_subset2, x="rank", y="spi", hue="league")
4.  #Plot-2 Combination of KDE and Rug Plot
5.  sns.kdeplot(data=soccer_subset, x="off")
6.  sns.rugplot(data=soccer_subset, x="off")
7.  #Plot-3 Combination of Scatter and Rug Plot with longer rug height
8.  sns.scatterplot(data=titanic, x="age", y="fare", hue="who")
9.  sns.rugplot(data=titanic, x="age", y="fare", hue="who",height=.2)
10. #Plot-4-8 Different types of Rug Plot on Offense, Defense, Perfor-
    mance and Ranking
11. sns.ecdfplot(data=titanic, x="fare", hue="class")
12. sns.ecdfplot(data=soccer_subset2, x="off", hue="league")
13. sns.ecdfplot(data=soccer_subset2, x="def", hue="league")
14. sns.ecdfplot(data=soccer_subset2, x="spi", hue="league")
15. sns.ecdfplot(data=soccer_subset2, x="rank", hue="league")
```

The following is the consolidated output:

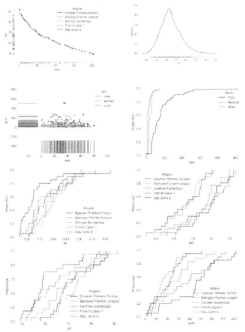

Figure 6.26: Seaborn soccer dataset of exercise 6-22: consolidated distributed plots

Let us try the other types of plots available in *Seaborn*.

Exercise 6-23: Use of histogram and KDE plots

We shall try different options available for plotting **kdeplot()** and **histplot()** in *Seaborn*. We leverage the soccer dataset for various plots – each with a single line of code.

The code looks as follows. We are using **hue** , **element**, **linewidth**, and **fill** parameters to plot different styles.

```
1.  sns.histplot(data=soccer_subset2)
2.  sns.histplot(data=soccer_subset2,x='spi',hue='league')
3.  sns.histplot(data=soccer_
       subset2,x='rank',hue='league',element="poly")
4.  sns.kdeplot(
5.      data=soccer_subset2, x="rank", hue="league",
6.      fill=True, common_norm=False,
7.      alpha=.5, linewidth=0,
8.  )
9.  sns.kdeplot(
10.     data=soccer_subset2, x="off", hue="league",
11.     fill=True, common_norm=False,
12.     alpha=.5, linewidth=0, multiple="fill"
13. )
```

The following is the consolidated output we get:

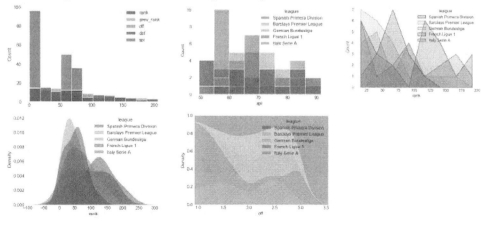

Figure 6.27: *Seaborn soccer dataset of exercise 6-23:
consolidated distributed plots – histogram and KDE plots*

Let us try some more plots such as Matrix plots heatmap and other regression plots.

Exercise 6-24: Use of Matrix plots – Heatmap()

In this exercise, we shall try some of the Matrix plots. We tried **clustermap()** earlier in this chapter. In this exercise, we shall try two types of **heatmap()**. One will be a standard **heatmap(),** and the second with a masked upper diagonal.

The code looks as follows:

```
1.  #Example-1 Let us build a random heatmap with a figure size
2.  fig, ax = plt.subplots(figsize=(16, 8))
3.  uniform_data = np.random.rand(12, 12)
4.  ax = sns.heatmap(uniform_data,annot=True)
5.  #Example-2 Let us build a random heatmap one diagonal blanked
6.  corr = np.corrcoef(np.random.randn(10, 200))
7.  mask = np.zeros_like(corr)
8.  mask[np.triu_indices_from(mask)] = True
9.  with sns.axes_style("white"):
10.     f, ax = plt.subplots(figsize=(7, 5))
11.     ax = sns.heatmap(corr, mask=mask, vmax=.3, square=True)
```

We get the following output:

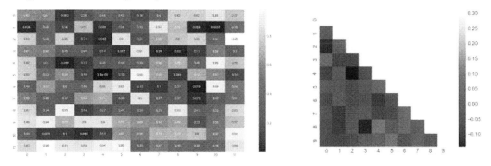

Figure 6.28: Seaborn heatmap example exercise 6-24

Exercise 6-25: Write a program to generate a heatmap on the stock market dataset

Note: This exercise needs to be tried out. The solution is available in the Python Notebook given along with this book.

Question: Use the Nifty stock market subset dataset we used earlier. Create a **heatmap()** of the columns with numerical values with an annotation of displaying the values and formatting options.

Exercise 6-26: Write a program to create jointplot() on the Titanic and soccer datasets

Note: This exercise needs to be tried out. The solution is available in the Python Notebook given along with this book.

Question 1: Use the Titanic dataset to create **jointplot()** with *age* in the x-axis, *fare* in the y-axis, and a hue on the *who*.

Question 2: Use the NIFTY stock market dataset to create a **jointplot()** with **price_earnings** in the x-axis, **market_cap** in the y-axis, and a hue on the *industry* column.

Exercise 6-27: Boxenplot() categorical plotting on Titanic dataset

In this exercise, we shall try some additional categorical plots in the form of **boxenplot()**. We can produce **boxenplot()** either using a direct function or bypassing the kind of plot as a **boxen** to **catplot()** function. The following is the code to produce two **boxenplot()** outputs:

```
1. ax = sns.boxenplot(x="age", y="class", data=titanic)
2. g = sns.catplot(y="age", x="survived",
3.                 hue="who", col="class",
4.                 data=titanic, kind="boxen",
5.                 height=4, aspect=.7);
```

We get the following output:

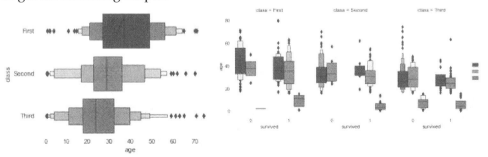

Figure 6.29: Seaborn boxenplot()example exercise 6-27

Exercise 6-28: Regression plots

In this exercise, we will try various types of regression plots such as a simple **lmplot()**, **lmplot()** with a hue parameter, **regplot()**, and **regplot()** using a log scale and **residplot()**.

The code looks like the following for seven different regression plots using the Titanic and soccer datasets we've been using:

```
1. g = sns.lmplot(x="fare", y="age", hue="class", data=titanic,
2.                 markers=["o", "x","."],  palette=dict(-
   First="g", Second="b", Third="r" ))
3. ax = sns.lmplot(x="def", y="off", hue="league", col="league",-
   data=soccer_subset2,
4.                 markers=["o", "x",".","p","+"])
5. ax = sns.lmplot(x="spi", y="rank", hue="league", col="league",-
   data=soccer_subset2,
6.                 markers=["o", "x",".","p","+"])
7. ax = sns.lmplot(x="rank", y="prev_
   rank", hue="league", col="league",data=soccer_subset2,
8.                 markers=["o", "x",".","p","+"])
9. ax = sns.regplot(x="def", y="off", data=soccer_subset2)
10.ax = sns.regplot(x="def", y="off", data=soccer_subset2,x_estima-
   tor=np.mean,color="g", logx=True)
11.ax = sns.residplot(x="def", y="off", data=soccer_subset2,col-
   or="m", label="league")
```

We get the following output for the soccer dataset plotting:

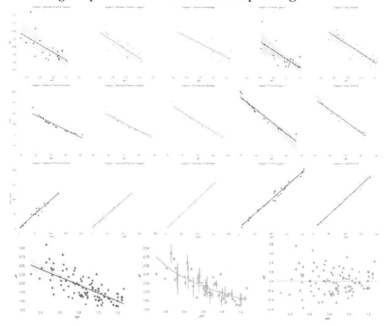

Figure 6.30: Seaborn regression plots example on the soccer dataset - exercise 6-28

And the following is the output for the Titanic dataset regression visualization based on the class of travel:

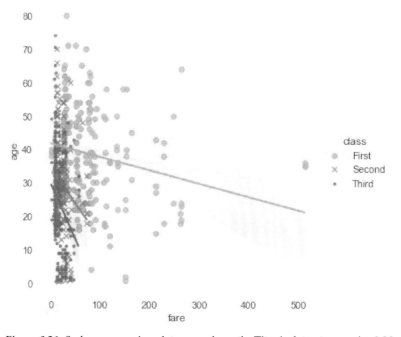

Figure 6.31: Seaborn regression plots example on the Titanic dataset - exercise 6-29

Let us do a bit of programming exercise.

Exercise 6-29: Write a program to create a jointplot() on the soccer dataset and kdeplot() on the Titanic dataset

Note: This exercise needs to be tried out. The solution is available in the Python Notebook given along with this book.

Question 1: Let us write a **jointplot()** on the soccer dataset using **kdeplot()**and **rugplot()** as marginal addition to **jointplot()**.

Question 2: Let us write code for **kdeplot()** on the Titanic dataset using *age* in x-axis with a hue of **who** and with a **fill** value of **True**, **common_norm** value of **False**, 50% transparency, and a **linewidth** of 0.

Exercise 6-30: A PairGrid on the soccer dataset

In this exercise, let us build:

- A **PairGrid()** on the soccer dataset with a hue on the league, and **histplot()**, **scatterplot(),** and **kdeplot()** along with the upper, diagonal, and bottom grids

- A **PairGrid()** split on parameters by passing x and y variables in an array

- **JointGrid()** by passing parameters

The code to do this work is given using the following few lines:

```
1.  # Build a PairGrid() on Soccer Dataset with a hue on the
    league, and histplot, scatterplot and kdeplot along with the uppe
    r, diagonal and bottom grids.
2.  g = sns.PairGrid(soccer_subset2, hue="league")
3.  g.map_diag(sns.histplot)
4.  g.map_offdiag(sns.scatterplot)
5.  g.map_diag(sns.kdeplot)
6.  g.add_legend()
7.  #Build a PairGrid() split on parameters by passing x and y vari-
    ables in an array
8.  x_vars = ["spi", "def", "off", "rank"]
9.  y_vars = ["spi"]
```

```
10. g = sns.PairGrid(soccer_subset2, hue="league", x_vars=x_vars, y_
    vars=y_vars)

11. g.map_diag(sns.kdeplot, color=".3")

12. g.map_offdiag(sns.scatterplot)

13. g.add_legend()

14. #Build a JointGrid() by passing parameters

15. g                             =                    sns.JointGrid(data=soccer_sub-
    set2, x="off", y="def", hue="league")

16. g.plot(sns.scatterplot, sns.histplot)

17. g.plot_marginals(sns.histplot, kde=True)
```

We get the following wonderful visualization for the data analyzed:

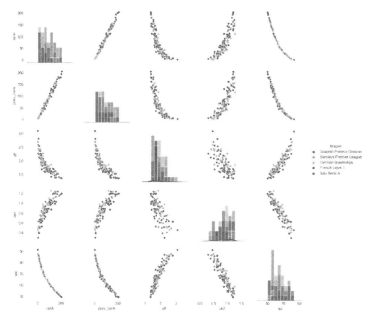

Figure 6.32: Seaborn PairGrid plot example on the soccer dataset - exercise 6-30

Let us see how the PairGrid plot for various leagues looks divided by SPI, defense, offense, and rank parameters.

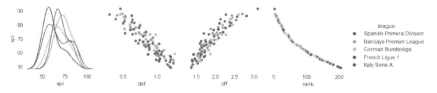

Figure 6.33: Seaborn PairGrid plot example on the
soccer dataset - exercise 6-30 in an array divided by variables

Let us see how the JointGrid looks like for the same dataset:

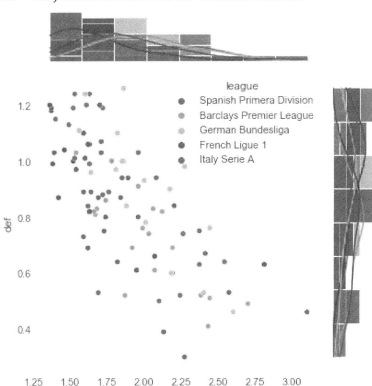

Figure 6.34: Seaborn JointGrid plot example on the soccer dataset - exercise 6-30

Let us complete the hands-on exercises with a programming exercise to try.

Exercise 6-32: Write a program to create a PairGrid() on the soccer dataset

Note: This exercise needs to be tried out. The solution is available in the Python Notebook given along with this book.

Tasks to Complete:

- Write a program to generate `PairGrid()` with a hue of league and corner=True
- Have a map of `kdeplot()` for the lower grid with no hue and ten levels
- Have a map of `scatterplot()` for the lower grid with marker type of 'x'
- Have a diagonal map of `histplot()` with element of `step` and `linewidth` of `0`, and `kde` of `True`
- Add a legend

- *Have the legend displayed to the anchor at .61 and .6*

This completes all our hands-on exercises for *Seaborn.* Let us check the resources available to enhance our skills further.

Seaborn resources

There are lots of resources available on the Internet to learn about *Seaborn*. The following is a curated list of some of the resources available for learning and understanding *Seaborn* for doing better Python coding and visualization:

Resource Name	Link
Seaborn official site	http://seaborn.pydata.org/
Seaborn tutorial	http://seaborn.pydata.org/tutorial.html
Seaborn API reference	http://seaborn.pydata.org/api.html
Seaborn example gallery	http://seaborn.pydata.org/examples/index.html
Seaborn introduction	http://seaborn.pydata.org/introduction.html
Seaborn quickstart	http://seaborn.pydata.org/installing.html#quickstart
Elite data science – Python Seaborn tutorial	https://elitedatascience.com/python-seaborn-tutorial
Visualization with Seaborn – Python data science handbook	https://jakevdp.github.io/PythonDataScienceHandbook/04.14-visualization-with-seaborn.html
Kaggle – Seaborn tutorial for beginners	https://www.kaggle.com/kanncaa1/seaborn-tutorial-for-beginners
Datacamp – Python Seaborn tutorial for beginners	https://www.datacamp.com/community/tutorials/seaborn-python-tutorial
YouTube video on Python for data visualization using Seaborn	https://www.youtube.com/playlist?list=PL998lXKj66MpNd0_XkEXwzTGPxY2jYM2d
YouTube – Visualization with Seaborn	https://www.youtube.com/playlist?list=PLE50-dh6JzC7X8VFX40yoIXnhctF2bR8F

Conclusion

So far, we have explored over 150 programs, including *Seaborn, Pandas, and Matplotlib,* to understand in-depth how to use *Python* to generate complex visualization and charting. As we can see from the examples in this chapter, *Seaborn* is very easy to use. We can do nice charting using just a single line of code compared to *Matplotlib* or *Pandas. Seaborn* is fast becoming a preferred library to use for advanced data visualization using *Python*. One aspect lacking currently in *Seaborn* is the interactive nature needed for plotting real-time data or the ability to visualize and filter the data progressively. The tools that can address this challenge shall be covered in the next two chapters. The *Bokeh* library covered in *Chapter 7* and libraries such as Plotly covered in *Chapter 8* is used extensively for dashboards and interactive visualization. Let us cover these libraries in *Chapter 7* and *Chapter 8*.

Questions

1. For what types of plotting will we choose the *Seaborn* library over *Matplotlib* and *Pandas?*

2. What are the benefits of *Seaborn* when we compare it with *Matplotlib?*

3. What are the benefits of *Seaborn* when we compare it with *Pandas?*

4. Is an interactive graph possible with *Seaborn?*

5. What are different types of visualization functions available in *Seaborn?*

Using Bokeh with Python

> "In school, we learn a lot about language and math. On the language side, we learn how to put words together into sentences and stories. With math, we learn to make sense of numbers. But these two sides are rarely paired. No one tells us how to tell stories with numbers ... this leaves us poorly prepared for an important task that is increasingly in demand."
>
> – *Cole Nussbaumer Knaflic*

We have covered some of the most popular plotting libraries for visualization using *Python*, namely, *Matplotlib, Pandas, and Seaborn*. Let us cover some of the other tools available for visualization in this *Chapter 7* on *Bokeh*. In *Chapter 8,* we shall cover *Plotly* and other tools. We shall be covering one of the most popular visualization tools with a good amount of interactive visualization capabilities in this chapter - *Bokeh*. We shall be covering the key features of *Bokeh* in good detail in this chapter.

Structure

In this chapter, we will cover the following topics:

- Introduction to *Bokeh*
- *Bokeh* plotting functions

- Examples and case studies for various types of visualizations using *Bokeh*

- *Bokeh* resources

Objective

This chapter aims to give Bokeh a basic introduction for experimenting with various data visualization elements such as charts and graphs. We will also touch upon details of how to use Bokeh elements for effective visualization. We shall start with simple examples of Bokeh and explore the libraries and various functions available before trying out some of the important charts and graphs we covered in earlier chapters. We shall conclude the chapter with some examples to try out and resources to consume.

Introduction to *Bokeh* visualization

Figure 7.1: The Bokeh logo

Bokeh *is* a powerful interactive visualization library compatible with modern web browsers providing an elegant outcome. It is useful for large-scale or real-time streaming datasets by providing a high-performing and optimal resource utilization to visualize interactive and versatile plotting. *Bokeh* takes away the pain of the need-to-know programming logic by easing how interactive plots and dashboards can be done with the underlying datasets. This feature makes it highly popular.

Bokeh, also known as "Boke," is a word from the Japanese language, meaning "blur." *Bokeh* is very popular as it makes the photographs visually aesthetic and appealing by redirecting viewers' focus on a particular area. *Bokeh* for plotting has a similar inclination to make the visualization appealing as well.

Bryan Van de Ven introduced *Bokeh* in 2013. Within a short time, it has enthralled the users due to the flexibility it offers.

Some of the benefits of using Bokeh include the following:

- Generation of images, regular grids, rectangular meshes, irregular 2D meshes, network, and graphs diagrams with a single library.

- Agility to leverage JavaScript and WebGL Libraries for high interaction as well as high-performance visualizations.

- Ability to generate output modes in a notebook or as HTML.

- Ability to run as a server application.

- Ability to embed plot outputs into web applications such as Django and flask. This allows us to extend interactivity.

Now let us see the key aspects of Bokeh visualization.

Introduction to *Bokeh* visualization

Let us see the key features of *Bokeh*.

Bokeh API modules and functions

- **bokeh.models** module - This is one of the widely used *bokeh* modules. It includes everything that makes a *bokeh* plot or an application. These include data sources, controls, tools and glyphs. It is sort of like a dictionary or a reference for *bokeh*.
    - o **bokeh.models** has the following functions:
        - ▪ bokeh.models.annotations(), / ->arrow_heads(), / ->axes(), / ->callbacks(), / ->expressions(), / ->filters(), / ->formatters(), / ->glyphs(), / ->graphs(), / ->grids(), / ->laWets(), / ->map_plots(), / ->mappers(), / ->markers(), / ->plots(), / ->ranges(), / ->renderers(), / ->scales(), / ->selections(), / ->sources(), / ->textures(), / ->tickers(), / ->tiles(), / ->tools(), / ->transforms(), / ->widgets.buttons(), / ->widgets.groups(), / ->widgets.icons(), / ->widgets.inputs(), / ->widgets.markups(), / ->widgets.sliders(), / ->widgets.tables(), / ->widgets.widget()

- **bokeh.plotting** module - This module/API is used like a *matplotlib.figure* command, and can be used for drawing rect(), arc(), image(), scatter(), text(), etc.
    - o **bokeh.plotting** has the following functions:
        - ▪ annular_wedge() / annulus() / arc() / geasterisk() / bezier() / circle() / circle_cross() / circle_dot() / circle_x() / circle_y() / cross() / dash() / diamond() / diamond_cross() / diamond_dot() / dot() / ellipse() / harea() / hbar() / hex() / hex_tile() / image() / image_rgba() / image_url() / inverted_triangle() / line() / multi_line() / multi_polygons() / oval() / patch() / patches() / plus() / quad() / quadratic() / ray() / rect() / segment() / square() / square_cross() / square_dot() / square_pin() / square_x() / step() / text() / triangle() / triangle_dot() / triangle_pin() / varea() / vbar() / wedge() / x() / y() / scatter() / bars-> hbar_stack(), vbar_stack() / lines -> hline_stack(), vline_stack() / areas -> harea_stack(), varea_stack() / hexbin()

- **bokeh.laWets** module - This module/API is used like a grid or subplots and is a way to combine multiple plots and controls in bokeh into a single document.

  o *bokeh.laWets has the following classes for use - GridSpec(nrows, ncols) and Spacer(*args, **kwargs)*

  o *bokeh.laWets has the following class functions and functions for use - apply_theme() , / dataspecs() , dataspecs_with_props() , / equals() , js_link() , js_on_change() , / laWet() , / lookup() , / on_change() , / properties() , / properties_containers() , / properties_with_refs() , / properties_with_values() , / query_properties_with_values() , / references(),remove_on_change() , / select() , / select_one() , / set_from_ json() , / set_select() , / themed_values() , / to_json() , / to_json_string() , / trigger() , / unapply_theme() , / update() , / update_from_json() , / column() , / grid() , / gridplot() , / laWet() , / row() , / widgetbox()*

- **bokeh.io** module - *bokeh.io* contains sub modules and functions for managing the bokeh documents and how and where they are shown and controlled such as load_notebook(), save_file() etc.

  o *bokeh.io has the following modules:*

    - bokeh.io.doc / bokeh.io.export / bokeh.io.notebook / bokeh. io.output / bokeh.io.saving / bokeh.io.showing / bokeh.io.state / bokeh.io.util

  o *bokeh.io modules and submodules have the following key functions to do various activities of visualization:*

    - curdoc() , / export_png() , / export_svgs() , / install_notebook_ hook() , / output_file() , / output_notebook() , / push_ notebook() , / save() , / show() , / set_curdoc() , / export_svg() , / get_laWet_html() , / get_screenshot_as_png() , / destroy_ server() , / get_comms() , / install_jupyter_hooks() , / install_ notebook_hook() , / load_notebook() , / publish_display_data() , / run_notebook_hook() , / show_app() , / show_doc() , / reset_output() , / curstate() , / default_filename() , / detect_ current_filename() , / temp_filename()

- **bokeh.palettes** module - Contains *palette* type definitions including *Matplotlib* palette styles, *D3* palette styles, *ColorBrewer* palette styles, and *Bokeh's* own palette styles - *Bokeh, ColorBlind,* and large palette styles

  o *bokeh.palettes has the following class functions and functions for use:*

    - cividis() , / diverging_palette() , / gray() , / grey() , / inferno() , / linear_palette() , / magma() , / viridis()

- **bokeh.settings** module - contains options and functions for configuring and setting all the global configuration by updating environment variables and settings that a bokeh component can access

  o *bokeh.settings* have the following functions for the *bokeh.settings* module:

    ▪ bokehjsdir(), / css_files(), / js_files(), / load_config(), / secret_key_bytes()

  o *bokeh.settings* functions can access and set the following settings in a *Bokeh* environment:

    ▪ allowed_ws_origin / auth_module / browser / version / cookie_secret / docs_cdn / docs_version / ignore_filename / log_level / minified / legacy / nodejs_path / validate_doc / pretty / py_log_level / resources / rootdir / secret_key / sign_sessions / simple_ids / ssl_certfile / ssl_keyfile / ssl_password / strict / xsrf_cookies

- Other key modules include the following:

  o bokeh.application / bokeh.client / bokeh.colors / bokeh.command / bokeh.core / bokeh.document / bokeh.driving / bokeh.embed / bokeh.events / bokeh.model / bokeh.protocol / bokeh.resources / bokeh.sampledata / bokeh.server / bokeh.sphinxext / bokeh.themes / bokeh.tile_providers / bokeh.transform / bokeh.util

We can see the usage of many of the functions and the methods outlined in the section above in our examples and exercises. Let us get to sample programs and see the visualizations in action.

Examples and case studies for various types of visualizations using Bokeh

Let us start with some of the basic aspects of *Bokeh*, just like we did with the earlier chapters. Let us start with a very simple plot.

A simple scatter chart

Let us take the example we referred to in *Chapter 4* on *Matplotlib* to plot a scatter plot that displays a message when scattered. The following program – with details as inline comments produces a scatter plot:

```
1.  #Import the Libraries
2.  import pandas as pd
3.  from bokeh.plotting import figure, output_file, show
```

```
4. from bokeh.io import output_notebook
5. from bokeh.models import ColumnDataSource
6. from bokeh.models.tools import HoverTool
7. import random
8.
9. #Let us define a random color function using hexadecimal value
10.def rand_color():
11.    return "#" + "".join(random.sample("0123456789abcdef", 6))
12.
13.#Define output to Jupyter Notebook
14.output_notebook()
15.#Load the scatter coordinates from a CSV file
16.#df  = pd.read_csv('drawpython.csv')
17.#Define the Pandas Dataframe
18.df  = pd.read_csv('https://raw.githubusercontent.com/kalilurrah-
   man/dvpkey/main/drawpython.csv?token=AM6ZPV5QTWCSCKO62Y767BC-
   736GNK')
19.source = ColumnDataSource(df) #Load to a Col-
   umn Data source for the plot
20.p = figure() #Define the Figure
21.p.circle(x='x', y='y',
22.          source=source,
23.          size=10, color=rand_color()) #Draw scatter us-
   ing CDS and random color function defined
24.p.title.text = 'A Sample Scatter Chart'
25.p.xaxis.axis_label = 'X Values'
26.p.yaxis.axis_label = 'Y Values'
27.hover = HoverTool() #Add a Hover tool
28.hover.tooltips=[
29.    ('X Value', '@x'),
30.    ('Y Value', '@y')
31.]
32.p.add_tools(hover) #Add the Hover tool
33.#output_file("scatterpython.html", title="Scatter Plot exam-
   ple") #If needed save into a file
```

34. `show(p)` *#Let us show the plot*`show(p)` *#Let us show the plot*

We get the following output for the program rendered:

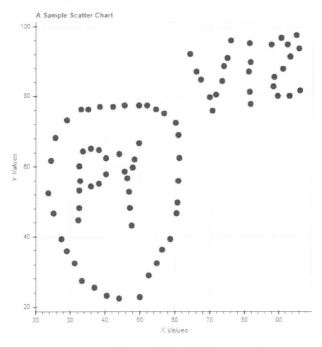

Figure 7.2: *The code for Bokeh scatter plot*

As we can see, the output is the same as what we saw in *Chapter 4* but in a different format and with different codes to produce the same output. Let us see an example of plotting a line plot using random values.

Line plot with a square pin marker

The following code is a simple example for plotting a line plot with a square pin marker. Let us see the code:

```
1. from bokeh.plotting import figure, output_notebook, show
2. import random
3. #Let us define a random color function using hexadecimal value
4. def rand_color():
5.     return «#» + «».join(random.sample("0123456789abcdef", 6))
6. N = 15
7. x = random.sample(range(10, 30), N)
8. y = random.sample(range(5, 42), N)
```

```
9.  randcolors=[]
10. for i in range(N):
11.    randcolors.append(rand_color())
12. output_notebook()
13. p = figure(title="Sample Scatter plot and Line", x_axis_label='x', y_
    axis_label='y')
14. p.square_pin(x, y, size=14, color=randcolors)
15. p.line(x,y)
16. show(p)
```

The function `rand_color()` returns a random color, and for each of the 15 elements of the array, we create a random color. For X and Y, we are choosing a number between the prescribed range. The line **p.line(x,y)** plots a line for the array. Hence, this program plots 15 lines per array for random X and Y coordinates created by the **random()** function.

The output will vary every time we run due to the random function. One of the outputs produced based on the random sample values generated looks as follows:

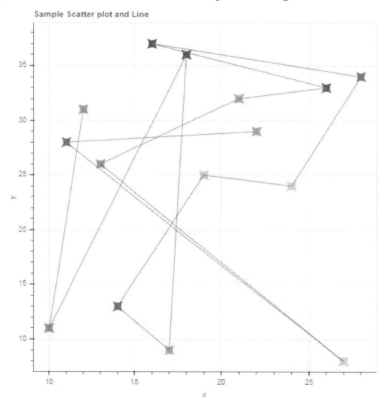

Figure 7.3: Bokeh line plot with markers

Now, let us see a bar chart using Bokeh.

Bar chart

For this, let us use the **hbar()** and **vbar()** functions. As the name say it, they produce horizontal and vertical bar chart for the data elements we pass.

```
1.  import random
2.  #Define the Array of Stocks and generate Random value for Shares
3.  stocks = ['Apple', 'Microsoft', 'Google', 'Amazon', 'Tes-
    la', 'NVidia']
4.  shares = random.sample(range(1, 100), 6)
5.  output_notebook() #Let us output the file to a notebook
6.  #Define a random color generation function
7.  def rand_color():
8.      return "#" + "".join(random.sample("0123456789abcdef", 6))
9.  N = 6
10. randcolors=[] #Let us generate random colors array
11. for i in range(N):
12.   randcolors.append(rand_color())
13. #Let us plot the first horizontal bar chart
14. p = figure(y_range=stocks, plot_height=250, ti-
    tle="Stocks Held - Horizontal Bar Chart")
15. p.hbar(y=stocks, right=shares, height=0.9, fill_color=randcolors)
16. p.x_range.start = 0
17. show(p)
18. #Let us plot the vertical bar chart
19. p1 = figure(x_range=stocks, plot_height=250, ti-
    tle="Stocks Held - Vertical Bar Chart")
20. p1.vbar(x=stocks, top=shares, width=0.9,fill_color=randcolors)
21. show(p1)
22. #Let us Sort and use the sorted value for plotting.  for descend-
    ing we us (reverse = True)
23. sorted_stocks = sorted(stocks, key=lambda x: shares[stocks.
    index(x)])
24. p2 = figure(x_range=sorted_stocks, plot_height=250, ti-
```

```
       tle="Stocks Held - Sorted Vertical Bar Chart")
25. p2.vbar(x=stocks, top=shares, width=0.9,fill_color=randcolors)
26. p2.xgrid.grid_line_color = None
27. p2.y_range.start = 0
28. show(p2)
```

This program produces the following diagram. The color combinations may be different for different runs, as we use random numbers for both colors and data generation for this program.

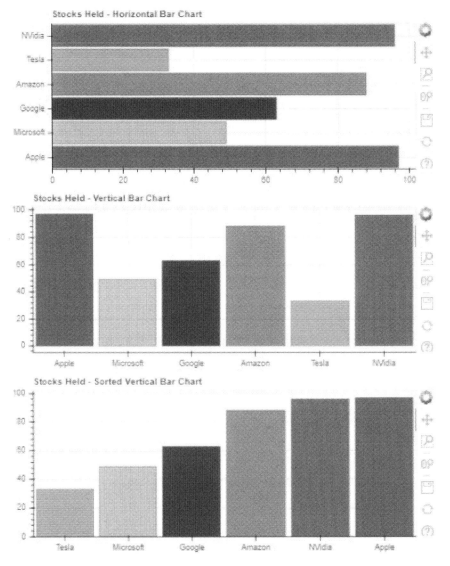

Figure 7.4: The Bokeh code output for horizontal and vertical bar charts

A simple mathematical formula plot

One of the big use cases for Python visualization is for scientific and engineering visualization. Let us try a simple trigonometric function along with random numbers. The colour combinations may be different for different runs, as we use random numbers for both colours and data generation for this program.

```
1. from bokeh.plotting import *
2. from numpy import *
3. import random
4. def rand_color():
5.     return "#" + "".join(random.sample("0123456789abcdef", 6))
6. output_notebook()
7. num = random.randint(1, 9)
8. x = linspace(-num, num, num*100)
9. y = (cos(x) - sin(x) )
10.p = figure(plot_height=250, title="Mathematical
   formula = cos(x) - sin(x)")
11.p.circle(x, y, color=rand_color())
12.show(p)
```

This program produces the following output. This output may vary based on the random numbers every time this is executed.

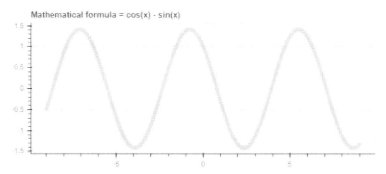

Figure 7.5: *An example for a Bokeh mathematical plot*

Use of patches

Let us see the use of patches to generate a visualization. We create an array – one each for x-region and y-region. We generate the number of elements based on a random integer generation. Once we create the array, we create a glyph using **figure()** and use **patches()** function to fill x and y regions.

```
1. from bokeh.io import output_file, show
2. from bokeh.plotting import figure
3. import random
4. import numpy as np
5. output_notebook()
6. rand_int = np.random.randint(5,15)
7. x_region = [random.sample(range(10, 40), rand_int),
8.             random.sample(range(-30, 10), rand_int+1),
9.             random.sample(range(40, 70), rand_int+2)]
10. y_region = [random.sample(range(10, 40), rand_int),
11.             random.sample(range(-30, 10), rand_int+1),
12.             random.sample(range(40, 70), rand_int+2)]
13. p = figure()
14. p.patches(x_region, y_region, fill_color = [rand_color(),rand_col-
    or(),rand_color()], line_color = rand_color())
15. show(p)
```

This program produces the following output:

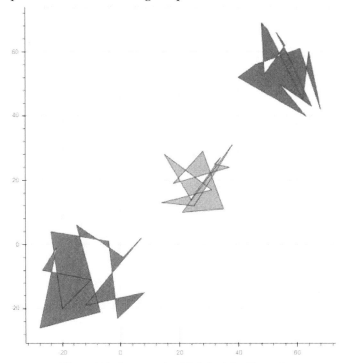

Figure 7.6: *An example of Bokeh plot with markers*

Use of grid plots and tool selects

The following example uses the **gridplot()** option and uses tool selects on a plot to use the renderer to replicate what is selected on one side of the grid on the other. The following code uses random values for the creation of the colors for plotting:

```
1.  from bokeh.models import ColumnDataSource
2.  from bokeh.laWets import gridplot
3.  from bokeh.laWets import column
4.  from bokeh.models import Slider
5.  from bokeh.plotting import figure, show
6.  from bokeh.io import output_file, show
7.  import random
8.  def rand_color():
9.      return "#" + "".join(random.sample("0123456789abcdef", 6))
10.
11. output_notebook()
12. num=random.randint(30,100)
13. #Let us create X axis dataset
14. x = list(range(-num+1, num))
15. k=random.randint(5,20)
16. #Let us generate y axis data set - one each for two columns
17. #Second one is a quadratic equation
18. y0, y1 = [abs(xx) for xx in x], [(abs(xx**2) + 2*xx + k) for xx i
    n x]
19. # create a ColumnDataSource for the plots to share
20. source = ColumnDataSource(data=dict(x=x, y0=y0, y1=y1))
21. #Use a lasso and box select tools
22. TOOLS = "box_select,lasso_select,help, reset"
23. # create a new plot and add a renderer
24. left = figure(tools=TOOLS, width=300, height=300)
25. left.circle('x', 'y0', source=source, color=rand_color())
26. # create another new plot and add a renderer
27. right = figure(tools=TOOLS, width=300, height=300)
28. right.circle('x', 'y1', source=source, color=rand_color())
```

```
29. #Use grid plot to link the renderer
30. p = gridplot([[left, right]])
31. #Show the plot
32. show(p)
```

This code produces the following output:

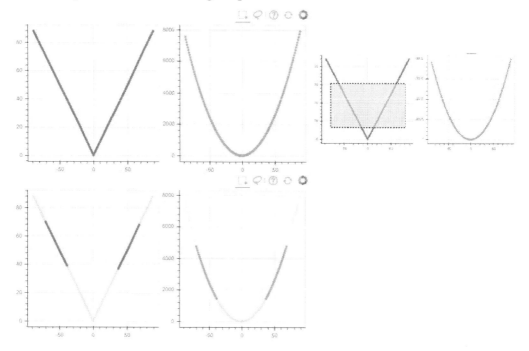

Figure 7.7: *A Bokeh example showing grid plot and tool-based area selects*

Simple mathematical plot

Let us see a simple mathematical plot using bokeh. Let us use random numbers to generate the sine and cosine plots. The following code is used for producing the plot:

```
1. import numpy as np
2. from bokeh.plotting import figure, show
3. from bokeh.io import output_file, show
4. output_notebook()
5. x = np.arange(0, 10.5, 0.2)
6. y = np.sin(x)
7. z = np.cos(x)
8. p = figure(plot_height=250, title="Simple Sine() and Co-
```

```
      sine() Waves using Bokeh")
9.  p.circle(x, y, color="navy")
10. p.circle(x, z, color="red")
11. show(p)
```

This program produces the following output:

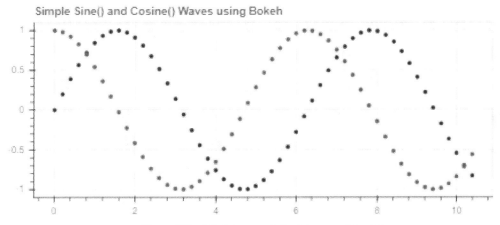

Figure 7.8: *A Bokeh example for trigonometric plot*

Use of data for a financial plotting

Let us use this to plot a real-life example of how financial plots use various visualization elements for plotting. For this example, we use the revenue numbers of Apple Inc. between 2008 to 2020, and we are hardcoding the data. Later in this book, we shall see how to leverage the finance libraries to ease the data collation and rendering. We include logic to change the bar's color when the revenue is lower than the preceding year. It has happened twice, as we can see. Let us see the following program:

```
1. #Let's put the years in an array for y axis
2. year = ['2008','2009','2010','2011','2012','2013','2014','2015','
   2016','2017','2018','2019','2020']
3. #Let's define the revenue in an array for x axis
4. revenue = [37.5,42.9,65.2,108.2,156.5,170.9,182.8,
   233.7,215.6,229.2,265.6,260.2,274.5]
5. #Let's build a bar chart with a purple color filling
6. output_notebook()
7.
8. color_list = []
```

```
9.  prev_val = 0
10. for i in revenue:
11.     if i > prev_val:
12.         color_list.append('green')
13.     else:
14.         color_list.append('red')
15.     prev_val = i
16.
17. p = figure(y_range=year, plot_height=250, title="Apple Reve-
    nue - HBAR")
18. p.hbar(y=year, right=revenue, color=color_list, height=0.9)
19. p.x_range.start = 0
20. show(p)
21.
22. p1 = figure(x_range=year, plot_height=250, title="Apple Reve-
    nue - VBAR")
23. p1.vbar(x=year, top=revenue, color=color_list, width=0.9)
24. show(p1)
```

This program produces the following output:

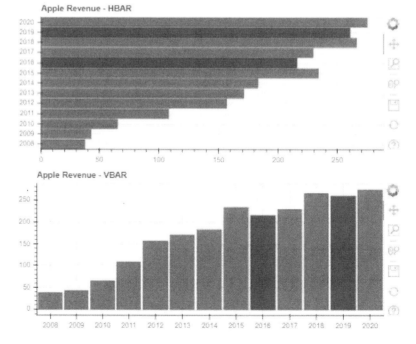

Figure 7.9: *A Bokeh example for a financial plot*

Let us see some more examples of categorical data using bar charts.

Multiple bar charts with the use of dodge

One of the challenges faced whilst using plotting libraries is the ability to group similar categories of data at the appropriate location whilst rendering the content. The use of *dodge* parameter whilst using x_range of the glyph allows us to render the bar charts effectively. Following the program, as shown in the inline comment leverages the *dodge* function to render a multi-category data in one type of rendering:

```
1.  from bokeh.io import output_file, show
2.  from bokeh.models import ColumnDataSource
3.  from bokeh.plotting import figure
4.  from bokeh.transform import dodge
5.  import random
6.  def rand_color():
7.      return "#" + "".join(random.sample("0123456789abcdef", 6))
8.  #Let's put the years in an array for x axis
9.  years = ['2008','2009','2010','2011','2012','2013','2014','2015',
    '2016']
10. #Let's define the revnue in an array for y axis
11. apple = [37.5,42.9,65.2,108.2,156.5,170.9,182.8,233.7,
    215.6,229.2,265.6,260.2]
12. msft = [60.42,58.44,62.48,69.94,73.72,77.85,86.83,93.58,85.32,89.
    95,110.36,125.84]
13. goog = [21.8,23.7,29.3,37.9,50.18,55.51,65.67,74.54,89.98,110.55,
    136.36,160.74]
14. amzn = [19.17,24.51,34.2,48.08,61.09,74.45,88.99,107.01,135.99,17
    7.87,232.89,280.52]
15. stocks = ['Apple', 'Microsoft', 'Google', 'Amazon']
16. data = {'stocks' : stocks,
17.         '2008'   : [int(apple[0]),int(msft[0]),int(-
    goog[0]),int(amzn[0])],
18.         '2009'   : [int(apple[1]),int(msft[1]),int(-
    goog[1]),int(amzn[1])],
19.         '2010'   : [int(apple[2]),int(msft[2]),int(-
    goog[2]),int(amzn[2])],
20.         '2011'   : [int(apple[3]),int(msft[3]),int(-
    goog[3]),int(amzn[3])],
```

```
21.         '2012'  : [int(apple[4]),int(msft[4]),int(-
    goog[4]),int(amzn[4])],
22.         '2013'  : [int(apple[5]),int(msft[5]),int(-
    goog[5]),int(amzn[5])],
23.         '2014'  : [int(apple[6]),int(msft[6]),int(-
    goog[3]),int(amzn[6])],
24.         '2015'  : [int(apple[7]),int(msft[7]),int(-
    goog[4]),int(amzn[7])],
25.         '2016'  : [int(apple[8]),int(msft[8]),int(-
    goog[5]),int(amzn[8])]
26. }
27. source = ColumnDataSource(data=data)
28. p = figure(x_range=stocks, y_range=(0, 300), plot_height=250, ti-
    tle="Revenues by the Year for top Stocks",
29.             toolbar_location=None, tools="")
30. p.vbar(x=dodge('stocks', -0.4, range=p.x_
    range), top='2008', width=0.1, source=source,
31.       color=rand_color(), legend_label="2008", line_col-
    or='white')
32. p.vbar(x=dodge('stocks',  -0.3,  range=p.x_
    range), top='2009', width=0.1, source=source,
33.       color=rand_color(), legend_label="2009",line_col-
    or='white')
34. p.vbar(x=dodge('stocks',  -0.2, range=p.x_
    range), top='2010', width=0.1, source=source,
35.       color=rand_color(), legend_label="2010",line_col-
    or='white')
36. p.vbar(x=dodge('stocks',  -0.1, range=p.x_
    range), top='2011', width=0.1, source=source,
37.       color=rand_color(), legend_label="2011",line_col-
    or='white')
38. p.vbar(x=dodge('stocks',  0.0, range=p.x_
    range), top='2012', width=0.1, source=source,
39.       color=rand_color(), legend_label="2012",line_col-
    or='white')
40. p.vbar(x=dodge('stocks',  0.1, range=p.x_
    range), top='2013', width=0.1, source=source,
41.       color=rand_color(), legend_label="2013",line_col-
```

```
   or='white')
42. p.vbar(x=dodge('stocks',  0.2, range=p.x_
    range), top='2014', width=0.1, source=source,
43.        color=rand_color(), legend_label="2014",line_col-
    or='white')
44. p.vbar(x=dodge('stocks',  0.3, range=p.x_
    range), top='2015', width=0.1, source=source,
45.        color=rand_color(), legend_label="2015",line_col-
    or='white')
46. p.vbar(x=dodge('stocks',  0.4, range=p.x_
    range), top='2016', width=0.1, source=source,
47.        color=rand_color(), legend_label="2016",line_col-
    or='white')
48. p.x_range.range_padding = 0.1
49. p.xgrid.grid_line_color = None
50. p.legend.location = "top_left"
51. p.legend.orientation = "horizontal"
52. show(p)
```

This program produces the following output:

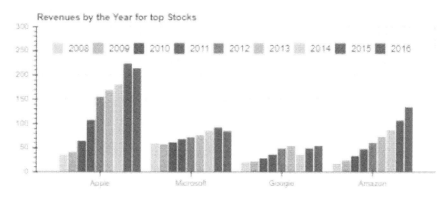

Figure 7.10: A Bokeh example showcasing grouped categorical data using a vertical bar chart

Dynamic line plot

Let us use the same dataset and use various **line**, **circle**, **circle_cross**, **diamond** plotting functions to render a different visualization:

```
1.  from bokeh.plotting import figure, output_file, show
2.  from bokeh.io import output_file, show
3.  from bokeh.models import ColumnDataSource
```

```
4.  from bokeh.plotting import figure
5.  import random
6.  def rand_color():
7.      return "#" + "".join(random.sample("0123456789abcdef", 6))
8.  #Let's put the years in an array for X axis
9.  years = ['2008','2009','2010','2011','2012','2013','2014','2015',
    '2016','2017','2018','2019']
10. #Let's define the revenue in an array for Y axis
11. apple    = [37.5,42.9,65.2,108.2,156.5,170.9,182.8,233.7,215.6,
    229.2,265.6,260.2]
12. msft = [60.42,58.44,62.48,69.94,73.72,77.85,86.83,93.58,85.32,89.
    95,110.36,125.84]
13. goog = [21.8,23.7,29.3,37.9,50.18,55.51,65.67,74.54,89.98,110.55,
    136.36,160.74]
14. amzn = [19.17,24.51,34.2,48.08,61.09,74.45,88.99,107.01,135.99,17
    7.87,232.89,280.52]
15. stocks = ['Apple', 'Microsoft', 'Google', 'Amazon']
16. output_notebook()
17. # create a new plot
18. p = figure(
19.     tools="pan,box_zoom,reset,save",
20.     title="Stock Market Data example",
21.     x_axis_label='Stocks', y_axis_label='Value'
22. )
23. # add some renderers
24. p.line(years, apple, legend_label="Apple")
25. p.circle(years, apple, legend_label="Apple", fill_color=rand_col-
    or(), size=8)
26. p.diamond(years, msft, legend_label="Microsoft", line_width=3)
27. p.line(years, msft, legend_label="Microsoft", line_color=rand_col-
    or())
28. p.cross(years, goog, legend_label="Google", fill_color=rand_col-
    or(), line_color=rand_color(), size=6)
29. p.line(years, goog, legend_label="Google", line_color=rand_col-
    or(), line_dash="4 4")
30. p.circle_cross(years, amzn, legend_label="Amazon", fill_color=rand_
```

```
    color(), line_color=rand_color(), size=6)
31. p.line(years, amzn, legend_label="Google", line_color=rand_col-
    or(), line_dash="6 4")
32. p.legend.location = 'top_left'
33. # show the results
34. show(p)
```

This program produces the following output:

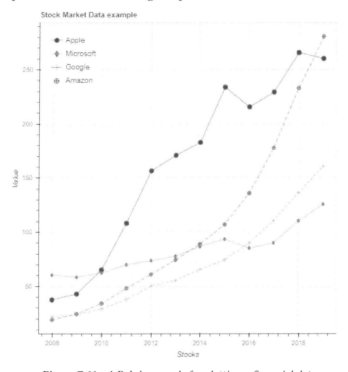

Figure 7.11: *A Bokeh example for plotting a financial data*

Scatter plot

Let us see the use of Bokeh libraries for creating a scatter plot. The following program uses two types of scatter plots. One with a radius for the scatter and another a basic scatter plot. Both the plots use random values for color and scatter datasets. As far as tools are concerned, various options are chosen that give the means to play around with the plot by selecting areas and datasets to analyze further. This is a very useful option in Bokeh.

```
1. import numpy as np
2. import random
3. from bokeh.plotting import figure, output_file, show
```

```
4.  np.random.seed(1968)
5.  #Define Number of points
6.  number = 1000
7.  #Assign the values to X & Y axis
8.  x = np.random.rand(number) * 100
9.  y = np.random.rand(number) * 100
10. #Choose a random color
11. radii = np.random.random(number) * 1.5
12. colors = [
13.    "#%02x%02x%02x" % (int(r), int(g), in-
    t(b)) for r, g , b in zip(50+2*x, 30+2*y, 30*x-20*y)
14. ]
15. TOOLS="hover,crosshair,pan,wheel_zoom,zoom_in,zoom_out,box_
    zoom,undo,redo,reset,tap,save,box_select,poly_select,lasso_se-
    lect,"
16. p = figure(tools=TOOLS)
17. p.scatter(x, y, radius=radii,
18.      fill_color=colors, fill_alpha=0.6,
19.      line_color=None)
20. show(p)
21. p1 = figure(tools=TOOLS)
22. p1.scatter(x, y)
23. show(p1)
```

This program produces the following output. The second plot is shown after the reflection of data selection using some of the tool choices.

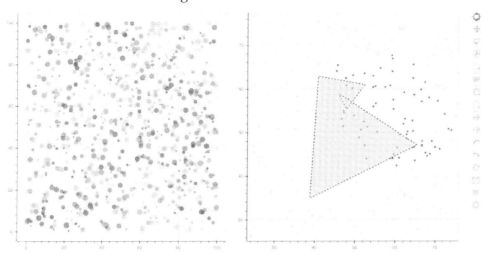

Figure 7 12: A Bokeh example showing scatter plot with the selection of an area using tools options

Use of colormap, colorbar, and linear colormap for plotting a scatter plot

Let use the **bokeh.models**, **bokeh.palettes**, **bokeh.transform** functions for a scatter plot. For this example, we use colormap to perform a linear colormap to generate the scatter plot. Let us see the example:

```
1.  import numpy as np
2.  import random
3.  from bokeh.plotting import figure, output_file, show, output_note-
    book
4.  from bokeh.models import ColorBar, ColumnDataSource
5.  from bokeh.palettes import Turbo256
6.  from bokeh.transform import linear_cmap
7.  output_notebook()
8.  TOOLS="hover,crosshair,pan,wheel_zoom,zoom_in,zoom_out,box_
    zoom,undo,redo,reset,tap,save,box_select,poly_select,lasso_se-
    lect,"
9.  p = figure(tools=TOOLS)
10. number = 500
11. x = np.random.rand(number) * number*2
12. y = np.random.rand(number) * number*2
```

```
13. ys = [i+2*x+(i*x)**3.2
14.      for i in range(number)]
15. #Use the field name of the column source
16. mapper = linear_cmap(field_name='y', palette=Tur-
    bo256,low=min(y) ,high=max(y))
17. source = ColumnDataSource(dict(x=x,y=y))
18. p = figure(plot_width=500, plot_height=500, title="Linear Col-
    or Map Based on Y values")
19. p.circle_cross(x='x', y='y', line_color=mapper,color=mapper, fill_
    alpha=1, size=12, source=source)
20. color_bar = ColorBar(color_mapper=mapper['trans-
    form'], width=8,  location=(0,0))
21. p.add_laWet(color_bar, 'right')
22. show(p)
```

This code produces the following output:

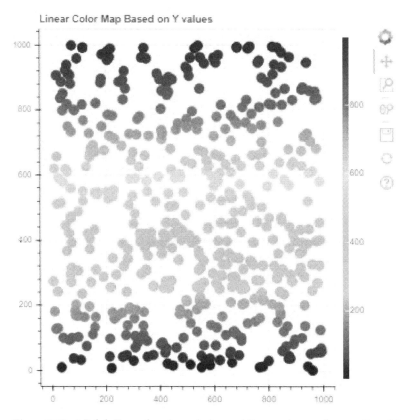

Figure 7.13: A Bokeh Example using colorbar and linear colormap for a scatter plot

Let us try a histogram next using Bokeh.

Histogram plot using Bokeh

Let us try a histogram next using Bokeh. The code has instructions on how we are building it:

```
1.  import numpy as np
2.  from bokeh.plotting import figure, output_file, show, output_notebook
3.  output_notebook()
4.  # Let us define my and Sigma
5.  mu, sigma = 0.1, 0.6
6.  # Let us build the normal distribution using mu and sigma
7.  measured = np.random.normal(mu, sigma, 999)
8.  # Let us build the histogram bins and edges
9.  hist, edges = np.histogram(measured, density=True, bins=99)
10. x = np.linspace(-3, 3, 777)
11. # Build a Probability and Cumulative Distribution Functions
12. pdf = 1/(sigma * np.sqrt(2*np.pi)) * np.exp(-(x-mu)**2 / (2*sigma**2))
13. cdf = (1+scipy.special.erf((x-mu)/np.sqrt(2*sigma**2)))/2
14. p = figure(title="Standard Histogram Normal distribu-
    tion (μ=0.1, σ=0.6)", tools='', background_fill_color="#faeffa")
15. p.quad(top=hist, bottom=0, left=edges[:-1], right=edges[1:],fill_
    color="navy", line_color="white", alpha=0.5)
16. p.line(x, pdf, line_color="gold", line_width=4, alpha=0.7, leg-
    end_label="Probability Density Function - PDF")
17. p.line(x, cdf, line_color="green", line_width=2, alpha=0.7, leg-
    end_label="Cumulative Distribution Function - CDF")
18. p.y_range.start = 0
19. p.legend.location = "top_left"
20. p.legend.background_fill_color = "#fefefe"
21. p.xaxis.axis_label = 'x'
22. p.yaxis.axis_label = 'Pr(x)'
23. p.grid.grid_line_color="white"
24. show(p)
```

This produces the following output:

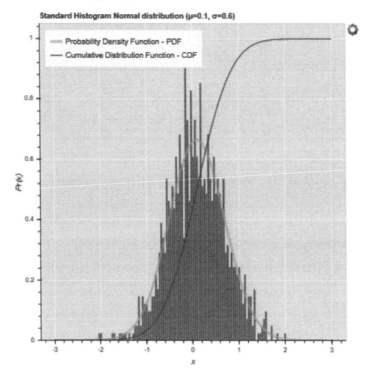

Figure 7.14: A Bokeh example of a histogram plot

As we can see, the probability distribution function is a gaussian bell curve. The cumulative distribution function is a cumulative line graph adding to 1 based on the histogram bins shown in the plot. The use of standard deviation (sigma σ) and mean (μ) determines the histogram representation. The number of bins determines the distribution of the histogram.

Let us see some examples of pie and donut charts.

Pie and donut charts in Bokeh

Let us see how the pie chart and donut chart are created in Bokeh. We shall use the same data set we used in our earlier *Chapter 5, Covering Pandas.*

Pie chart code

Let us see the first example for the creation of a pie chart using Bokeh:

```
01.   from math import pi
02.   import pandas as pd
03.   from bokeh.io import output_file, show
04.   from bokeh.palettes import Colorblind
05.   from bokeh.plotting import figure
06.   from bokeh.transform import cumsum
07.   output_notebook()
08.   brands = {'Samsung' : 30.25,
09.               'Apple' : 26.53,
10.               'Huawei' : 10.44,
11.               'Xiaomi' : 9.67,
12.               'Oppo' : 4.83,
13.               'Others' : 18.28
14.               }
15.   data = pd.Series(brands).reset_index(name='brandshare').rename(columns={'index':'brand'})
16.   data['angle'] = data['brandshare']/data['brandshare'].sum() * 2*pi
17.   data['color'] = Colorblind[len(brands)]
18.   p = figure(plot_height=350, title="Pie Chart", toolbar_location=None,
19.               tools="hover", tooltips="@brand: @brandshare", x_range=(-0.5, 1.0))
20.   p.wedge(x=0, y=1, radius=0.4,
21.           start_angle=cumsum('angle', include_zero=True), end_angle=cumsum('angle'),
22.           line_color="white", fill_color='color', legend_field='brand', source=data)
23.   p.axis.axis_label=None
24.   p.axis.visible=False
25.   p.grid.grid_line_color = None
26.   show(p)
```

Figure 7.15: *A Bokeh example for a pie chart*

We get the following output:

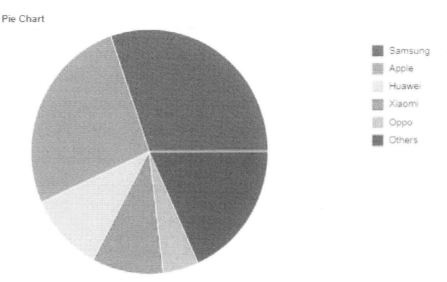

Figure 7.16: *A Bokeh example – code output of a pie chart*

Donut chart code

Let us see the first example for the creation of a donut chart using Bokeh:

```
01.  from math import pi
02.  import pandas as pd
03.  from bokeh.io import output_file, show
04.  from bokeh.palettes import Colorblind
05.  from bokeh.plotting import figure
06.  from bokeh.transform import cumsum
07.  output_notebook()
08.  brands = {'Samsung' : 30.25, 'Apple' : 26.53, 'Huawei' : 10.44, 'Xiaomi' : 9.67,
09.          'Oppo' : 4.83, 'Others' : 18.28 }
10.  data = pd.Series(brands).reset_index(name='brandshare').rename(columns={'index':'brand'})
11.  data['angle'] = data['brandshare']/data['brandshare'].sum() * 2*pi
12.  data['color'] = Colorblind[len(brands)]
13.  p = figure(plot_height=350, title="Donut Chart", toolbar_location=None,
14.          tools="hover", tooltips="@brand: @brandshare", x_range=(-0.5, 1.0))
15.  p.annular_wedge(x=0, y=1, inner_radius=0.2, outer_radius=0.4,
16.          start_angle=cumsum('angle', include_zero=True), end_angle=cumsum('angle'),
17.          line_color="white", fill_color='color', legend='brand', source=data)
18.  p.axis.axis_label=None
19.  p.axis.visible=False
20.  p.grid.grid_line_color = None
21.  show(p)
```

Figure 7.17: *A Bokeh example – code for a donut chart*

We get the following output:

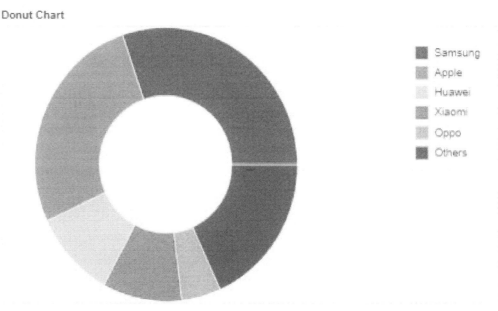

Figure 7.18: *A Bokeh example – code output of a donut chart*

Let us see some examples of area charts

Area charts

The following program produces a simple area chart using random colors and are based on random values against a leap year value in x axis:

```
1.  import numpy as np
2.  import pandas as pd
3.  from bokeh.palettes import brewer
4.  from bokeh.plotting import figure, output_file, show
5.  import random
6.  #Let us define a random color function using hexadecimal value
7.  def rand_color():
8.      return «#» + «».join(random.sample("0123456789abcdef", 6))
9.  output_notebook()
10. year= np.arange(start=2000, stop=2020, step=4)
11. numbers_1 = np.random.randint(40, size=len(year))
12. p = figure(title='Bokeh Area Chart', plot_width=800, plot_
    height=600,
13.              x_axis_label=›Year›, y_axis_label=›Number')
14. p.varea(x=year, y1=numbers_1, y2=0, color=rand_color(), al-
    pha=0.8)
15. show(p)
```

This program produces the following output:

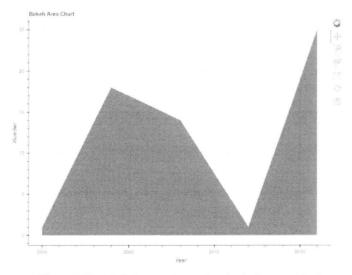

Figure 7.19: *A Bokeh example – code output of an area chart*

If we extend the program a bit by adding more areas in the form of a simple dataframe as executed in the following program, we can build a vertically stacked area chart.

```
1.  import numpy as np
2.  import pandas as pd
3.  from bokeh.palettes import brewer
4.  from bokeh.plotting import figure, output_file, show
5.  from bokeh.models import ColumnDataSource
6.  import random
7.  #Let us define a random color function using hexadecimal value
8.  def rand_color():
9.      return "#" + "".join(random.sample("0123456789abcdef", 6))
10. output_notebook()
11. years=np.arange(start=2000, stop=2024, step=4)
12. data = {
13.     "year": years,
14.     "numbers_1": np.random.randint(40, size=len(years)),
15.     "numbers_2": np.random.randint(40, size=len(years)),
16.     "numbers_3": np.random.randint(40, size=len(years)),
17.     "numbers_4": np.random.randint(40, size=len(years))
18. }
19. cds = ColumnDataSource(data=data)
20. p = figure(title='Bokeh Stacked Area Chart', plot_width=600, plot_
    height=400,
21.         x_axis_label='Year', y_axis_label='Number')
22. p.varea_stack(["numbers_1","numbers_2","numbers_3","num-
    bers_4"],x="year",
23.     color=[rand_color(), rand_color(), rand_color(), rand_color()],
24.     legend_label=["Area 1","Area 2","Area 3","Area 4"], source=cds)
25. p.legend.location = "top_left"
26. show(p)
```

This program produces the following output:

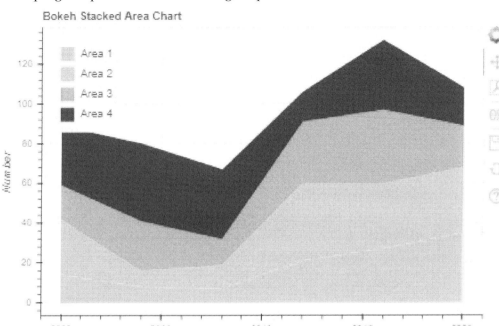

Figure 7.20: A Bokeh example – code output of a stacked area chart

Let us use the scatter plot to build an outline of a map using Bokeh.

Scatter plot to build a map outline

Let us build repetition of the *Exercise 5-69* from *Chapter 5* using *Bokeh* - creation of an approximate outline of India map using scatter plot. The code for creation of the map is as follows:

```
1.  import pandas as pd

2.  import random

3.  #Let us define a random color function using hexadecimal value

4.  def rand_color():

5.      return "#" + "".join(random.sample("0123456789abcdef", 6))

6.  output_notebook()

7.  #Let us read a file that has the lat long coords and popula-
    tion of top cities

8.  cities = pd.read_csv('https://raw.githubusercontent.com/kalilur-
    rahman/datasets/main/in2merged.csv')
```

```
9.  #Let us load the data from the file
10. latitude, longitude = cities['lat'], cities['lng']
11. #Let us load the Population and Proper Population (of metro area)
12. population, properpop = cities['population'], cities['population_
    proper']
13. #Let us Convert the Population into multiples of a million
14. properpop = properpop/1000000
15. colors=[]
16. for city in population:
17.   colors.append(rand_color())
18. TOOLS="hover,crosshair,pan,wheel_zoom,zoom_in,zoom_out,box_
    zoom,undo,redo,reset,tap,save,box_select,poly_select,lasso_se-
    lect,"
19. #Let us define the figure for rendering and use scat-
    ter plot and size as population
20. p = figure(plot_height=800, plot_width=600,tools=TOOLS)
21. p.scatter(longitude, latitude, radius=np.log10(properpop),
22.           fill_color=colors, fill_alpha=0.6,
23.           line_color=None)
24. p.title.text= 'Creating an India Map outline through Popula-
    tion data'
25. p.xaxis.axis_label = 'longitude of the City'
26. p.yaxis.axis_label = 'latitude of the City'
27. show(p)show(p)
```

We get the following output. Similar outlines can be created purely using a scatter plot using various latitudes and longitudes.

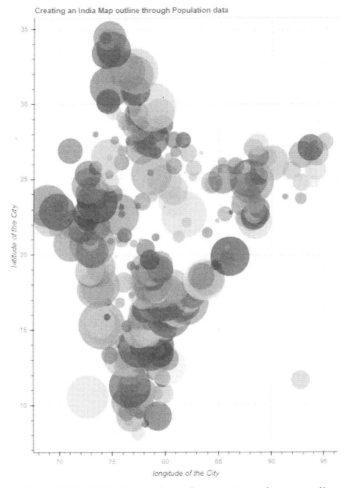

Figure 7.21: *A Bokeh example – code output to render map outline using latitude and longitude data with scatter bubble on another datapoint*

Let us build a hex-tile chart using Bokeh.

Hex tile plot

The following program produces a hex tile chart using Bokeh. It uses the *axial_to_cartesian* library to determine the values of an array for x and y axis values mapped to a hexagonal unit – akin to a scatter in a scatter plot.

```
1.  import numpy as np
2.  from bokeh.io import output_file, show
3.  from bokeh.plotting import figure
```

```
4. from bokeh.util.hex import axial_to_cartesian
5. output_notebook()
6. xvalues = np.ar-
   ray([0,  0,  0, -1, -1,  1, 1,  1, -1,  1, 2, 2,  0,
   2, -1, 2, 1,  0,  2])
7. yvalues = np.array([0,  -1,  1,  0,  1, -1, 0,  2,  2,
   1, 1, 2,  2, -1, -1, 0, -2, -2, -2])
8. p = figure(plot_width=400, plot_height=400,
   toolbar_location=None)
9. p.grid.visible = False
10.p.hex_tile(xvalues, yvalues, size=1, fill_col-
   or=["red"]*1+["green"]*6 + ["navy"]*6 + ["gold"]*6,
11.            line_color="yellow", alpha=0.9)
12.x, y = axial_to_cartesian(xvalues, yvalues, 1, "pointytop")
13.p.text(x, y, text=["(%d, %d)" % (xvalues,yvalues)
   for (xvalues, yvalues) in zip(xvalues, yvalues)],
14.        text_baseline="middle", text_align="center")
15.show(p)
```

This program produces the following output:

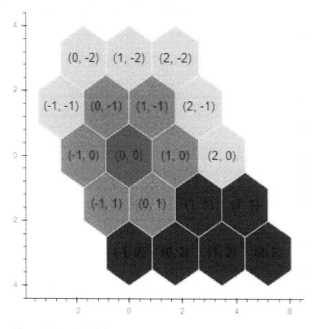

Figure 7.22: *A Bokeh example – code output to create a hex tile plot*

Let us try a dynamic plotting example using Bokeh.

Dynamic plotting using widgets in Bokeh

In the introduction section, we saw how widgets and plugins can be leveraged by the Bokeh plotting library. Let us build a dynamic plot using *bokeh* using the widgets available for usage:

```
1.  from bokeh.io import show
2.  from bokeh.plotting import figure
3.  from bokeh.laWets import column
4.  from bokeh.models import ColumnDataSource, CustomJS,
    Spinner, Select, ColorPicker, Panel, Tabs
5.  from bokeh.models.tools import HoverTool
6.  import pandas as pd
7.  import numpy as np
8.  import random
9.  #Define a Random Color Defintion function
10. def rand_color():
11.     return "#" + "".join(random.sample("0123456789abcdef", 6))
12. #Define the number of elements to plot
13. N = random.randint(10,100)
14. #Define the Data frame and assign to a Column Data Source
15. df = pd.DataFrame({'2017': np.random.random(size=N) * 100,
16.                    '2018': np.random.random(size=N) * 100,
17.                    '2019': np.random.random(size=N) * 100,
18.                    '2020': np.random.random(size=N) * 100},
19.               index=np.arange(0,N*5,5))
20. cds = ColumnDataSource(df)
21. #Define the first scatter plot using
    datasource and random colors assign to a tab
22. p1 = figure(plot_width=500, plot_height=500)
23. p1.add_tools(HoverTool(tooltips=[("y", "@index")]))
24. points = p1.scatter('2017', 'index', source=cds,
    size=4, marker="square",color=rand_color())
25. tab1 = Panel(child=p1, title="scatter")
26. #Define a line plot connected by diamond using
```

```
       datasource and random colors assign to a tab
27. p2 = figure(plot_width=500, plot_height=500)
28. line_plot=p2.line('2017', 'index', source=cds, line_color=rand_
    color())
29. diamond_plot=p2.diamond_
    cross('2017', 'index', source=cds, color=rand_color(),size=4)
30. tab2 = Panel(child=p2, title="line + diamond")
31. #Define a circle scatted plot using datasource and
    random colors assign to a tab
32. p3 = figure(plot_width=500, plot_height=500)
33. circle_plot=p3.circle('2017', 'index', source=cds, color=rand_
    color())
34. tab3 = Panel(child=p3, title="circle")
35. #Define a spinner widget and link to the specific
    bokeh glyphs in the 3 plots
36. spinner = Spinner(title="Marker Size", low=0, high=100,
    step=1, value=4, width=80)
37. spinner.js_link('value', points.glyph, 'size')
38. spinner.js_link('value', diamond_plot.glyph, 'size')
39. spinner.js_link('value', circle_plot.glyph, 'size')
40. spinner.js_link('value', line_plot.glyph, 'line_width')
41. #Define a Color Picker widget and link to the specific
    bokeh glyphs in the 3 plots
42. picker = ColorPicker(title="Color")
43. picker.js_link('color', line_plot.glyph, 'line_color')
44. #Define the column laWet and define how the tabs and
    widgets are mapped
45. laWet = column(Tabs(tabs=[tab1, tab2, tab3]) , spinner, picker)
46. #show the laWet interactively
47. show(laWet, notebook_handle = False)
```

This program produces the following output as in *Figure 7.23* Based on the interactive values chosen in the *ColorPicker* and the *spinner,* the glyphs for the programs and the tabs configured changes. We can program other widgets available in *bokeh* in a similar manner. When used with a *Bokeh*.server, the interactive features can be rendered as a web application through an HTML page rendered.

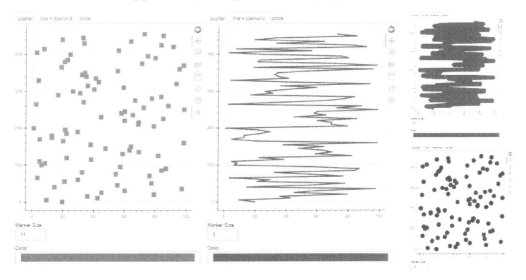

Figure 7.23: *A Bokeh example –for using widgets to change plot characteristics dynamically*

Given that we have done many examples in a standalone format let us try some examples in a case study format.

Bokeh case study

Let us use a freely available dataset at Harvard dataverse site. We shall be leveraging the US presidential vote data set from 1976 to 2016 across the various US States. We shall be tabulating data for the top two parties across the years. For the first exercise, we shall build a pivot table on the data and plot the trends:

```
1.  from bokeh.io import show
2.  from bokeh.plotting import figure
3.  from bokeh.laWets import column
4.  from bokeh.models import ColumnDataSource, CustomJS,
    Spinner, Select, ColorPicker, Panel, Tabs
5.  from bokeh.models.tools import HoverTool
6.  import pandas as pd
7.  import numpy as np
8.  import random
9.  #Define a Random Color Defintion function
```

```
10. def rand_color():
11.     return "#" + "".join(random.sample("0123456789abcdef", 6))
12. #Define the number of elements to plot
13. N = random.randint(10,100)
14. #Define the Data frame and assign to a Column Data Source
15. df = pd.DataFrame({'2017': np.random.random(size=N) * 100,
16.                    '2018': np.random.random(size=N) * 100,
17.                    '2019': np.random.random(size=N) * 100,
18.                    '2020': np.random.random(size=N) * 100},
19.                 index=np.arange(0,N*5,5))
20. cds = ColumnDataSource(df)
21. #Define the first scatter plot using datasource and random col-
    ors assign to a tab
22. p1 = figure(plot_width=500, plot_height=500)
23. p1.add_tools(HoverTool(tooltips=[("y", "@index")]))
24. points = p1.scatter('2017', 'index', source=cds, size=4, mark-
    er="square",color=rand_color())
25. tab1 = Panel(child=p1, title="scatter")
26. #Define a line plot connected by diamond using datasource and ran-
    dom colors assign to a tab
27. p2 = figure(plot_width=500, plot_height=500)
28. line_plot=p2.line('2017', 'index', source=cds, line_color=rand_
    color())
29. diamond_plot=p2.diamond_cross('2017', 'index', source=cds, col-
    or=rand_color(),size=4)
30. tab2 = Panel(child=p2, title="line + diamond")
31. #Define a circle scatted plot using datasource and random col-
    ors assign to a tab
32. p3 = figure(plot_width=500, plot_height=500)
33. circle_plot=p3.circle('2017', 'index', source=cds, color=rand_
    color())
34. tab3 = Panel(child=p3, title="circle")
35. #Define a spinner widget and link to the specific bo-
    keh glyphs in the 3 plots
36. spinner = Spinner(title="Mark-
```

```
    er Size", low=0, high=100, step=1, value=4, width=80)
37. spinner.js_link('value', points.glyph, 'size')
38. spinner.js_link('value', diamond_plot.glyph, 'size')
39. spinner.js_link('value', circle_plot.glyph, 'size')
40. spinner.js_link('value', line_plot.glyph, 'line_width')
41. #Define a Color Picker widget and link to the specific bo-
    keh glyphs in the 3 plots
42. picker = ColorPicker(title="Color")
43. picker.js_link('color', line_plot.glyph, 'line_color')
44. #Define the column LaWet and define how the tabs and wid-
    gets are mapped
45. laWet = column(Tabs(tabs=[tab1, tab2, tab3]) , spinner, picker)
46. #show the LaWet interactively
47. show(laWet, notebook_handle = False)
```

This program produces the following output:

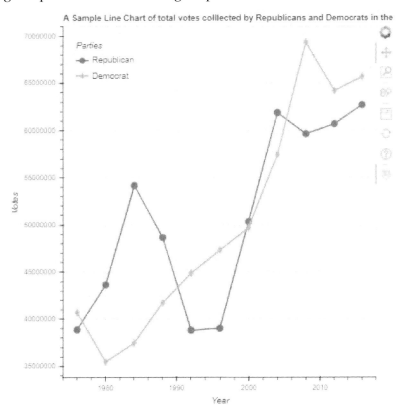

Figure 7.24: *A Bokeh example – from a dataset used for case study - line plots*

For the next chart, let us use the bar chart and use the *dodge* feature of the vertical bar chart to render the summary, along with a line plot to show the trend.

Bar chart and difference in data

The following program leverages the power of pandas, builds a new column for the difference in votes, and uses it to plot the vertical bar chart to show the trend over the years:

```
1.  import numpy as np
2.  output_notebook()
3.  #Define a function to calculate absolute difference
4.  def abs_min(a, b): # a, b is input arrays
5.      return np.abs(a[:,None]-b).min(axis=0)
6.  #Define a function to calculate difference
7.  def diff_min(a, b): # a, b are input arrays
8.      return (a-b)
9.  #Convert the pivot table to a pandas Dataframe
10. table31_df = pd.DataFrame(table3.to_records())
11. #Find the difference between democrats and republicans
12. diffs = diff_min(table31_df.republican.values, table31_df.demo-
    crat.values)
13. #Create a new column with difference in votes
14. table31_df.insert(3, "difference", diffs, True)
15. # Let us choose the top Republican states
16. table3_df = table31_df.sort_values(by='republican', ascending=-
    False).head(15)
17. states = table3_df['state']
18. # Convert the votes as multiples of millions
19. republican = table3_df['republican']/1000000
20. democrat = table3_df['democrat'] / 1000000
21. difference = table3_df['difference'] / 1000000
22. # Build a dataset for plotting
23. data = {'states' : states, 'republican' : republican,
24.         'democrat' : democrat, 'difference' : difference }
25. source = ColumnDataSource(data=data)
```

```
26. #Plot a vertical bar chart with dodge by a parameter
27. p2 = figure(plot_height=1500, plot_width=1200,x_range=states,
28.              y_range=(difference.min(),max(republican.
    max(), democrat.max())),
29.              title="State wise Votes - vote size in millions")
30. p2.vbar(x=dodge('states', -0.25, range=p2.x_
    range), top='republican', width=0.2,
31.         source=source, color="#ff0011", legend_
    label="Republican")
32. p2.vbar(x=dodge('states', +0.0, range=p2.x_
    range), top='democrat', width=0.2,
33.         source=source, color="#1100ff", legend_label="Democrat")
34. p2.vbar(x=dodge('states', +0.25, range=p2.x_
    range), top='difference', width=0.2,
35.         source=source, color="gold", legend_label="Difference")
36. #Plot a line plot
37. p2.line(x=dodge('states', -0.25, range=p2.x_
    range), y='republican',
38.         source=source, line_width=2, color='red',legend_
    label='Republican')
39. p2.circle_dot(x=dodge('states', -0.25, range=p2.x_
    range), y='republican',
40.         source=source, size=4, color=rand_color(),legend_
    label='Republican')
41. p2.line(x='states', y='democrat',
42.         source=source, line_width=2, color='navy',legend_
    label='Democrat')
43. p2.diamond_cross(x='states', y='democrat',
44.         source=source, size=4, color=rand_color(),legend_
    label='Democrat')
45. p2.line(x=dodge('states', +0.25, range=p2.x_
    range), y='difference',
46.         source=source, line_width=2, color='gold',legend_
    label='Difference')
47. p2.diamond_dot(x=dodge('states', +0.25, range=p2.x_
    range), y='difference',
```

```
48.            source=source, size=4, color=rand_color(),legend_la-
   bel='Difference')
49. #Add Formatting aspects
50. p2.x_range.range_padding = 0.1
51. p2.xgrid.grid_line_color = None
52. p2.legend.location = "top_right"
53. p2.legend.orientation = "vertical"
54. p2.yaxis.formatter=NumeralTickFormatter(format="00")
55. p2.xaxis.major_label_orientation = math.pi/2
56. #Add Hover
57. hover = HoverTool()
58. hover.tooltips=[('States', '@states')]
59. p2.add_tools(hover)
60. #Show the plot
61. show(p2)
```

We get the following output for the program:

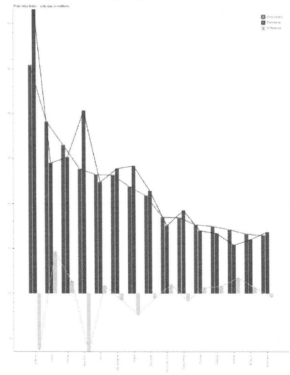

Figure 7.25: *A Bokeh example – from a dataset used for case study – comparative bar and line plots*

For the third exercise, let us see how both the parties performed in one of their bellwether states over the years. We shall take one state for each party to plot the performance and show the trend. The following code allows us to do the use case:

```
1.  from bokeh.models import FixedTicker
2.  from bokeh.palettes import Turbo256
3.  table41_df = pd.DataFrame(table.to_records())
4.  diffs = abs_min(table41_df.republican.values, table41_df.demo-
    crat.values)
5.  table41_df.insert(3, "difference", diffs, True)
6.  table4_df = table41_df.sort_values(by='democrat', ascending=-
    False)
7.  states = table4_df['state']
8.  #Change the values in 1000s of vote
9.  republican = table4_df['republican']/1000
10. democrat = table4_df['democrat'] / 1000
11. difference = table4_df['difference'] / 1000
12. year = table4_df['year'].sort_values(ascending=True).unique()
13. table4_df.republican.fillna(0)
14. table4_df.difference.fillna(0)
15. table4_df.democrat.fillna(0)
16. tab4_pivot = pd.pivot_table(table4_df, values=['republican','dem-
    ocrat','difference'],
17.                             index=['year'], col-
    umns=['state'], aggfunc=np.sum, margins=True)
18. flat_tab4_df = pd.DataFrame(tab4_pivot.to_records())
19. tabcols = [flat_tab4_df.columns]
20. years = table4_df['year']
21. states = table4_df['state']
22. republican = table4_df['republican']/1000
23. democrat = table4_df['democrat'] / 1000
24. difference = table4_df['difference'] / 1000
25. votegroup = ['democrat', 'republican','difference']
26. source = ColumnDataSource(data=dict(x=tabcols, democrat=demo-
    crat, republican=republican, difference=difference,))
```

```
27.p4 = figure(width=900, height=800) #, x_axis_type="datetime")
28.years = flat_tab4_df.year
29.values = flat_tab4_df["('democrat', 'California')"]
30.rvalues = flat_tab4_df["('republican', 'California')"]
31.#Plotting for a democrat state - California
32.p4.vbar(years, top = values, width = .9, fill_alpha = .5,line_
   alpha = .5,
33.        fill_color = rand_color(), line_color=rand_color(), line_
   dash='dashed')
34.p4.line(years,rvalues,line_width=4,line_color="red",line_
   dash="dotted")
35.p4.circle(years,rvalues,radius=.2,fill_color='yellow',line_
   color=rand_color())
36.hover = HoverTool()
37.hover.tooltips=[('Votes', '@top'),('Year',  '@x')]
38.p4.x_range.range_padding = 0.1
39.p4.xgrid.grid_line_color = None
40.p4.yaxis.formatter=NumeralTickFormatter(format="00")
41.p4.xaxis.major_label_orientation = math.pi/2
42.p4.add_tools(hover)
43.show(p4)
44.
45.p5 = figure(width=900, height=800)
46.years = flat_tab4_df.year
47.#Plotting for a republican state - Texas
48.values = flat_tab4_df["('republican', 'Texas')"]
49.dvalues = flat_tab4_df["('democrat', 'Texas')"]
50.divalues = flat_tab4_df["('difference', 'Texas')"]
51.p5.vbar(years, top = values, width = .9, fill_alpha = .5,line_al-
   pha = .5,
52.        fill_color = rand_color(), line_color=rand_color(), line_
   dash='dotted')
53.p5.line(years,dvalues,line_width=4,line_color="navy",line_
   dash="dotted")
```

```
54. p5.circle(years,dvalues,radius=.2,fill_color='yellow',line_col-
    or=rand_color())
55. p5.line(years,divalues,line_width=2,line_color=rand_color(),line_
    dash="dashdot")
56. hover = HoverTool()
57. hover.tooltips=[('Votes', '@top'),('Year',   '@x')]
58. p5.x_range.range_padding = 0.1
59. p5.xgrid.grid_line_color = None
60. p5.yaxis.formatter=NumeralTickFormatter(format="00")
61. p5.xaxis.major_label_orientation = math.pi/2
62. p5.add_tools(hover)
63. show(p5)
```

The output is as follows. It can be seen that the Democrats have last won Texas in 1976 and Republicans won California in 1988, and their political rival has been winning the states continuously since the last win. This is one example to showcase how a good visualization helps us draw insights very quickly.

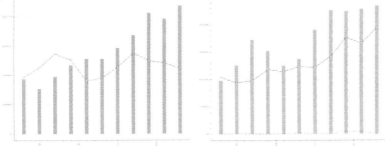

Figure 7.26: A Bokeh example – from a dataset used for case study – data insight for a subset of states

More examples are given in the Jupyter Notebook that comes with this book to play around with the data and generate more insightful visualizations. As a question, what would be the visualizations we will undertake for this dataset? What are the different ways to render meaningful visualizations for this dataset?

Now let us focus on some of the resources available for Bokeh to understand the features better.

Bokeh – additional resources

In this chapter, we covered a good amount of introduction to data visualization. There are plenty of excellent resources on *Bokeh* that we can refer to. Some of the resources to consider and leverage are as follows. Please note that *Bokeh* has a module called *resources,* and this section is not for the details of this module.

Resource	Purpose
Bokeh landing site	https://docs.bokeh.org/en/latest/index.html
Bokeh installation guide	https://docs.bokeh.org/en/latest/docs/installation.html
User guide	https://docs.bokeh.org/en/latest/docs/user_guide.html
Examples gallery	https://docs.bokeh.org/en/latest/docs/gallery.html
Reference guide	https://docs.bokeh.org/en/latest/docs/reference.html
Developers guide	https://docs.bokeh.org/en/latest/docs/dev_guide.html
Bokeh tutorial	https://mybinder.org/v2/gh/bokeh/bokeh-notebooks/master?filepath=tutorial%2F00%20-%20Introduction%20and%20Setup.ipynb
Bokeh user community forum	https://discourse.bokeh.org/
Visualizing data with Bokeh and Pandas	https://programminghistorian.org/en/lessons/visualizing-with-bokeh
Building a server app using Flask and Bokeh	https://github.com/realpython/flask-bokeh-example/blob/master/tutorial.md

Conclusion

In this chapter, we covered a good amount of introduction to Data Visualization elements using *Bokeh*. We got introduced to various functions within *Bokeh* and how to leverage them effectively. We covered a lot of programs to see how we can emulate various visualizations using *Bokeh*. We also evaluated a few interactive plotting options in Bokeh. In the next chapter, we shall explore other visualization libraries for interactive visualization and dashboard using Python. This gives us an understanding of various tools available and the flexibility to choose the best approach for the visualization tasks. We shall be covering *Plotly, Folium, MPLFinance, Altair,* and other libraries available to do visualization. We cover more libraries, only a few examples, and no extensive exploration as we did for *Matplotlib, Pandas, Seaborn,* and *Bokeh* in the past four chapters.

Questions

1. For the US presidential election dataset shared, what will be the best visualization for sharing the trends over the past 20 years?

2. What charts can we create using the US presidential dataset?

3. How can we add interactions to the *Bokeh* chart?

4. What are various types of functions available in the *bokeh.resources* module?

5. What are the different ways to update *glyphs* in *bokeh?*

6. How can we build a *bokeh* server application?

7. What can we use to output the visualization to a Jupyter Notebook? What is the benefit of saving a file?

8. What is the main difference between *bokeh* and *seaborn?*

9. What is the main difference between *bokeh* and *pandas?*

10. What is the main difference between *bokeh* and *matplotlib?*

11. What are some gaps in using *bokeh* for plotting compared to commercial applications such as *Tableau, Qlik Sense,* and others?

Using Plotly, Folium, and Other Tools for Visualization

> "There are two goals when presenting data: convey your story and establish credibility." and "The single biggest threat to the credibility of a presentation is cherry-picked data."
>
> *- Edward Tufte*

We have looked at some of the tools available for visualization using Python so far. We've looked at the library that started it all and one of the most popular – *Matplotlib*. We also looked at one of the best data analysis tools for plotting capabilities as well – *Pandas*. We explored the statistical capabilities of *Seaborn* and the interactive capabilities of *Bokeh* over *Chapter 6, Using Seaborn for Visualization*, and *Chapter 7, Using Bokeh with Python*. Now, we shall look at some of the advanced libraries and tools that have a specific purpose for their extensions or toolkits to take it to the next level. While we have 100's of libraries available as an extension with a specific purpose, we shall take a look at some of the best in this chapter as each of the libraries may need a chapter, if not a book of their own.

Structure

- Introduction to other popular libraries – *Plotly, Folium, MPLFinance, etc.*
- Examples for various types of visualizations using *Plotly*
- Examples for various types of geographic visualizations using *Folium*

- Examples for various types of stock and finance data visualizations using *MPLFinance*
- Other examples
- Resources

Objective

This chapter aims to give a basic introduction to interactive plotting using Plotly, geographic plotting using Folium, financial plotting example using MPLFinance, and few additional libraries such as Altair. We shall be exploring some of the important features with examples to try out and resources to consume. Given we have quite a few libraries to cover, we shall be using a few examples per library. The Jupyter Notebook and this book will have additional exercises and examples to practice your visualization skills.

Introduction to other popular libraries – Plotly, Folium, MPLFinance

Like we covered in *Chapter 3, Various Data Visualization Elements and Tools*, there are many libraries available for data visualization using Python. These include:

- *matplotlib, Plotly,* or *bokeh* - Core Python visualization packages
- *pandas, xarray, hvplot, cufflinks,* or *pdvega* - Shared API packages that are built on *Python or JavaScript libraries*
- *seaborn, Altair, holoviews, Plotly express, chartify, AutoViz, plotnine, pygal, bqplot, or SciVis* - High-level libraries focusing on a particular theme using core *Python or JavaScript libraries*
- *pyqtgraph, glue,* or *Chaco* - Native GUI libraries
- *mayavi, vispy, pyvista* or *glumpy* - Scientific libraries
- *GeoPandas, folium, Cartopy, ipyleaflet, geoplot* or *Geoplotlib* - Geospatial libraries
- *network, Graphviz,* or *pyvis* - Network and graphs plotting libraries
- *scikit-image, missingno, scikit-plot, MetPy, yt* or *facets* - Domain or capability specific libraries
- *datashader, mpl-scatter-density,* or *vaex* - Tools for rendering large datasets
- *bokeh, dash, panel, streamlit, flask, and voila* - Libraries for creating nice dashboards
- *palettable, colorcet, cmocean* or *viscm* - Tools specifically for building colormaps for colorful visualizations

Additionally, *holoviz* offers a set of capabilities to visualize your data. As the number of possibilities is huge, we shall cover some of the tools in this chapter, namely *Plotly, Plotly express, folium,* and a few other tools as a quick functional reference.

Now, let us start with Plotly as a tool.

Examples for various types of visualizations using Plotly

Figure 8.1: The Plotly logo

Plotly is an open-source library and toolkit for web-centric visualizations. We can run a Plotly program from a Jupyter Notebook or as a program through a web-based application as it has an API capability. *Plotly* has many nice visualization capabilities such as statistical plots, AI/ML centric charts, financial charts, 3D plots, animated scatter plots, and a whole suite of libraries that make it second to none. It also can plot against multiple axes and other good features such as subplots and contour plots. We can also add custom controls to the visualizations.

Plotly can be installed using a simple command:

```
pip install Plotly
```

or

```
conda install -c plotly.
```

If you want to upgrade to the latest version, you can use the following command:

```
pip install --upgrade Plotly
```

or

```
pip install –U Plotly
```

Let us see the plot types we can visualize using Plotly and Plotly Express libraries.

Plotly chart types

With Plotly, we have features to plot following charts ➔ scatter, line, area, bar, funnel, timeline. pie, sunburst, treemap, funnel_area, histogram, box, violin, strip, density_heatmap, density_contour, imshow, scatter_3d, line_3d, scatter_matrix, parallel_coordinates, parallel_categories, scatter_mapbox, line_mapbox, choropleth_mapbox, density_mapbox, scatter_geo, line_geo, choropleth, scatter_polar, line_polar, bar_polar, scatter_ternary, and line_ternary.

A majority of the plots from the list are covered in earlier chapters. We shall not be replicating every possible chart in our exercises. We will cover a few charts. Additional charts are included in the notebook addendum for this chapter.

Let us start with some basic charts for Plotly.

Simple Plotly scatter plot

Let us try a simple plot with the **scatter()** function:

```
1.  # x and y given as array_like objects
2.  import plotly.express as px
3.  import random
4.  x = random.sample(range(30, 80), 50)
5.  y = random.sample(range(20, 99), 50)
6.  z = random.sample(range(51, 110), 50)
7.  plot = px.scatter(x, y, size=z, hover_data=[x,y])
8.  plot.show()
```

This program produces an output as follows:

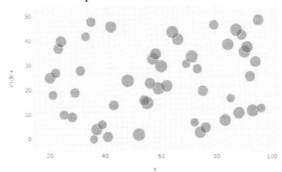

Figure 8.2: A simple Plotly scatter plot

Let us see a mathematical plot using **line()** function.

Simple mathematical plot

```
1.  import plotly.express as px
2.  import numpy as np
3.  t = np.linspace(0, np.pi, 20)
4.  fig = px.line(x=t, y=np.sin(t), labels={'x':'t', 'y':'sin(t)'})
5.  fig.show()
```

This program produces an output as follows:

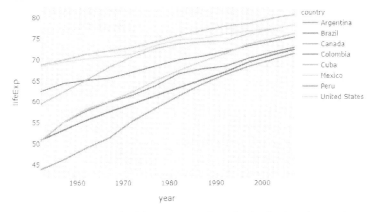

Figure 8.3: A simple Plotly mathematical plot

Let us create a dynamic line chart using a popular dataset. Plotly has different datasets for visualization. One of the most popular ones is the *gapminder* dataset.

Line plot using the gapminder() dataset

Using the **gapminder** dataset, let us plot a line plot for life expectancy for some of the big countries in the Americas region. We create a pandas dataframe using a filter on continent and then on the countries we want to plot for.

1. ```import plotly.express as px```

2. ```df = px.data.gapminder().query("continent == 'Americas'")```

3. ```filt1   =df['country'].isin(['Argentina','Brazil','Mexico','United States','Canada','Peru','Colombia','Cuba'])```

4. ```fig = px.line(df[filt1], x='year', y='lifeExp', color='country')```

5. ```fig.show()```

This program produces an output as follows:

Figure 8.4: A gapminder life expectancy line plot for the Americas region

Let us plot a scatter plot using markers and size as a parameter.

Scatter plot using markers and size

Let us generate a random array and give a size of the scatter value as a parameter:

```
1.  # x and y given as array_like objects
2.  import plotly.express as px
3.  import plotly.graph_objects as go
4.  import random
5.  def rand_color():
6.     return "#" + "".join(random.sample("0123456789abcdef", 6))
7.  N = 50
8.  x = random.sample(range(30, 30+N), N)
9.  y = random.sample(range(20, 30+N), N)
10. z = random.sample(range(1, 30+N), N)
11. fig = go.Figure(data=[go.Scatter(
12.    x=x, y=y, fillcolor=rand_color(),
13.    mode='markers',
14.    marker_size=z)
15. ])
16. fig.show()
```

This program produces an output as follows:

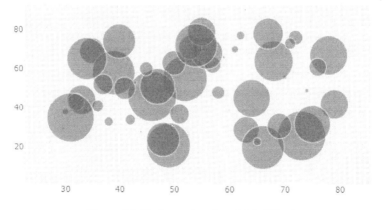

Figure 8.5: Plotly scatter plot with bubble sizes

Using the *gapminder* dataset, let us plot a pie chart and donut chart examples.

Pie chart and donut charts using the gapminder dataset

The following snippet of code has three Jupyter Notebook cells and covers four aspects of pie and donut charts. A simple pie chart, a formatted pie chart, a donut chart, and a pie chart with exploded pie. The simple lines of code can be expanded further for various types of formatting using Plotly:

```
1.  #Program-1 for a simple Pie Chart
2.  import plotly.express as px
3.  df = px.data.gapminder().query("year == 2007").query
    ("continent == 'Asia'")
4.  df.loc[df['pop'] < 1.e8, 'country'] = 'Other countries'
5.  fig = px.pie(df, values='pop', names='country', title=
    'Population of Asian continent')
6.  fig.show()
7.
8.  #Program-2 Pie Chart with colors and value embedded
9.  import plotly.graph_objects as go
10. from random import randint
11. def rand_color():
12.   return "#" + "".join(random.sample("0123456789abcdef", 6))
13. color = [rand_color(),rand_color(),rand_color(),rand_color()]
14. label = ['Tesla','Apple','Google','Amazon']
15. value = [ randint(10, 20), randint(20, 30), randint(10, 20),rand-
    int(20, 40)]
16. fig = go.Figure(data=[go.Pie(labels=label,values=value)])
17. fig.update_traces(hoverinfo='label+percent', textinfo='val-
    ue', textfont_size=20,
18.                   marker=dict(colors=color, line=dict(color=ran
    d_color(), width=2)))
19. fig.show()
20.
21. #Program-3 Donut Chart and a Pie Chart with a pie exploded
22. import plotly.graph_objects as go
23. from random import randint
```

```
24. def rand_color():
25.    return "#" + "".join(random.sample("0123456789abcdef", 6))
26.
27. color = [rand_color(),rand_color(),rand_color(),rand_color()]
28. label = ['Tesla','Apple','Google','Amazon']
29. value = [ randint(10, 20), randint(20, 30), randint(10, 20),rand-
    int(20, 40)]
30. fig = go.Figure(data=[go.Pie(labels=label,values=val-
    ue,  hole=.5)])
31. fig.show()
32. fig2 = go.Figure(data=[go.Pie(labels=label,values=val-
    ue,  pull=[0, 0, 0.2, 0])])
33. fig2.show()
```

These programs produce the four outputs as shown in the following image collage:

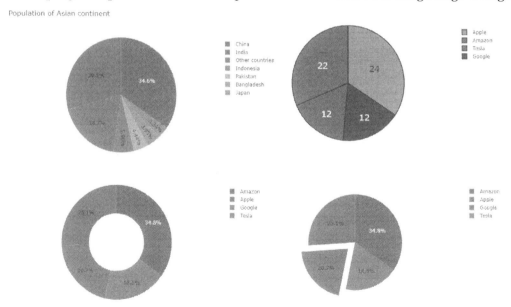

Figure 8.6: *Plotly examples for pie, donut charts, and exploration of options*

Let us see the use of Plotly for bar charts.

Use of bar charts in Plotly

Let us see build simple bar chart using random number generation:

```
1.  import plotly.graph_objects as go
2.  import random
3.  fig = go.Figure(data=go.Bar(y=random.sample(range(3, 99), 5)))
4.  fig.show()
```

This program produces the code as follows:

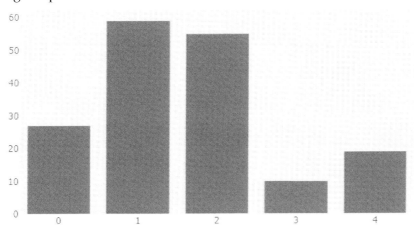

Figure 8.7: *Plotly simple bar chart*

If we want to try a little bit advanced plotting, we can leverage the *gapminder* dataset and use various options to generate three distinct bar charts – comparative bar chart, stacked bar chart, and faceted bar chart on the country parameter:

```
1.  import plotly.express as px
2.  data_pop = px.data.gapminder().query("country in ( 'India',
    'China', 'Indonesia','United States')")
3.  fig = px.bar(data_pop, x='year', y='pop', color="country",
    barmode='group')
4.  fig.show()
5.  fig2 = px.bar(data_pop, x='year', y='pop', color="country")
6.  fig2.show()
7.  fig3 = px.bar(data_pop, x="year", color="country", y='pop',
    barmode='group',height=700,
8.         title="A Grouped Bar Chart Python using Plotly",
    facet_col="country")
9.  fig3.show()
```

This program produces the following output:

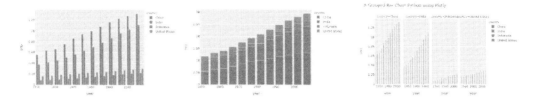

Figure 8 8: Plotly simple bar chart using the gapminder datasets

Let us try 3D plots now.

3D Scatter chart and 3D line chart

The following code produces two charts – a 3D Scatter chart and 3D line chart. Plotly gives us an option to rotate and navigate the 3D plot produced using its wonderful interaction capabilities.

```
1.  #Let us try a 3d scatter chart. We shall use plotly
    carshare dataset
2.  import plotly.express as px
3.  df = px.data.carshare()
4.  fig = px.scatter_3d(df, x = 'centroid_lat',
5.          y = 'centroid_lon',
6.          z = 'car_hours',
7.          color = 'peak_hour')
8.  fig.show()
9.  #Let us try a 3D Line chart
10. import plotly.express as px
11. df = px.data.carshare()
12. fig = px.line_3d(df, x="centroid_lat", y="centroid_lat", z="peak_
    hour")
13. fig.show()
```

The code produces the two charts shown in the image below. One on the left is the 3D scatter chart, and the one on the right is the 3D line chart using the car share data across locations and peak hour of usage and car hours usage.

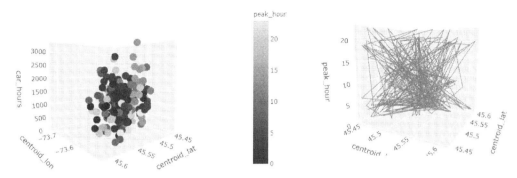

***Figure 8.9:** Plotly examples with 3D plots*

Let us use the skills gained to apply in a case study. Given 2020 has been impacted by COVID-19, we shall leverage the good dataset provided by Johns Hopkins University, available in GitHub.

Case study - Use of Plotly for the COVID-19 dataset analysis

The following code produces seven charts in total, analysing the data loaded and wrangled. We use good number of *Pandas*-driven data analysis and use basic functions of *Plotly*. This outlines the power of *Plotly*.

```
1.  import plotly.express as px

2.  import pandas as pd

3.  import plotly.graph_objs as go

4.  #Load the Dataset

5.  df = pd.read_csv('https://raw.githubusercontent.com/CSSEGISand-
    Data/COVID-19/master/csse_covid_19_data/csse_covid_19_daily_re-
    ports/12-24-2020.csv',index_col = 'Combined_Key')

6.  #Chart-1 Build a Pie chart for all confirmed cases

7.  fig = px.pie(df, values='Confirmed', names='Country_Region',

8.              title='COVID-19 Impact across Nations',

9.              hover_data=['Country_Region'], labels={'Country/Re-
    gion':'Country_Region'})

10. fig.update_traces(textposition='inside')

11. fig.show()

12. #Chart-2 Build a Bar chart for Deaths

13. df2=df.sort_values(by='Deaths', ascending=False)
```

```
14. fig2 = px.bar(df2, x='Country_Region', y = 'Deaths', color='Coun-
    try_Region', title ='Number Deaths across countries')

15. fig2.show()

16. #Perform Data wrangling and modifications

17. df.rename(columns={"Country_Region": "country", "Province_
    State": "province",

18.                      "Last_Update" : "Date"}, inplace=True)

19. gr_df = df.fillna('NA').groupby(['country','province','Date'])['Con-
    firmed'].sum().groupby(['country','province']).max().sort_values().
    groupby(['country']).sum().sort_values(ascending = False)

20. gr2_df = df.fillna('NA').groupby(['country','province','Date'])
    ['Deaths'].sum().groupby(['country','province']).max().sort_val-
    ues().groupby(['country']).sum().sort_values(ascending = False)

21. #Create new dataframes for top-20 confirmed and deaths

22. top20 = pd.DataFrame(gr_df).head(20)

23. top20d = pd.DataFrame(gr2_df).head(20)

24. #Chart-3 Build a Bar chart for COnfirmed cases sorted by numbers

25. fig3 = px.bar(top20, x=top20.index, y='Confirmed', la-
    bels={'x':'Country'},

26.              color="Confirmed", color_continuous_scale=px.colors.
    sequential.Rainbow)

27. fig3.update_layout(title_text='Confirmed COVID-19 cases by coun-
    try')

28. fig3.show()

29. #Chart-4 Build a Bar chart for Deaths sorted by numbers

30. fig4 = px.bar(top20d, x=top20d.index, y='Deaths', la-
    bels={'x':'Country'},

31.              color="Deaths", color_continuous_scale=px.colors.
    sequential.Inferno)

32. fig4.update_layout(title_text='COVID-19 Deaths by country')

33. fig4.show()

34. #Let us use timeseries dataset available for global con-
    firmed, deaths and recovery and story in dataframes

35. URL = 'https://raw.githubusercontent.com/CSSEGISandData/COVID-19/
    master/csse_covid_19_data/csse_covid_19_time_series/time_series_
    covid19_confirmed_global.csv'
```

```
36. data1 = pd.read_csv(URL).drop(['Lat', 'Long'], axis=1).melt(id_
    vars=['Province/State', 'Country/Region'],var_name='date', val-
    ue_name='TotalConfirmed').astype({'date':'datetime64[ns]', 'Total-
    Confirmed':'Int64'}, errors='ignore')

37. data1['Province/State'].fillna('<all>', inplace=True)

38. data1['TotalConfirmed'].fillna(0, inplace=True)

39. URL = 'https://raw.githubusercontent.com/CSSEGISandData/COVID-19/
    master/csse_covid_19_data/csse_covid_19_time_series/time_series_
    covid19_deaths_global.csv'

40. data2 = pd.read_csv(URL).drop(['Lat', 'Long'], axis=1).melt(id_
    vars=['Province/State', 'Country/Region'],var_name='date', val-
    ue_name='TotalDeaths').astype({'date':'datetime64[ns]', 'Total-
    Deaths':'Int64'}, errors='ignore')

41. data2['Province/State'].fillna('<all>', inplace=True)

42. data2['TotalDeaths'].fillna(0, inplace=True)

43. URL = 'https://raw.githubusercontent.com/CSSEGISandData/COVID-19/
    master/csse_covid_19_data/csse_covid_19_time_series/time_series_
    covid19_recovered_global.csv'

44. data3 = pd.read_csv(URL).drop(['Lat', 'Long'], axis=1).melt(id_
    vars=['Province/State', 'Country/Region'],var_name='date', val-
    ue_name='TotalRecovery').astype({'date':'datetime64[ns]', 'Total-
    Recovery':'Int64'}, errors='ignore')

45. data3['Province/State'].fillna('<all>', inplace=True)

46. data3['TotalRecovery'].fillna(0, inplace=True)

47. #Merge all datasets

48. allData =  data1.merge(data2).merge(data3)

49. countries = allData['Country/Region'].unique()

50. #Sort the data

51. countries.sort()

52. #Chart-5 - plot a line chart for confirmed cases

53. fig5 = px.line(allData, x='date', y='TotalConfirmed', color='Coun-
    try/Region')

54. fig5.show()

55. #Chart-6 - plot a line chart for Death cases

56. fig6 = px.line(allData, x='date', y='TotalDeaths', color='Country/
    Region')
```

```
57. fig6.show()
58. #Chart-7 - plot a line chart for Recovery cases
59. fig7 = px.line(allData, x='date', y='TotalRecovery', color='Coun-
    try/Region')
60. fig7.show()
```

We get the following seven plots for the preceding code. As you can see, the data can be visualized in multiple ways. You can play around with the code provided along with the book to check and modify it further.

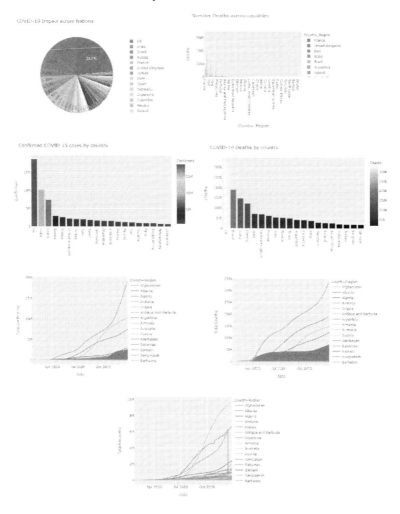

Figure 8.10: Plotly examples for the COVID-19 datasets

Let us try some animation with Plotly that it is popular for. Let us leverage the *gapminder* dataset for the same.

Plotly animation

The following three lines of code gives a nice animation output using the *gapminder* dataset:

1. ```
   import plotly.express as px
   ```

2. ```
   df = px.data.gapminder()
   ```

3. ```
   fig = px.scatter(df, x="lifeExp", y="pop", animation_frame="-
   year", animation_group="country",
   ```

4. ```
              size="gdpPercap", color="continent", hover_name="coun-
   try",## facet_col="continent",
   ```

5. ```
          log_y=True, size_max=65, range_y=[50000,2000000000], range_
   x=[33,99])
   ```

6. ```
   fig.show()
   ```

The output plot produced for the snippet of code looks as follows:

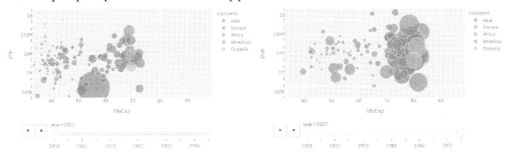

***Figure 8.11:** Plotly examples for animation using the gapminder datasets*

Let us see the scatter matrix plotting capability of *Plotly*.

Scatter matrix plotting capability of *Plotly*

We shall see two dataset examples; one line of code is enough for producing a nice scatter matrix capability of Plotly. We use the *gapminder* and *carshare* datasets for this example.

1. ```
   import plotly.express as px
   ```

2. ```
   #Fig 1 Gapminder dataset scatter matrix
   ```

3. ```
   df = px.data.gapminder()
   ```

4. ```
   fig = px.scatter_matrix(df, dimensions=['pop' , 'lifeExp' ,
   'gdpPercap'], color='continent')
   ```

5. ```
   fig.show()
   ```

6. ```
   #Fig 2 Carshare dataset scatter matrix
   ```

```
7. df = px.data.carshare()
8. fig2 = px.scatter_matrix(df, dimensions=['centroid_lat', 'centroid_
   lon', 'car_hours'], color='peak_hour')
9. fig2.show()
```

This program produces the following output:

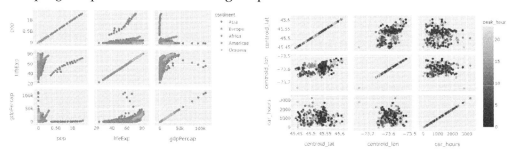

Figure 8.12: *Plotly examples for scatter matrix using the gapminder and carshare datasets*

Let us try and build a treemap using *Plotly*.

Treemap using *Plotly*

We shall use the *gapminder* dataset to build a nice *treemap* using Plotly. We used the *squarify* library to build the treemap in earlier chapters. Plotly comes with an implicit function to do this in a nice manner.

```
1. #!pip install --upgrade plotly
2. import plotly.express as px
3. import numpy as np
4. #Let us plot a treemap using the data set
5. df = px.data.gapminder().query("year == 2007")
6. fig = px.treemap(df, path=['continent', 'country'], values='pop',
7.                   color_discrete_sequence=px.colors.qualitative.
   Alphabet,
8.                   color='pop', hover_data=['iso_alpha'])
9. fig.show()
```

Let us see the output of this code:

Figure 8.13: Plotly examples for treemap using the gapminder dataset

With this, we shall conclude the exercises using *Plotly*. Like *Seaborn, Bokeh, Matplotlib*, and other libraries, we can write a comprehensive book on Plotly to showcase its capabilities.

Let us look at one of the most widely used data visualization features – geographic visualization using the Folium library.

Examples for various types of geographic visualizations using Folium

Folium

Figure 8.14: The Folium logo

folium is a library available in Python that allows us to merge the power of both Python data-wrangling power and the might of geographic visualization power of the **leaflet.js** library. *folium* allows us to bind data from python for maps through the choropleth visualizations and bypassing rich HTML or Vector info as markers on the map. *folium* also supports various types of map tile sets such as Stamen (*Terrain, Toner,* and *Watercolor*), *MapBox* (*Bright* and *Control Room*), *CloudDB, CartoDB* (*positron* and *dark_matter*), and *OpenStreetMaps*. We can overlay JSON content, images, videos, and geographic or topographic JSON (GeoJSON/TopoJSON) to be overlaid. We can also leverage *Flask* applications to render *folium* output in real-time in a web application or an HTML page.

folium can be installed using:

```
pip install folium
```

Or

```
conda install folium -c conda-forge
```

folium needs the following libraries as a pre-requirement - *Branca, jinja2, requests,* and it may require *numpy, pandas, geopandas, Altair* for some of the rendering.

folium features

The key features to evaluate in a *folium* application are *markers, overlays, choropleth maps, map styling, layers, and plugins.* We shall see some of these features in the examples in this section.

The following are the core functions and features of ***folium***:

Library	Key functions
folium.folium • *Contains the main function for map rendering*	*GlobalSwitches,* **Map**
folium.map • *Core functions to manage the map information display*	*CustomPane, FeatureGroup, FitBounds, Icon, Layer, LayerControl, Marker, Popup, and Tooltip*
folium.vector_layers • *Useful for building unique polygon and special visualizations*	*BaseMultiLocation, Circle, CircleMarker, PolyLine, Polygon, Rectangle, and path_options*
folium.raster_layers • *Useful for adding images, video, and additional tiles*	*ImageOverlay, TileLayer, VideoOverlay, and WmsTileLayer*

Let us see the examples in action.

Simple world map

We can generate a simple world map with one line of code **folium.map()** without any parameters.

```
1. #!pip install --upgrade plotly
2. import plotly.express as px
3. import numpy as np
4. #Let us plot a treemap using the data set
```

```
5. df = px.data.gapminder().query("year == 2007")
6. fig = px.treemap(df, path=['continent', 'country'], values='pop',
7.                   color_discrete_sequence=px.colors.qualitative.
   Alphabet,
8.                   color='pop', hover_data=['iso_alpha'])
9. fig.show()
```

This produces the following output:

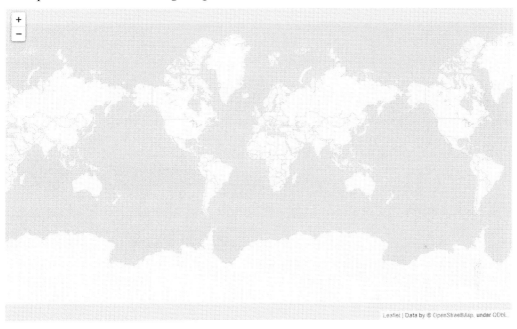

***Figure 8.15:** folium example for a world map output*

Let us see some advanced examples using Folium. Let us plot a Stamen Toner Map using North America coordinates passed:

```
1. # create a Stamen Toner map of the world
   centred around North America
2. NA_map = folium.Map(location=[46.130, -106.35], tiles=
   'Stamen Toner', zoom_start=4)
3. # display map
4. NA_map
```

We would get the following output:

Figure 8.16: *folium example for "Stamen Toner" based the US map*

When we change tiles to *'Stamen Terrain,'* we get the following output:

NA_map = folium.Map(location=[46.130, -106.35], tiles='Stamen Terrain', zoom_start=4)

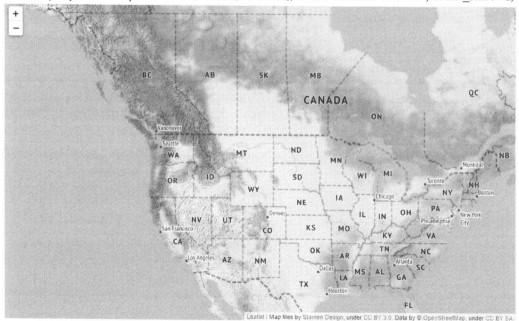

Figure 8.17: *folium example for "Stamen Terrain" based on the US map*

For the next example, we will build a map using GeoJSON (Geographic JSON file) containing outlines of various maps. We shall use US GEO JSON file to render our visualization.

```
1.  import json
2.  import requests
3.  #Load the United States JSON file
4.  url = 'https://raw.githubusercontent.com/python-visualization/fo-
    lium/master/examples/data'
5.  us_states = f'{url}/us-states.json'
6.  #Load the data
7.  geo_json_data = json.loads(requests.get(us_states).text)
8.  #Create a Stamen Toner US Folium Map
9.  JSON_US_Map = folium.Map([43, -100], zoom_start=4, tiles="stamen-
    toner")
10. #Add the GeoJSON data to the map and Show
11. folium.GeoJson(geo_json_data).add_to(JSON_US_Map)
12. JSON_US_Map
```

We get the following output:

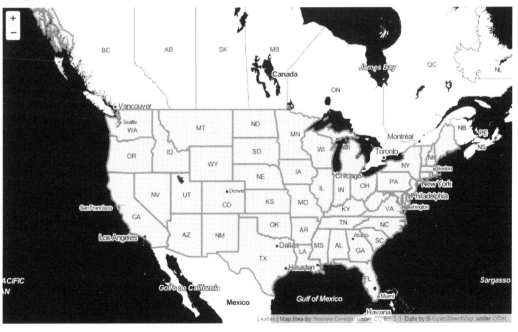

Figure 8.18: folium example for geoJSON based on the US map

Now let us try a featuregroup, layer control, and marker configuration in folium¶. We shall try all the features mentioned above on a single map and try key attractions in New Delhi, India and around. Let us see the code:

```
1.  import random
2.  #Let us define a random array Font Awesome Icons https://
    fontawesome.com/icons?d=gallery&m=free
3.  #Please note that not all the icons are render-
    able on all platforms and depends on what Folium library has.
4.  icon_array = ['500px' #...lots of elements
5.                            ,'zhihu',]
6.  #Let us generate a random icon. We shall be us-
    ing this in out next plot
7.  print(random.choice (icon_array))
8.  icon_col_array = ['red', 'blue', 'green', 'purple', 'or-
    ange', 'darkred', 'lightred', 'beige', 'darkblue', 'dark-
    green', 'cadetblue', 'darkpurple', 'pink', 'lightblue', 'light-
    green', 'gray', 'black', 'lightgray']
9.  print(random.choice (icon_col_array))
10. #Let us define a random color function using hexadecimal value
11. def rand_color():
12.     return random.choice (icon_col_array)
13. from folium import FeatureGroup, LayerControl, Map, Marker
14. #Start by creating a Feature Group Map Base
15. ND_FeatureGroupMap = Map(
16.     location=[28.6321, 77.2194],
17.     zoom_start=12,
18.     tiles=›Stamen Terrain›
19. )
20. #Define the Feature Group
21. feature_group = FeatureGroup(name='Some icons')
22. #Start Defining the Location MArkers, Use Folium.Icons
23. Marker(location=[28.6321, 77.2194],
24.        popup=›Connaught Place›).add_to(feature_group)
25. Marker(location=[27.1751, 78.0421],
26.        popup=›Taj Mahal›,
27.        icon=folium.Icon(color=rand_color(),
28.                         icon_color='white',
29.                         icon='fa-street-view',
```

```
30.                       angle=0, prefix='fa')).add_to(feature_
    group)
31. Marker(location=[28.6172, 77.2082],
32.         popup=›Parliament›,
33.         icon=folium.Icon(color=rand_color(),
34.                          icon_color='white',
35.                          icon='fa-university',
36.                          angle=0, prefix='fa')).add_to(feature_
    group)
37. Marker(location=[28.6129, 77.2295],
38.         popup=›India Gate›,
39.         icon=folium.Icon(color=rand_color(),
40.                          icon_color='white',
41.                          icon='fa-street-view',
42.                          angle=0, prefix='fa')).add_to(feature_
    group)
43. Marker(location=[28.5535, 77.2588],
44.         popup=›Lotus Temple›,
45.         icon=folium.Icon(color=rand_color(),
46.                          icon_color='white',
47.                          icon='fa-tree',
48.                          angle=0, prefix='fa')).add_to(feature_
    group)
49. Marker(location=[28.5245, 77.1855],
50.         popup=›Qutub Minar›,
51.         icon=folium.Icon(color=rand_color(),
52.                          icon_color='white',
53.                          icon='fa-street-view',
54.                          angle=0, prefix='fa')).add_to(feature_
    group)
55. Marker(location=[28.6271, 77.2166],
56.         popup=›Jantar Mantar›,
57.         icon=folium.Icon(color=rand_color(),
58.                          icon_color='white',
59.                          icon='fa-street-view',
60.                          angle=0, prefix='fa')).add_to(feature_
    group)
61. Marker(location=[28.6406, 77.2495],
```

```
62.          popup=›Raj Ghat›,
63.          icon=folium.Icon(color=rand_color(),
64.                            icon_color='white',
65.                            icon='fa-university',
66.                            angle=0, prefix='fa')).add_to(feature_
     group)
67. Marker(location=[28.6143, 77.1994],
68.          popup=›Rashtrapati Bhavan›,
69.          icon=folium.Icon(color=rand_color(),
70.                            icon_color='white',
71.                            icon='fa-university',
72.                            angle=0, prefix='fa')).add_to(feature_
     group)
73. Marker(location=[28.5562, 77.1000],
74.          popup=›IG Int. Airport›,
75.          icon=folium.Icon(color=rand_color(),
76.                            icon_color='white',
77.                            icon='plane',
78.                            angle=0, prefix='fa')).add_to(feature_
     group)
79. Marker(location=[28.6127, 77.2773],
80.          popup=›Akshardam Temple›,
81.          icon=folium.Icon(color=rand_color(),
82.                            icon_color='white',
83.                            icon='bell',
84.                            angle=0, prefix='fa')).add_to(feature_
     group)
85. Marker(location=[28.6379, 77.2432],
86.          popup=›Feroze Shah Kotla Stadium›,
87.          icon=folium.Icon(color=rand_color(),
88.                            icon_color='white',
89.                            icon='fa-university',
90.                            angle=0, prefix='fa')).add_to(feature_
     group)
91. #Add the Feature Group and the Layer Control
92. feature_group.add_to(ND_FeatureGroupMap)
93. LayerControl().add_to(ND_FeatureGroupMap)
94. #Show the map
95. ND_FeatureGroupMap
```

We get the following output:

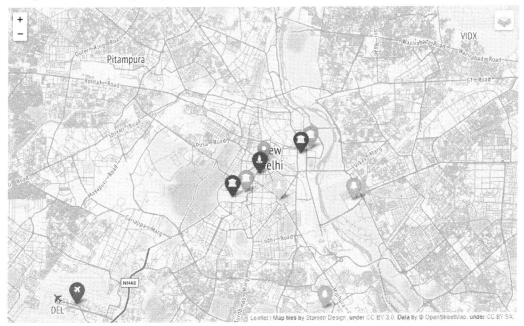

Figure 8.19: *folium example using markers and icons for the map of New Delhi*

Let us see how we can build a custom marker (a compass navigator) for our maps:

```
1. from folium.plugins import FloatImage
2. url = ('https://raw.githubusercontent.com/SECOORA/static_assets/'
3.         'master/maps/img/rose.png')
4. floatImageMap = folium.Map([56.12,0.0], zoom_start=5)
5. FloatImage(url, bottom=70, left=70).add_to(floatImageMap)
6. floatImageMap
```

The code above produces the following output:

Figure 8.20: folium example using custom float images

Let us build a heatmap output animation that changes with time.

Folium heatmap with time animation

For this program, we shall focus on a central part of a map and then build a heatmap that changes coordinates with time. The heatmap is generated using a random number. This can be real data as well.

```
1.  import folium
2.  import folium.plugins as plugins
3.  import numpy as np
4.  #Define a random seed
5.  np.random.seed(3141592)
6.  Number=50
7.  #Generate random data around latitude = 23 (Tropic of Can-
    cer) longitude of 77
8.  initial_data = (
9.      np.random.normal(size=(Number, 2)) * np.array([[1, 1]]) +
10.     np.array([[23, 77]])
11. )
```

```
12. #Generate Heatmap movement dataset
13. move_data = np.random.normal(size=(Number, 2)) * 0.02
14. data = [(initial_data + move_data * i).
    tolist() for i in range(Number)]
15. weight = 1  # default value
16. for time_entry in data:
17.     for row in time_entry:
18.         row.append(weight)
19. #Define the Folium Map
20. hmwtMap = folium.Map([23., 77.], tiles='OpenStreetMap', zoom_
    start=4)
21. #Add the Heatmap data to HeatMapWithTime plugin
22. hmwtPlugin = plugins.HeatMapWithTime(data)
23. hmwtPlugin.add_to(hmwtMap)
24. #Render the Finished Map
25. hmwtMap
```

The program above produces the following output at the start and end of the animation:

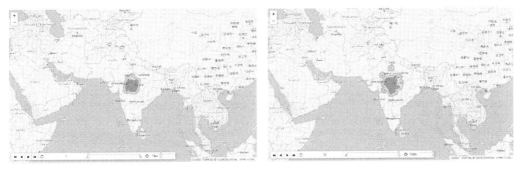

Figure 8.21: folium example using heatmap with time animation

Let us see a simple heatmap function.

Simple Heatmap

The following code produces a simple heatmap:

```
1. from folium.plugins import HeatMap
2. import numpy as np
3. data = (
```

```
4.    np.random.normal(size=(100, 3)) *
5.    np.array([[1, 1, 1]]) +
6.    np.array([[28, 77, 1]])
7. ).tolist()
8. SimpleHmDataMap = folium.Map([28., 77.], tiles='OpenStreet-
   Map', zoom_start=6)
9. HeatMap(data).add_to(SimpleHmDataMap)
10.SimpleHmDataMap
```

The output produced is as follows:

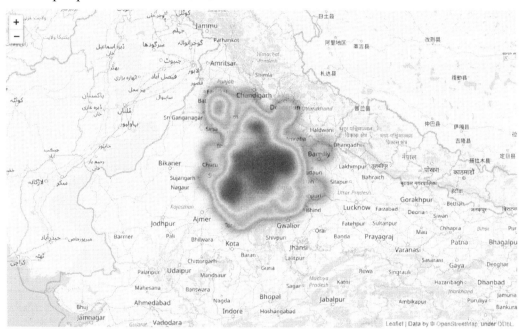

Figure 8.22: folium example using a simple heatmap

Let us try some of the folium features such as cluster maps, fast cluster maps, popups, dual maps, and measure control maps.

The following code (shown as four distinct cells in the Jupyter book attached) produces simple outputs based on the feature explored. The code is explained inline.

```
1. #Visualization - 1 Mapping Cluster Maps and Fast Cluster Maps
2.
3. import numpy as np
4. size = 1000
5. lons = np.random.randint(74, 89, size=size) + np.random.rand-
```

```
    int(0, 1000, size=size)/1000
6.  lats = np.random.randint(10, 33, size=size) + np.random.rand-
    int(0, 1000, size=size)/1000
7.  locations = list(zip(lats, lons))
8.  popups = ['lon:{}<br>lat:{}'.for-
    mat(lon, lat) for (lat, lon) in locations]
9.  from folium.plugins import MarkerCluster
10. from folium.plugins import FastMarkerCluster
11. fmClusterMap = folium.Map(
12.     location=[np.mean(lats), np.mean(lons)],
13.     tiles='Cartodb Positron',
14.     zoom_start=5
15. )
16. FastMarkerCluster(data=list(zip(lats, lons))).add_to(fmCluster-
    Map)
17. folium.LayerControl().add_to(fmClusterMap)
18. fmClusterMap
19.
20. #Visualization - 2 Code for Cluster Marker and Popup
21. N = 100 #Number of Popups
22. #Generate Random Datasets
23. data = np.array(
24.     [
25.         np.random.uniform(low=11, high=33, size=N),
26.         np.random.uniform(low=70, high=88, size=N),
27.     ]
28. ).T
29. popups = [str(i) for i in range(N)] # Popups texts are sim-
    ple numbers.
30. #Create a Map
31. randomPopupMarker_Map = folium.Map([27, 77], zoom_start=4)
32. plugins.MarkerCluster(data, popups=popups).add_to(randomPopup-
    Marker_Map)
33. randomPopupMarker_Map
34.
35. #Visualization 3 Dual Map Example
```

```
36. dualMap = folium.plugins.DualMap(loca-
    tion=(39.7392, -104.9903), tiles=None, zoom_start=8)
37. folium.TileLayer('openstreetmap').add_to(dualMap.m1)
38. folium.TileLayer('cartodbpositron').add_to(dualMap.m2)
39. folium.LayerControl(collapsed=False).add_to(dualMap)
40. dualMap
41.
42. #Visualization 4 Folium Measure Control
43. from folium.plugins import MeasureControl
44. measureControlMap = folium.Map([28.6321, 77.2194], zoom_start=10)
45. measureControlMap.add_child(MeasureControl())
46. measureControlMap
```

This program produces the following output:

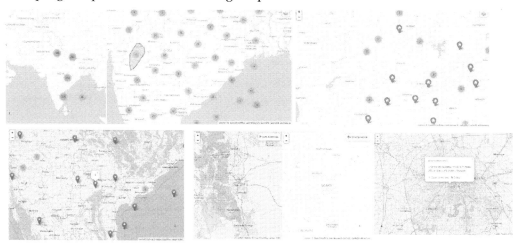

Figure 8.23*: folium example using marker cluster,*
fast marker cluster, popups, icons, dual maps and measure control options

Let us try a tour of a nation using Folium using PolyLineOffset and other plugins and features available in folium. For the first program, we shall build a tour of key cities in India using *PolyLineOffset* to plot a visualize navigation in a visually impactful manner. Let us see the code:

```
1. import folium.plugins as plugins
2. loc = 'India Tour in a Folium Map'
3. title_html = '''
4.              <h3 align=»center» style=»font-size:16px»><b>{}</
   b></h3>
```

```
5.                    <>>.format(loc)
6.  #Define the map
7.  IndiaTourMap = folium.Map(location=[24.0, 77.0], zoom_
    start=4, tiles="cartodbpositron")
8.  #Define the coordinates
9.  coords = [
10.     [13.09,80.28],[10.7704,79.15],[9.92,78.12],[8.5,76.95],[11,76
    .95],[12.31,76.66],[12.9,74.85],[12.97,77.56],
11.     [13.6504,79.42],[14.47,75.92],[15.36,75.125],[15.492,73.818],
    [15.865,74.505],[16.7,74.22],[17.4,78.48],[17.73,83.305],
12.     [18.1204,83.5],[18.53,73.85],[19.017,72.857],[20.7197,70.9904
    ],[21.2,72.84],[23.0301,72.58],[20.0004,73.78],
13.     [22.7151,75.865],[22.2304,84.83],[20.2704,85.8274],[22.495,88
    .3247],[23.8004,86.42],[23.25,77.41],[24.8,85],
14.     [25.33,83],[25.453,78.5575],[25.455,81.84],[25.625,85.13],[26
    .1204,85.3799],[26.23,78.1801],[26.2918,73.0168],
15.     [26.7504,83.38],[26.855,80.915],[27.15,78.3949],[27.1704,78.0
    15],[27.5,77.67],[27.8922,78.0618],[28.4104,77.8484],
16.     [28.4333,77.3167],[28.45,77.02],[28.6,77.2],[28.67,77.23],[28
    .9,76.58],[30.72,76.78],[31.64,74.87],[32.7118,74.8467],
17.     [31.1,77.1666],[34.1,74.815],[23.0301,72.58],
18. ]
19. #Let us add color code connects for each coordinate
20. plugins.PolyLineOffset(
21.     coords, weight=2, dash_array="5,10", color="red", opacity=1
22. ).add_to(IndiaTourMap)
23. plugins.PolyLineOffset(coords, color="#00f", opacity=1, off-
    set=-5).add_to(IndiaTourMap)
24. plugins.PolyLineOffset(coords, color="#080", opacity=1, off-
    set=5).add_to(IndiaTourMap)
25. #Let us show the map
26. IndiaTourMap.get_root().html.add_child(folium.Element(title_
    html))
27. IndiaTourMap
```

When we execute this code, we get the following output:

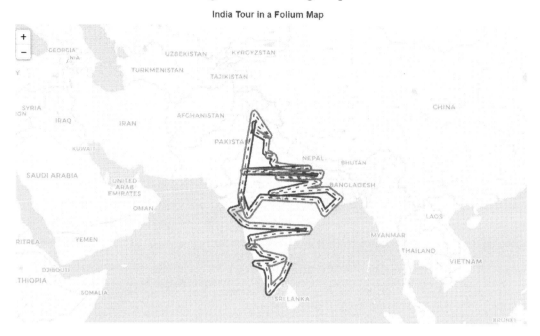

Figure 8.24: folium example using PolyLineOffest feature to show an India Tour

Let us use the logic to build a tour of the US continental map by traveling to all the capital cities of the continental US:

```
1.  import numpy as np  # use-
    ful for much scientific computing in Python
2.  import pandas as pd # primary data structure library
3.  import folium
4.  from folium im-
    port FeatureGroup, LayerControl, Map, Marker, features
5.  import folium.plugins as plugins
6.  from folium.plugins import FloatImage, HeatMap, MarkerCluster,
    FastMarkerCluster, MeasureControl, MousePosition
7.  from folium.features import DivIcon
8.
9.
10. loc = 'Continental USA Tour traversal in a Foli-
    um Map in a non-overlapping manner'
11. title_html = '''
12.              <h2 align=»center» style=»font-size:18px»><b>{}</
    b></h2>
```

```
13.                   <>>.format(loc)
14. # Let us define a map with the US in the center and a reason-
    able Zool Level with an Open StreetMap
15. ContinentalUSTourMap = folium.Map(location=[40.0, -100], zoom_
    start=4, tiles="OpenStreetMap")
16.
17. # Let us define Locations of the states to traverse in sequence.
18. # These states are as per the US Map. We can also use an algo-
    rithm on Latitude & Longitude for this as well
19. #
20.
21. Locations = ['WA', 'OR', 'CA','NV','AZ','UT','ID','MT','WY','CO',
22.                'NM','TX','OK','KS','NE','SD','ND','MN','IA','MO',
23.                'AR','LA','MS','AL','TN','IL','WI','MI','IN','KY','
    OH',
24.                'WV','PA','NY','VT','ME','NH','MA','RI','CT','NJ','
    DE',
25.                'DC','MD','VA','NC','SC','GA','FL',
26.                ]
27.
28. #Let us define the corresponding Latitudes and Longi-
    tudes for the capital cities of these states
29. coords = [
30.      [47.042418,-122.893077],[44.931109,-123.029159],
31.      [38.555605,-121.468926],[39.160949,-119.753877],
32.      [33.448457,-112.073844],[40.7547,-111.892622],
33.      [43.613739,-116.237651],[46.595805,-112.027031],
34.      [41.145548,-104.802042],[39.7391667,-104.984167],
35.      [35.667231,-105.964575],[30.266667,-97.75],
36.      [35.482309,-97.534994],[39.04,-95.69],
37.      [40.809868,-96.675345],[44.367966,-100.336378],
38.      [46.8083,-100.7837],[44.95,-93.094],
39.      [41.590939,-93.620866],[38.572954,-92.189283],
40.      [34.736009,-92.331122],[30.4515, -91.1871],
41.      [32.320,-90.207],[32.361538,-86.279118],
42.      [36.165,-86.784],[39.783250,-89.650373],
43.      [43.074722,-89.384444],[42.7335,-84.5467],
```

```
44.     [39.790942,-86.147685],[38.197274,-84.86311],
45.     [39.962245,-83.000647],[38.349497,-81.633294],
46.     [40.269789,-76.875613],[42.659829,-73.781339],
47.     [44.26639,-72.57194], [44.323535,-69.765261],
48.     [43.220093,-71.549127],[42.2352,-71.0275],
49.     [41.8240,-71.4128],[41.767,-72.677],
50.     [40.221741,-74.756138],[39.161921,-75.526755],
51.     [38.972945,-76.501157],[38.913,-77.013],
52.     [37.54,-77.46],[35.771,-78.638],
53.     [34.000,-81.035],[33.76,-84.39],
54.     [30.4518,-84.27277],
55. ]
56.
57. Capitals = ['Olympia','Salem','Sacramento','Carson City','Phoe-
    nix','Salt Lake City','Boise','Helena',
58.           'Cheyenne','Denver','Santa Fe','Austin','Oklaho-
    ma City','Topeka','Lincoln','Pierre',
59.           'Bismarck','Saint Paul','Des Moines','Jeffer-
    son City','Little Rock','Baton Rouge','Jackson','Montgomery',
60.           'Nashville','Springfield','Madison','Lansing','India-
    napolis','Frankfort','Columbus','Charleston',
61.           'Harrisburg','Albany','Montpelier','Augusta','Con-
    cord','Boston','Providence','Hartford',
62.           'Trenton','Dover','Washington D.C','Annapolis','Rich-
    mond','Raleigh','Columbia','Atlanta','Tallahassee',
63. ]
64. Population = [46478,174365,513624,55916,1680992,200567,
    228959,32315,64235,727211,
65.           84683,978908,655057,125310,289102,13646,73529,30809
    6,214237,42838,
66.           197312,220236,160628,198525,670820,114230,259680,11
    8210,876384,27679,
67.           898553,46536,49528,96460,7855,18681,43627,692600,17
    9883,122105,83203,
68.           38079,39174,230436,474069,131674,506811,194500,3211
    3,345064,
69. ]
70. tiles = ['stamenwatercolor', 'cartodbpositron', 'openstreet-
    map', 'stamenterrain','stamentoner']
```

```
71. for tile in tiles:
72.     folium.TileLayer(tile).add_to(ContinentalUSTourMap)
73. #feature_group = FeatureGroup(name='Some icons')
74. folium.LayerControl().add_to(ContinentalUSTourMap)
75. #Let us iterate and add the markers for the capital cit-
    ies of each state we are traversing
76. iterlength = len(coords)
77. iteratorno = 0
78. iconc = folium.Icon(color="red",icon="fa-car", prefix='car',icon_
    size=(20, 20))
79. while iteratorno < iterlength:
80.     my_string = ' 2019 Population   : :<b> {} </b> <br>'.for-
    mat(Population[iteratorno])
81.     my_string = my_string + ' State   : :<b> {} </b> <br>'.for-
    mat(Locations[iteratorno])
82.     tootip_str = " Capital City <b>" + Capitals[iteratorno] + "</
    b><br>" + my_string
83.     ContinentalUSTourMap.add_child(
84.         folium.Marker(
85.             location=[coords[iteratorno][0], coords[iteratorno]
    [1]],
86.             popup=my_string,
87.             icon=DivIcon(icon_size=(50,50),html='<div style="-
    font-size: 6pt; color : blue">' + str(iteratorno+1) + '</div>',),
88.             tooltip = tootip_str,
89.             radius=10+Population[iteratorno]/100000,
90.             color='black',
91.             fill=True,
92.             fill_color='yellow',
93.             fill_opacity=0.2,
94.         )
95.     )
96.     ContinentalUSTourMap.add_child(
97.         folium.CircleMarker(
98.             location=[coords[iteratorno][0], coords[iteratorno]
    [1]],
99.             radius=10+Population[iteratorno]/100000,
100.                color='black',
```

```
101.                    fill=True,
102.                    fill_color='yellow',
103.                    fill_opacity=0.2,
104.            )
105.        )
106.        iteratorno = iteratorno + 1
107.
108.    #feature_group.add_to(ContinentalUSTourMap)
109.    LayerControl().add_to(ContinentalUSTourMap)
110.    plugins.PolyLineOffset(
111.        coords, weight=2, dash_array="5,10", color="red", opac-
    ity=1
112.    ).add_to(ContinentalUSTourMap)
113.    plugins.PolyLineOffset(coords, color="#00f", opaci-
    ty=1, offset=-3).add_to(ContinentalUSTourMap)
114.    plugins.PolyLineOffset(coords, color="#080", opaci-
    ty=1, offset=3).add_to(ContinentalUSTourMap)
115.    ContinentalUSTourMap.get_root().html.add_child(folium.Ele-
    ment(title_html))
116.    ContinentalUSTourMap.save("Continental_US_Tour_Map.html")
117.    ContinentalUSTourMap
```

When we execute this code, we get the following output:

***Figure 8.25**: folium example using PolyLineOffset
to feature popups, markers for a continental US tour map*

If you look at the code, we have added a tiles array to the map, which gives us a choice to choose the tile we want to render dynamically.

```
1. tiles = ['stamenwatercolor', 'cartodbpositron', 'openstreet-
   map', 'stamenterrain','stamentoner']
2. for tile in tiles:
3.     folium.TileLayer(tile).add_to(ContinentalUSTourMap)
```

As a result, when we choose different tiles form the link on the top right corner, we get different maps as follows:

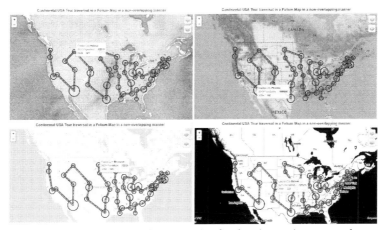

Figure 8.26: folium example using TileLayer option for choosing various types of map rendering

In the Jupyter Notebook for the chapter, there are other examples included that cover some additional maps, including using the pandas dataset used to display meaningful information. A collage of some of the visualization is included below:

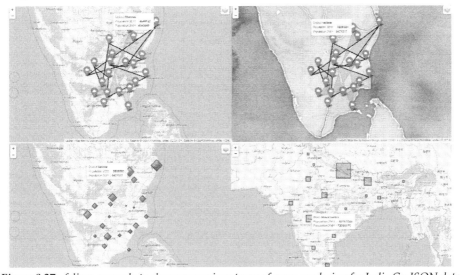

Figure 8.27: folium example to showcase various types of maps rendering for India GeoJSON data

Let us try some financial visualization options using MPLFinance now.

Examples for various types of stock and finance data visualizations using MPLFinance

Matplotlib Finance is an API available to create nice financial plots by leveraging the power of *Pandas* dataframes. We can create good *OHLC (Open-High-Low-Close)* and Moving Average trends for stocks using *candle, line,* and *volume* options available. Other libraries known as *matplotlib.finance* and *mpl_finance* are getting deprecated and merged onto *mplfinance.*

Let us see how to install mplfinance:

```
#!pip install mplfinance
```

Now we can try some examples using *mplfinance.* In the first example, we shall use the following:

- OHLC, candle, and line type charts

- Classic, brasil, checkers and Charles style plotting

- Showing of shares traded and non-trading days in two different charts

We shall use the dataset downloaded for Apple stock to plot the preceding types of charts:

```
1. import pandas as pd
2. import warnings
3. warnings.filterwarnings('ignore')
4. apple_df = pd.read_csv('https://raw.githubusercontent.com/kali-lurrahman/datasets/main/AAPL.csv', index_col=0,parse_dates=True)
5. dt_range = pd.date_range(start="2020-01-01", end="2020-03-31")
6. apple_df = apple_df[apple_df.index.isin(dt_range)]
7. import mplfinance as fplt
8.
9. fplt.available_styles()
10. fplt.plot(apple_df, type='candle', title='Apple - 2020',ylabel='Price ($)')
11. fplt.plot(apple_df,type='ohlc', style='classic', title='Apple - 2020',ylabel='Price ($)')
```

12. `fplt.plot(apple_df, style='brasil', type='candle', title='Ap-`
    `ple - 2020',ylabel='Price ($)')`

13. `fplt.plot(apple_df, style='checkers', type='candle', title='Ap-`
    `ple - 2020',ylabel='Price ($)')`

14. `fplt.plot(apple_df, style='charles', type='candle', title='Ap-`
    `ple - 2020',ylabel='Price ($)')`

15. `fplt.plot(apple_df, style='charles', type='candle', title='Ap-`
    `ple - 2020',ylabel='Price ($)',volume=True,ylabel_lower='Shares\`
    `nTraded')`

16. `fplt.plot(apple_df, style='charles', type='candle', title='Ap-`
    `ple - 2020',ylabel='Price ($)',volume=True,ylabel_lower='Shares\`
    `nTraded',show_nontrading=True)`

We get the following outputs for the preceding program:

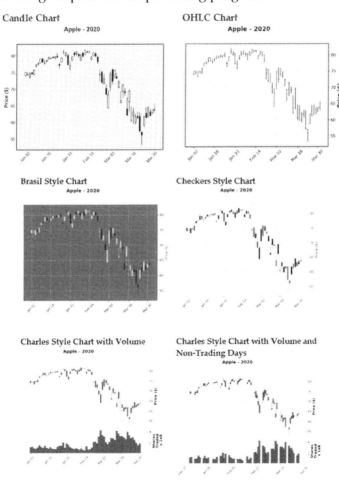

Figure 8.28: MPLFinance examples for various types of charts

We have a few more examples and outputs in the Jupyter Notebook for the chapter. We shall conclude this section with an example comparing the performances of some key global technology stocks in 2020.

The code is as follows:

```
1.  import pandas as pd
2.  import mplfinance as mpf
3.  from tkinter import *
4.  #!pip install tkcalendar mpl_finance
5.  from tkcalendar import DateEntry
6.  import datetime as dt
7.  import pandas_datareader as web
8.  import matplotlib.pyplot as plt
9.  import matplotlib.dates as mdates
10. from mpl_finance import candlestick_ohlc
11. import warnings
12. warnings.filterwarnings('ignore')
13. start_dt = '2020-01-01'
14. end_dt = '2020-12-28'
15. aapl = web.DataReader('AAPL','yahoo',start_dt,end_dt)
16. goog = web.DataReader('GOOG','yahoo',start_dt,end_dt)
17. spy  = web.DataReader('SPY','yahoo',start_dt,end_dt)
18. amzn = web.DataReader('AMZN','yahoo',start_dt,end_dt)
19. msft = web.DataReader('MSFT','yahoo',start_dt,end_dt)
20. nvda = web.DataReader('NVDA','yahoo',start_dt,end_dt)
21. tsla = web.DataReader('TSLA','yahoo',start_dt,end_dt)
22. #Convert Volume to 100Ks
23. aapl['Volume'] = aapl['Volume'] /100000
24. goog['Volume'] = goog['Volume'] /100000
25. amzn['Volume'] = amzn['Volume'] /100000
26. msft['Volume'] = msft['Volume'] /100000
27. spy['Volume'] = spy['Volume'] /100000
28. tsla['Volume'] = tsla['Volume'] /100000
29. #Define the two figures
30. fig = mpf.figure(figsize=(18,12),style='yahoo')
31. fig2 = mpf.figure(figsize=(18,12),style='yahoo')
```

```
32. # First we set the kwargs that we will use for all of these exam-
    ples:
33. kwargs = dict(type='candle',mav=(2,4,6),volume=True,figra-
    tio=(11,8),figscale=2.2)
34. ax1 = fig.add_subplot(2,3,1)
35. av1 = fig.add_subplot(3,3,7,sharex=ax1)
36. mpf.plot(aapl,type='candle',ax=ax1,volume=av1,axtitle=
    'Apple Stock',style='blueskies',mav=(20,40,60))
37. ax2 = fig.add_subplot(2,3,2)
38. av2 = fig.add_subplot(3,3,8,sharex=ax2)
39. mpf.plot(goog,type='candle',ax=ax2,volume=av2,axtitle=
    'Google Stock',style='starsandstripes',mav=(4,8,12))
40. ax3 = fig.add_subplot(2,3,3)
41. av3 = fig.add_subplot(3,3,9,sharex=ax3)
42. mpf.plot(msft,type='candle',ax=ax3,volume=av3,axtitle=
    'Microsoft Stock',style='yahoo',mav=(2,4,6))
43. ax4 = fig2.add_subplot(2,3,1)
44. av4 = fig2.add_subplot(3,3,7,sharex=ax4)
45. mpf.plot(amzn,type='candle',ax=ax4,volume=av4,axtitle=
    'Amazon Stock',style='checkers',mav=(10,20,30))
46. ax5 = fig2.add_subplot(2,3,2)
47. av5 = fig2.add_subplot(3,3,8,sharex=ax5)
48. mpf.plot(tsla,type='candle',ax=ax5,volume=av5,axtitle='Tesla
    Stock',style='charles',mav=(5,10,15))
49. ax6 = fig2.add_subplot(2,3,3)
50. av6 = fig2.add_subplot(3,3,9,sharex=ax6)
51. mpf.plot(spy ,type='candle',ax=ax6,volume=av6,axti-
    tle='S&P 500 Index',style='brasil',mav=(3,6,9))
52. fig.tight_layout(pad=1.0)
53. fig2.tight_layout(pad=1.0)
54. fig
55. fig2
```

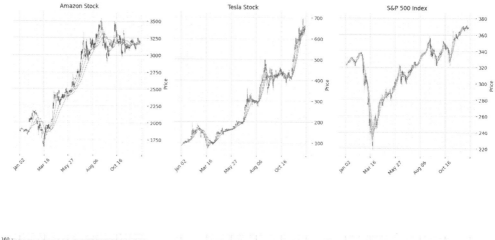

Figure 8.29: *MPLFinance examples – subplots of Amazon, Tesla, and S&P 500 index in 2020*

Let us see the second chart:

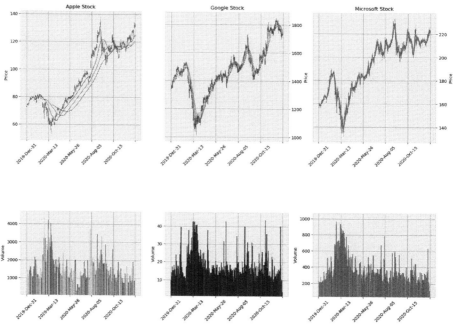

Figure 8.30: *MPLFinance examples – subplots of Apple, Google, and Microsoft stocks in 2020*

Let us conclude this chapter with an example to leverage WordCloud and image masking to do some interesting visualization.

Other examples

Let us try an interesting example to conclude this chapter. The code has inline information. The following are the steps to follow:

1. Download a book.

2. Generate a WordCloud.

3. Download the map for outline purposes.

4. Create a WordCloud from the book.

5. Generate a mask from the geographical country map (India).

6. Apply the WordCloud mask.

7. Recreate the WordCloud.

8. Display the outcome.

Let us see the program:

```
1.  # download file and save as Tagore.txt
2.  !wget --quiet https://www.gutenberg.org/files/7164/7164.txt -O Tag-
    ore.txt
3.  %matplotlib inline
4.  # open the file and read it into a variable Tagore's Gitanjali
5.  tagore_gitanjali = open('Tagore.txt', 'r').read()
6.  print ('File downloaded and saved!')
7.  # import package and its set of stopwords
8.  from wordcloud import WordCloud, STOPWORDS
9.  print ('Wordcloud is installed and imported!')
10. stopwords = set(STOPWORDS)
11. # instantiate a word cloud object
12. tagore_wc = WordCloud(
13.     background_color='white',
14.     max_words=2000,
15.     stopwords=stopwords
16. )
17. # generate the word cloud
18. tagore_wc.generate(tagore_gitanjali)
19. import matplotlib.pyplot as plt
```

```
20. fig = plt.figure()
21. fig.set_figwidth(14) # set width
22. fig.set_figheight(18) # set height
23. # display the cloud for test
24. plt.imshow(tagore_wc, interpolation='bilinear')
25. plt.axis('off')
26. plt.show()
27. import numpy as np   # useful for many scientific computing in Py-
    thon
28. import pandas as pd # primary data structure library
29. from PIL import Image # converting images into arrays
30. import urllib
31. #Load the Map for using outline and masking
32. URL    ='https://raw.githubusercontent.com/kalilurrahman/datasets/
    main/IndiaMap.jpg'
33. urllib.request.urlretrieve(URL, "map.png")
34. img = Image.open("map.png")
35. img.show()
36. #Let us show the map
37. India_mask = np.array(img)
38. print('Image downloaded and saved!')
39. # instantiate a word cloud object
40. India_wc = WordCloud(background_color='white', max_
    words=4000, mask=India_mask, stopwords=stopwords)
41. # generate the word cloud
42. India_wc.generate(tagore_gitanjali)
43. # display the word cloud
44. fig = plt.figure()
45. fig.set_figwidth(28) # set width
46. fig.set_figheight(36) # set height
47. #Show the map
48. plt.imshow(India_wc, interpolation='bilinear')
49. plt.axis('off')
50. plt.show()
```

This program produces the following final output:

Figure 8.31: An example using maps, masks, WordCloud for a visualization

As reiterated multiple times in the book, we have multiple libraries available to build visualizations using Python. The key focus should be on getting good practice, understanding visualization needs and focus, using the data, the end state expectations, and using libraries to simplify the tasks.

Resources

The following are some of the good resources for Plotly, Folium, and other key libraries:

Resource	Link
Plotly	
Plotly express course	**https://www.coursera.org/projects/data-visualization-plotly-express**
Plotly tutorial at Kaggle	**https://www.kaggle.com/kanncaa1/plotly-tutorial-for-beginners**
Plotly videos	**https://www.youtube.com/watch?v=j0wvKWb337A**

Plotly cheatsheet	https://images.plot.ly/plotly-documentation/images/python_cheat_sheet.pdf
Plotly basics resources	https://learn.co/lessons/plotly-basics
Plotly Dash – Enterprise dashboarding	https://dash.plotly.com/
Folium	
Folium bluebook	https://lyz-code.github.io/blue-book/coding/python/folium/
Folium – hands-on tutorial	https://analyticsindiamag.com/hands-on-tutorial-on-folium-python-library-for-geographical-data-visualization/
MPLFinance	
MPL Finance reference	https://github.com/matplotlib/mplfinance
Altair	
Altair for Python visualization	https://altair-viz.github.io/index.html
Time Series with Altair – Google developers	https://developers.google.com/earth-engine/tutorials/community/time-series-visualization-with-altair
Data visualization with Altair	https://huppenkothen.org/data-visualization-tutorial/13-walkthrough-altair/index.html
PyGal	
PyGal charting	http://www.pygal.org/en/stable/
Complete tutorial on PyGal	https://analyticsindiamag.com/complete-tutorial-on-pygal-a-python-tool-for-interactive-and-scalable-visualization/

There are multiple resources available to learn and master data visualization using *Python*, and it is a never-ending list. It is always important to keep learning and fine-tune one's skills to develop the career further.

Conclusion

In this chapter, we covered the key essentials of an important library – *Plotly*. We explored the might of *Plotly* with its capability to build nice visualizations with very simple code to render, the ability to create three-dimensional plots and animations with very simple API to leverage. We also covered the capabilities of geographical data visualization using folium and covered a decent amount of financial plotting capabilities using mplfinance. We also covered some interesting plots for exploration and some excellent resources to consider.

Over the last eight chapters, we covered the importance of data visualization, key elements to consider while doing visualization, introduction to various libraries, hands-on examples covering various key aspects of different libraries, such as *matplotlib, pandas, Seaborn, Bokeh, Plotly, folium,* and others. We have tried various case studies to build visualization using very simple coding. With the libraries available – programmers can build visualization easily. In the next chapter, we shall be leveraging all the learning we have had so far to try some hands-on exercises.

Hands-on Visualization Exercises, Case Studies, and Further Resources

"The ability to visualize data is an essential piece to the puzzle of data exploration and use ... the fear data providers have of having their data trivialized, misunderstood, or misrepresented also apply to the process of making visualizations, even simple ones ... Visualizing data changes how data is understood and increases interest in data generally, which will encourage more and better data to be developed."

– Robert Kosara

As mentioned in the conclusion of the previous chapter *(Chapter 8, Using Plotly, Folium, and other tools for visualization)*, we can get better by doing more hands-on programming. Given we had 100's of examples covered from Chapters 4-8, it is good to try some of the features independently. This chapter will give some case studies and example datasets to leverage and build a visualization by leveraging the power of various libraries we have covered so far. This chapter is 100% hands-on. Towards the end, we shall cover some good resources to lean on to propel our knowledge further.

Structure

- Case study and exercises – Using Seaborn – Driving/Insurance dataset
- Case study and exercises – Using Bokeh – Titanic dataset

- Case study and exercises – Using Plotly – Gapminder dataset
- Case study and exercises – Using Folium Choropleths - Denver traffic accidents dataset
- Open case study – Use any library – Air travel data
- Open case study – Using Altair
- Resources and conclusion

Objective

This chapter aims at covering all the key functionalities we explored so far in this book till *Chapter 8* in a hands-on manner. The cast studies and exercises will be explained in this chapter, and the solved solutions are available in the Jupyter Notebook created for this chapter. The examples can be further extended for better visualizations and usage.

Case studies and examples using Seaborn

In this case study, we have the following tasks to accomplish:

Exercise - 1:

- Load the US States JSON file (*'us-states.json'*) from *https://github.com/python-visualization/folium/tree/master/examples/data* or the folder specified in the Jupyter Notebook
- Load a dataset called a state-wide car crashes (*'car_crashes.csv'*) in the same folder
- Create a US Choropleth Map using the JSON file and state dataset. Use the following for the folium map:
    a. Columns to choose = columns=['abbrev', 'ins_premium']
    b. Key On key_on='feature.id'
    c. Legend Name legend_name='Insurance Premium(%)'

The following is an example of the output produced:

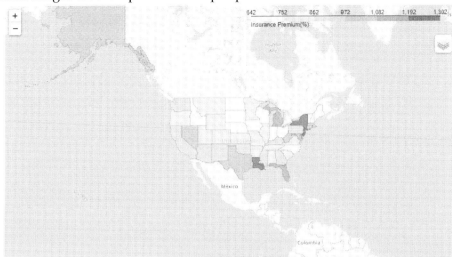

Figure 9.1: Exercise-1 output produced – US map

Exercise – 2:

- Correlate on *State_data* using the *corr()* function
- Using *Seaborn*, generate a *heatmap()*

The following is an example of the output produced:

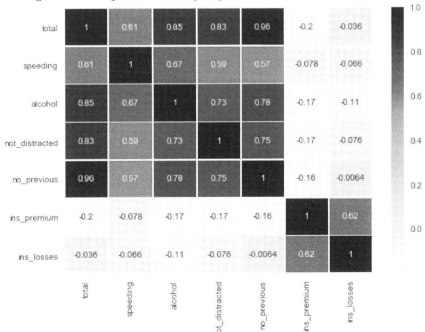

Figure 9.2: Exercise-2 output produced – heatmap

- **Exercise-3:**
  - a. Create a distplot on State_data for *speeding*
  - b. Create a distplot on State_data for *alcohol*
  - c. Create a distplot on State_data for *total*
  - d. How does the plot look?

The following is an example of the output produced:

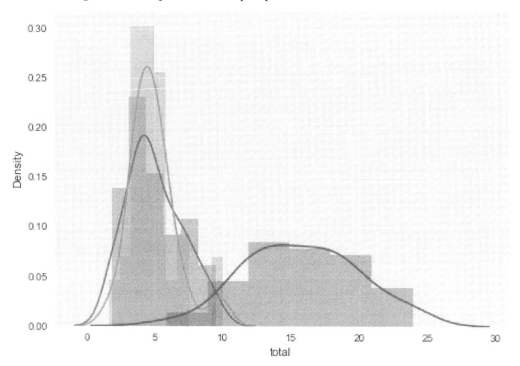

Figure 9.3: Exercise-3 output produced – distplot

Exercise-4:

- Create a bar plot using state abbreviation (*abbrev*) as x coordinate and *speeding* as y coordinate with a vertical orientation.
- Use *xticks(rotation=?)* to ensure that the axis values are not overlapping

The following is an example of the output produced:

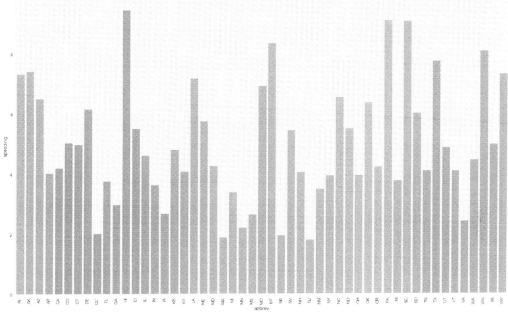

***Figure 9.4**: Exercise-4 output produced – bar charts*

Exercise-5:

   a. Part-1

      i. Create a function to plot kernel density estimate plot – kdeplot() based on parameters passed

   b. Part-2

      i Using the **kdeplot** function created in Part-1, plot a kdeplot for all the relevant columns in the dataset

   c. Part-3

      i. Correlate the columns of relevance

      ii. Create a heatmap() for all the columns having a correlation

   d. Part-4

      i. Create a pairplot() for the relevant columns. Use *hue on alcohol, diagonal plot as kde,* and palette type as *hsv*

The following are the output produced by the solution:

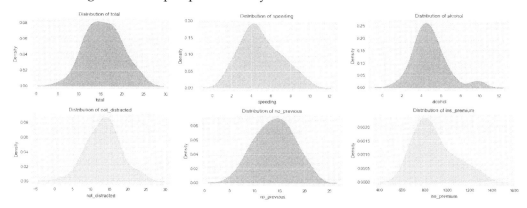

Figure 9.5: Exercise-5 output produced – KDE plots

The following is the second part of the output – a heatmap:

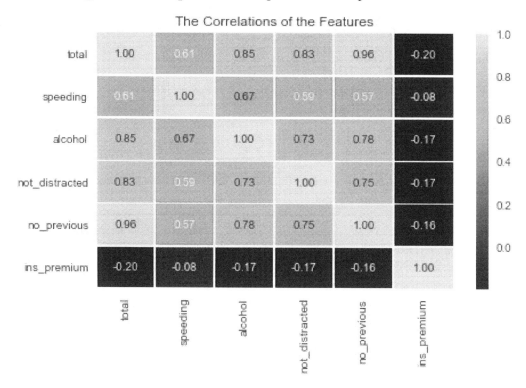

Figure 9.6: Exercise-5 output produced part-2 – a heatmap

The following is the third part of the output – a pairplot:

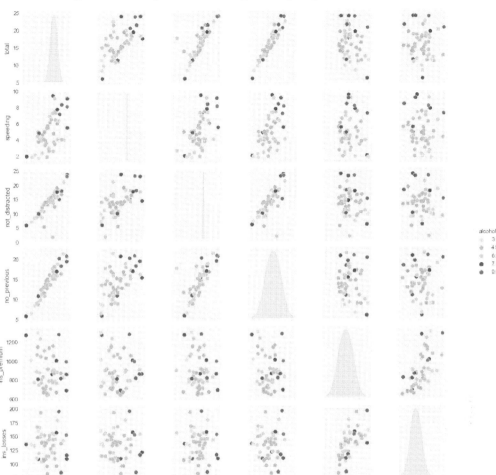

Figure 9.7: *Exercise-5 output produced part-3 – a pairplot using car crashes dataset*

Exercise-6:

a. Create two joint plots

    i. The first one with x values of *total* and y values of *alcohol*

    ii. The second one with y values of *total* and x values of *alcohol* and a hue on *ins_losses* with a palette type as *hsv*

    iii. What differences do you see in the two plots?

The following are the outputs produced by the solution:

Part-1 of the output looks as follows:

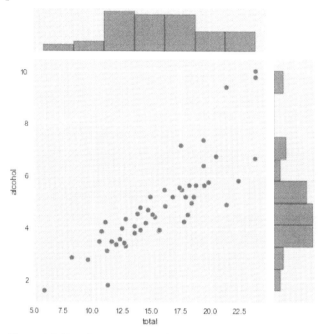

Figure 9.8: *Exercise-6 output produced part-1 – a normal jointplot*

Part-2 of the output looks as follows:

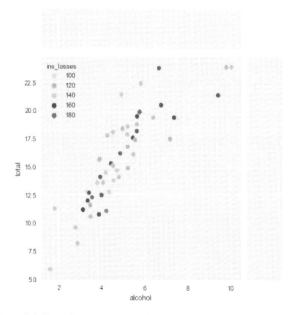

Figure 9.9: *Exercise-6 output produced part-2 – a formatted jointplot*

Exercise-7:

    a. Create a pairplot with a hue on *total* with a palette type as *Accent*

        The following is the output produced by the solution:

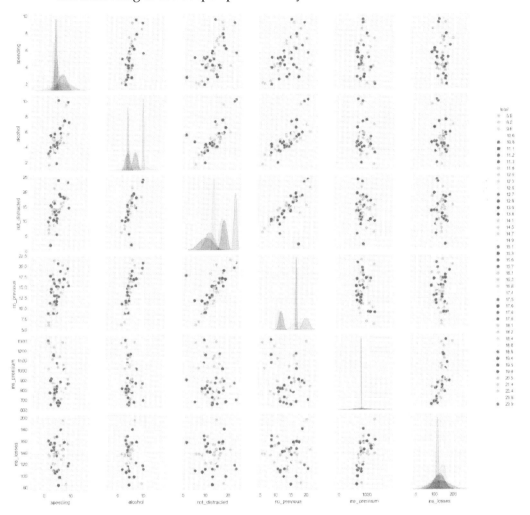

Figure 9.10: Exercise-7 output produced pairplot

Exercise-8:

    a. Create a US choropleth map using the JSON file and state dataset. Use the following for the folium map:

        i. Columns to choose = `columns=['abbrev', 'speeding']`

        ii. Key On `key_on='feature.id'`

        iii. Legend Name `legend_name='Speeding(%)'`

A sample output for this exercise is almost similar to the output for Exercise-1 except for the scale and legend_name.

Exercise-9:

a. Create a US choropleth map using the JSON file and state dataset. Use the following for the folium map:

   i. Columns to choose = `columns=['abbrev', 'alcohol']`

   ii. Key On `key_on='feature.id'`

   iii. Legend Name `legend_name='Alcohol(%)'`

A sample output for this exercise is almost similar to the output for Exercise-1 except for the scale and legend_name.

Let us now see some case studies and examples using Bokeh.

Case studies and examples using Bokeh

For this case study, we shall be using the Titanic dataset in the form of a CSV file. This file contains information about all the passengers of the fateful Titanic ship. The columns it contains are - {*'PassengerId', 'Survived', 'Pclass', 'Name', 'Sex', 'Age', 'SibSp', 'Parch', 'Ticket', 'Fare', 'Cabin', 'Embarked'*}. We shall be using this dataset for our visualization.

Exercise-1:

a. Create a bokeh plot showcasing the scatter on 'age' and 'fare.'

b. Use the "square" plotting function to check the outcome.

c. Play around with other bokeh marker types to see various outputs. Check on changing the size, color, transparency through alpha, setting the font sizes for axes, alignment, tick marks, data range start, etc.

A sample output for this exercise is as follows:

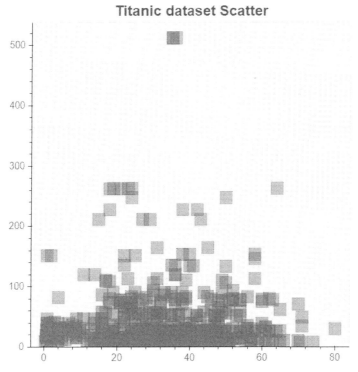

Figure 9.11: *A Bokeh case study - exercise-1 Titanic dataset scatter plot*

Exercise-2:

a. Create a scatter plot on age and fare with a legend field on Pclass.

b. Use a marker array for various classes and map the travel class as 1, 2, 3.

c. Use a factor colormap of Viridis256 on the travel class

A sample output for this exercise is as follows:

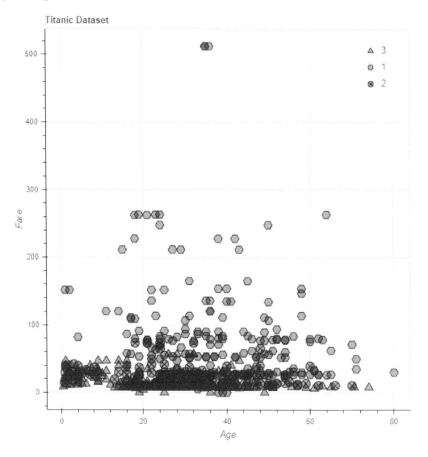

Figure 9.12: A Bokeh case study - exercise-2 Titanic dataset scatter plot with different markers

Exercise-3:

a. Create a ColumnDataSource on the Titanic dataset

b. Create a CDSView (Column Data Source View) with an IndexFilter at 10,50,90 and 130

c. Define tools to be displayed box_select, hover, and reset

d. Create a plot with a height and width of 300 pixels and pass tools setting

e. Create a circle scatter plot with the x-axis of age and y-axis of fare and hover color of "purple."

f. Create a filtered plot with the same setting

g. Create a filtered scatter plot with the filter created above

h. Show a grid plot with both the scatter plots - regular and filtered

A sample output for this exercise is as follows:

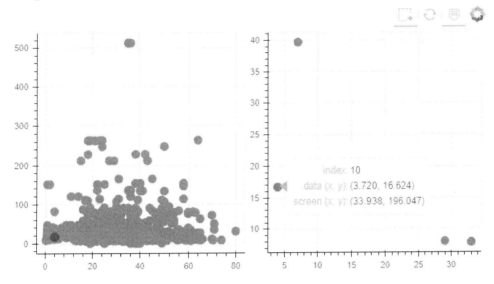

Figure 9.13: A Bokeh case study - exercise-3 Titanic dataset with interconnected filtered scatter plot

Exercise-4:

a. Create a plot with three grids to showcase:

    i.   The first plot will be a circle scatter plot of the age and fare columns of the dataset. You can choose the color and transparency (alpha) of your choice

    ii.   The second plot will be a triangle scatter plot of the fare and age columns of the dataset. You can choose the color and transparency (alpha) of your choice

    iii.   The third   plot will be a square scatter plot of class and age columns of the dataset. You can choose the color and transparency (alpha) of your choice

b. Create a gridplot with a 2x2 matrix with two plots in the first row, an empty first column in the second row, and the third plot in the final column

c. Play around with the choices; what do you see?

A sample output for this exercise is as follows:

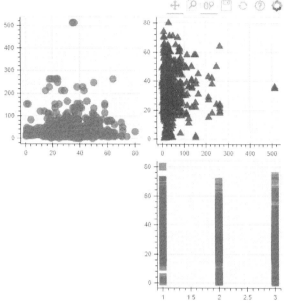

Figure 9.14: A Bokeh case study - exercise-4 Titanic dataset a grid-based scatter plot

Exercise-5:

a. Group all the data under travel class *Pclass*

b. Plot a vertical bar chart based on *Passenger Travel Class* - Pclass that we grouped by

A sample output for this exercise is as follows:

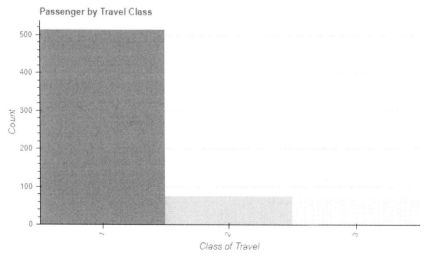

Figure 9.15: A Bokeh case study - exercise-5 Titanic dataset – bar chart on the class of travel

Exercise-6:

    a. Build an array based on the place of embarkation for the passengers

    b. Count the total number of passengers embarking on different stations

    c. Use a *ColumnDataSource* with color options for each of the category

    d. Plot a vertical bar chart based on embarkation location

A sample output for this exercise is as follows:

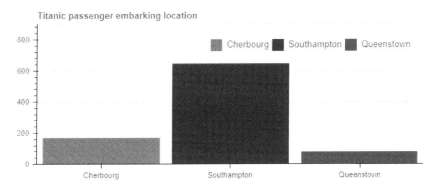

Figure 9.16: *A Bokeh case study - exercise-6 Titanic dataset – bar chart on the location of* **embarkation**

Exercise-7

    a. Import the *bokeh.transform* function for *jitter*

    b. Build a *Dataframe* of the class of travel *Pclass* and *fare*

    c. Plot a scatter chart with *fare* and jitter on *Pclass*

    d. What do you see?

A sample output for this exercise is as follows:

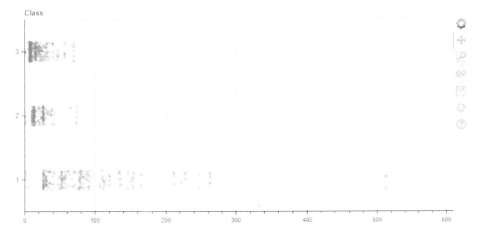

Figure 9.17: *A Bokeh case study - exercise-7 Titanic dataset – scatter plot with jitters*

Exercise-8:

a. Create a correlation of all values in the Titanic dataset

b. Set the index of the columns and set the index in the tight format for the correlation dataframe

c. Assign the correlated values to a linear color mapper through the LinearColorMapper function

d. Define a set of tools such as box_select, lasso_select, pan, wheel_zoom, box_zoom, reset, hover, and help

e. Create a figure with x_range and y_range values defined by the list of the unique column, and row values defined earlier

f. Create a heatmap using the rect function. Use the ColumnDataSource of the correlation dataframe and pass the indexed columns for X and Y values

g. Define a color bar and assign it to the tickers

h. Show the plot

A sample output for this exercise is as follows:

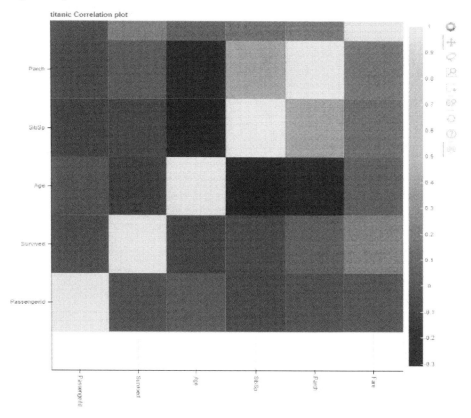

Figure 9.18: A Bokeh case study - exercise-8 Titanic dataset – Bokeh correlation chart - heatmap

Exercise-9:

a. Load Gapminder dataset for population, life expectancy, and per capita GDP of nations

b. Create a scatter plot with gdpPerCap and lifeExp as X and Y parameters

c. Play around with other scatter charts, change the X and Y values, and give a hue based on a parameter. What do you see?

A sample output for this exercise is as follows:

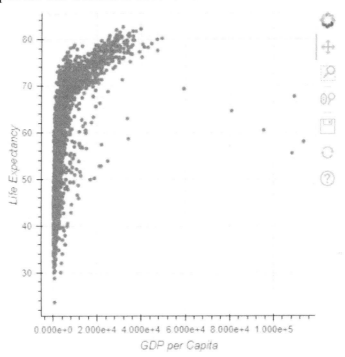

Figure 9.19: *A Bokeh case study - exercise-9 gapminder dataset – scatter plot*

Exercise-10:

a. Build arrays with the following code:

```
factors = [("Scheduled", "United"), ("Scheduled", "Amer-
ican"), ("Scheduled", "Delta"),("Scheduled", "South-
west"),("Operated", "United"), ("Operated", "Ameri-
can"), ("Operated", "Delta"),("Operated", "Southwest"),("-
Cancelled", "United"), ("Cancelled", "American"), ("Can-
celled", "Delta"),("Cancelled", "Southwest"),]

years = ['y19', 'y20']

colors = ["#c9d9d3", "#e84d60"]
```

```
values2019 = [ 1571.404,    111.039,    766.033,    363.946,
1533.942, 2057.523, 1754.095, 1330.324, 37.462, 53.516, 11
.938, 33.622]

values2020 = [  675.539,    1026.695,    789.47,    762.595,
623.808, 946.122, 746.237, 686.051,51.731, 80.573, 43.233
, 76.544]

h = [8091.684, 7938.055,53.629 ]

adj_h = [8092/2,7938/2,53/2]
```

   b. Build a vertically stacked bar chart and a line chart using the data provided above.

   c. What do you see?

A sample output for this exercise is as follows:

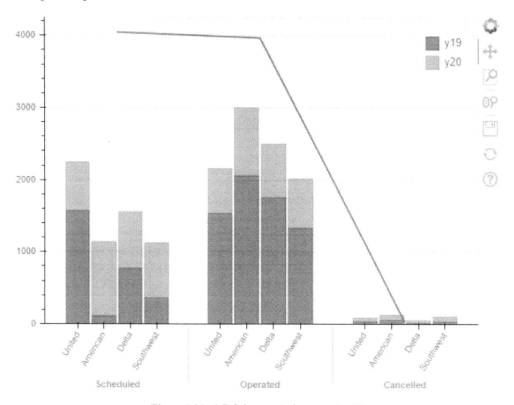

Figure 9.20: *A Bokeh case study - exercise-10*
stacked bar chart with a line plot combination for flight statistics

Let us now see some case studies and examples using Plot.ly.

Case studies and examples using Plotly

We shall be using the available datasets in Plot.ly for our plotting.

Exercise-1:

- We shall be using the gapminder dataset and query on year==2007 to subset the dataset
- Build a choropleth with locations as iso_alpha that gives countries and coloring based on life expectancy with a hover on country
- Let us build a *sequential.Plasma* colormap to the continuous color scale. This allows us to color code based on the values.

A sample output for this exercise is as follows:

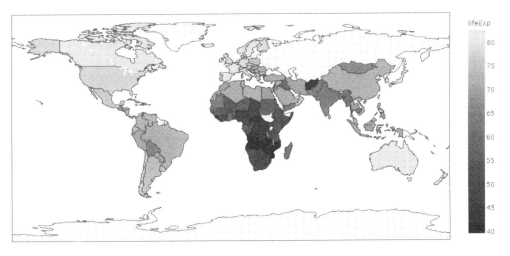

Figure 9.21: *A Plotly case study - exercise-1 gapminder dataset – animation on life expectancy*

Exercise-2:

- Build a choropleth with locations as iso_alpha that gives countries, and coloring based on GDP Per Cap *gdpPerCap* with a hover on country
- Let us build a sequential.Plasma colormap to a continuous color scale. This allows us to color code based on the values.

A sample output for this exercise is as follows:

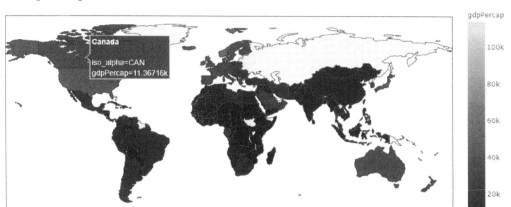

Figure 9.22: A Plotly case study - exercise-2 gapminder dataset – GDP per capita

Exercise-3:

- Build a *scatter_matrix* with *gapminder* dataset with dimensions of **['lifeExp', 'pop', 'gdpPerCap']** and color on *continent.*

A sample output for this exercise is as follows:

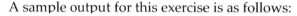

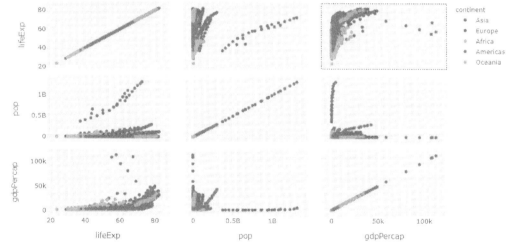

Figure 9.23: A Plotly case study - exercise-3 gapminder dataset – scatter matrix

Exercise-4:

- Build a *scatter_matrix* with *medals_wide* dataset with dimensions of *["gold", "silver", "bronze"]* and color on *nation*
- What difference do you see against the previous example?

A sample output for this exercise is as follows:

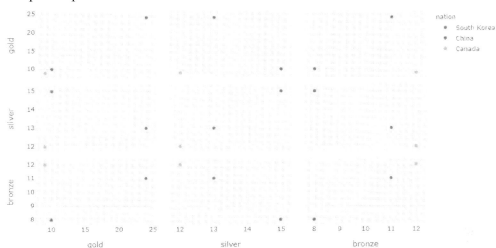

Figure 9.24: A Plotly case study - exercise-4 Olympic medals dataset – scatter matrix

Exercise-5:

- Build a **sunburst** plot with gapminder dataset for the year 2007
- Use path parameter as continent followed by the country
- Values are given as *pop* or population, color on life expectancy or *lifeExp*, and hover on country or *iso_alpha*

A sample output for this exercise is as follows:

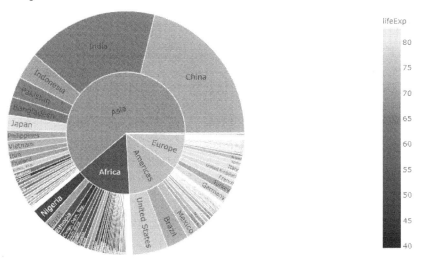

Figure 9.25: A Plotly case study - exercise-5 gapminder dataset – sunburst chart

Exercise-6:

- Build a **Treemap** plot with gapminder dataset for the year 2007
- Use path parameter as continent followed by the country
- Values are given as *gdpPerCap* or GDP Per Cap. Use same for color and hover on country or *iso_alpha*
- Use a discrete color sequence on Dark24.
- What do you infer from this treemap?

A sample output for this exercise is as follows:

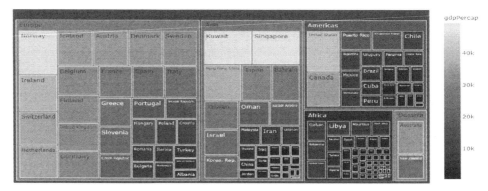

Figure 9.26: A Plotly case study - exercise-6 gapminder dataset – treemap

Let us see the case studies and examples in Folium.

Case studies and examples using Folium

For the Folium case study, we shall do a simple project using a traffic accident dataset from the Denver Police Department. The ¶source dataset is available at the following URL - **https://www.denvergov.org/media/gis/DataCatalog/traffic_accidents/csv/traffic_accidents.csv**

For the case study, we shall be performing the following tasks:¶

- Load the dataset into a Dataframe
- Check the first five items in the Dataframe
- The following are the columns in the dataset:
  - 'OBJECTID_1','INCIDENT_ID','OFFENSE_ID','OFFENSE_CODE','OFFENSE_CODE_EXTENSION','TOP_TRAFFIC_ACCIDENT_OFFENSE','FIRST_OCCURRENCE_DATE','LAST_OCCURRENCE_DATE','REPORTED_DATE','INCIDENT_ADDRESS','GEO_X','GEO_Y','GEO_LON','GEO_

LAT','DISTRICT_ID','PRECINCT_ID','NEIGHBORHOOD_ ID','BICYCLE_IND','PEDESTRIAN_IND','HARMFUL_EVENT_ SEQ_1','HARMFUL_EVENT_SEQ_2','HARMFUL_EVENT_ SEQ_3','ROAD_LOCATION','ROAD_DESCRIPTION','ROAD_ CONTOUR','ROAD_CONDITION','LIGHT_CONDITION','TU1_ VEHICLE_TYPE','TU1_TRAVEL_DIRECTION','TU1_VEHICLE_ MOVEMENT','TU1_DRIVER_ACTION','TU1_DRIVER_ HUMANCONTRIBFACTOR','TU1_PEDESTRIAN_ACTION','TU2_ VEHICLE_TYPE','TU2_TRAVEL_DIRECTION','TU2_ VEHICLE_MOVEMENT','TU2_DRIVER_ACTION','TU2_ DRIVER_HUMANCONTRIBFACTOR','TU2_PEDESTRIAN_ ACTION','SERIOUSLY_INJURED','FATALITIES','FATALITY_ MODE_1','FATALITY_MODE_2','SERIOUSLY_INJURED_ MODE_1','SERIOUSLY_INJURED_MODE_2'

- Check for the shape of the Dataframe

- Load 200 or 1000 Data items for plotting

- Build a Dataframe for fatal accidents

- Define the Denver latitude and longitude values (39.7392, -104.9903)

- **Task-1** Create a Denver map and display it

- **Task-2** Create a Feature group of the incidents and display

- **Task-3** Create a circle marker and display the same

- **Task-4** Create a marker cluster and display the same

- **Task-5** Create a marker cluster for fatal accidents

- **Task-6** Include offense details, report details, and fatalities as popup and tooltip

- **Additional Tasks** – Using the columns available for the dataframe, what other analysis can you perform? What about

  o Driving under influence accidents?

  o Pedestrian involvement information from the accident data?

  o Serious injury count?

  o What is your summary assessment?

A sample output for this exercise is as follows (Each image refers to an out of a task):

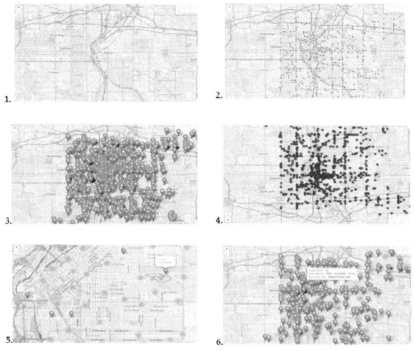

Figure 9.27: *A Folium case study - exercise-1-6 outputs for traffic violations dataset*

Folium - more choropleth examples

Exercise-7:

- Use a custom Icon for a marker
- Use Popups
- Use New Delhi - Chandni Chowk location as the location with a zoom level start of 12.
- Use Stamen Terrain as the tile

A sample output for this exercise is as follows:

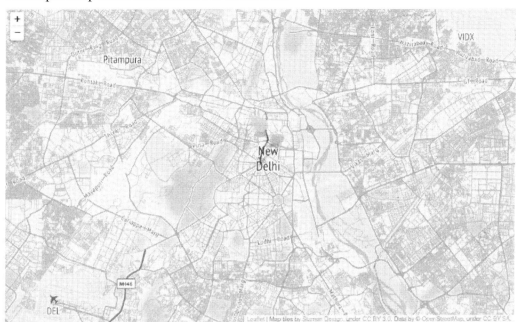

Figure 9.28: A Folium case study - exercise-7 output for new Delhi map choropleth

Exercise-8:

- Use Popups
- Use Stamen Terrain as the tile
- Use LayerControl feature for plotting
- Plot top-10 locations in New Delhi using an array
- Data to use is as follows:

```
Latitudes = [28.6321, 27.1751,  28.6172, 28.6129,
28.5245,  28.5535,  28.6271,  28.6406,  28.6143,
28.5562,28.6127, 28.6379]

Longitudes = [77.2194, 78.0421, 77.2082, 77.2295,
77.1855, 77.2588, 77.2166, 77.2495, 77.1994, 77.1000,
77.2773, 77.2432]

Locations = ['Connaught Place', 'Taj Mahal', 'Indi-
an Parliament', 'India Gate', 'Qutub Minar', 'Lotus
Temple', 'Jantar Mantar' , 'Raj Ghat', 'Rashtrapati
Bhavan', 'Indira Gandhi International Airport', 'Ak-
shardam Temple', 'Feroz Shah Kotla Stadium']
```

A sample output for this exercise is as follows:

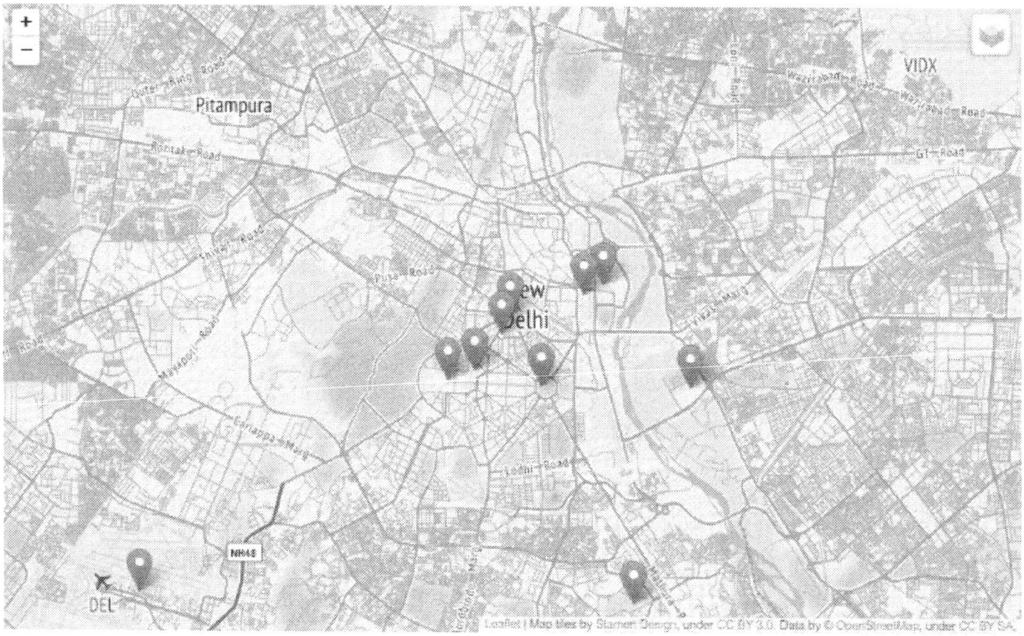

Figure 9.29: *A Folium case study – exercise-8 output for new Delhi map choropleth with markers*

Exercise-9:

- Generate a random scatter point location
- Use the *Vincent* library
- Generate a scatter chart using the *vincent.Scatter* function
- Convert the scatter chart to a JSON
- Use the JSON created as popups for random locations plotted in a Folium Map
- Use different popup widths – default, zero, and a high number
- Use the *folium.Vega* function to add popups to the *Folium* Map
- What difference do you see?

A sample output for this exercise is as follows:

Figure 9.30*: A Folium case study – exercise-9*
output for folium markers with vincent vega markers for mapping

Exercise-10:

- Load datasets for districts and states in India

- Load datasets for census data in 2001 and 2011

- Load GEO JSON dataset for India map

- Add a TileLayer for various tile types

- Add JSON state borders for the Indian states

- Add marker and popup information for state information using the data loaded

A sample output for this exercise is as follows:

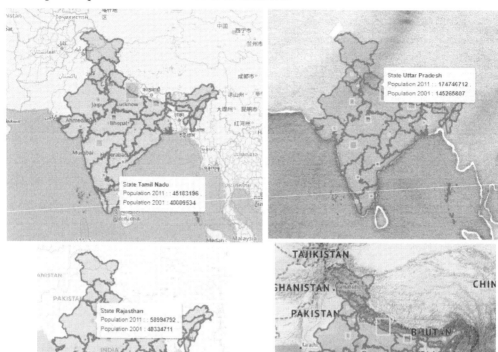

Figure 9.31: *A Folium case study – exercise-10 output for folium JSON overlay for the Indian states with popups and tooltip info for various state wise datasets*

Let us now see a case study on air travel. This can be solved using any library. The standard solution given in the Jupyter Notebook uses Bokeh. The case study can be solved using any library of choice.

Air travel data case study - Use Bokeh, Matplotlib, Plotly, or any choice

For this case study, you can choose any of the libraries you like to use.

- We shall be using a dataset modified from **https://www.bts.gov/sites/bts. dot.gov/files/docs/data-spotlight/232556/scheduled-canceled-operated-**

flights-jan2019-sept2020.xlsx by taking relevant data and removing the unnecessary headers

- The cleaned data is available at **https://raw.githubusercontent.com/ kalilurrahman/datasets/main/USFlightTravel201920.tsv**

- **Case Study Tasks**

   o **Task-1:** Load the Dataset

   o **Task-2:** Reindex the data with columns on Year, Month, Category, TotalFlights, Alaska, Allegiant, American, Delta, Frontier, Hawaiian, JetBlue, Southwest, Spirit, United

   o **Task-3:** Create three dataframes based on status as canceled, operated, scheduled

   o **Task-4:** Create a random color generation function

   o **Task-5:** Create a column data source (if you are using Bokeh)

   o **Task-6:** Create a line plot for all the airlines having data

   o **Task-7:** Add mute function for the lines added (if you are using Bokeh)

   o **Task-8:** Convert the date field to YYYY-MM-DD format and add a new column

   o **Task-9:** Calculate the average flights per month using the mean() function

   o **Task-10:** Plot a bar chart using the data calculated in Task-9

   o **Task-11:** Create a line plot for the data created in Task-9 for any airline

   o **Task-12:** Create a pivot table calculating the total canceled, operated, and scheduled flights count per airlines

   o **Task-13:** Generate a stacked bar chart for each of the airlines' flight status

A sample output for this exercise is as follows:

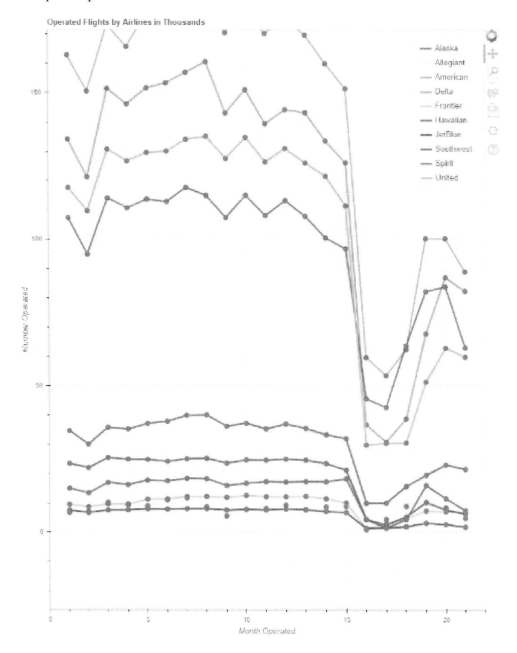

Figure 9.32: *Air travel database case study – output-1 for line chart of flights operated*

Let us see the following output:

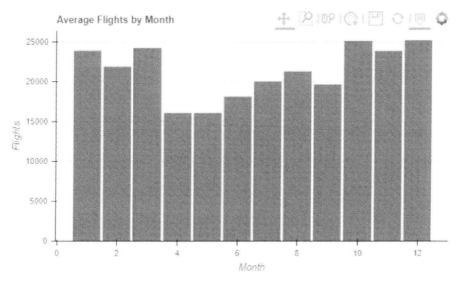

Figure 9.33: *Air travel database case study – output-2 bar chart of average flights operated per month*

Let us see the following output:

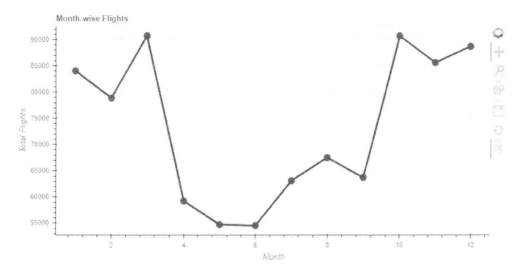

Figure 9.34: *Air travel database case study – output-3 line chart of flights operated by United*

Let us see the following output:

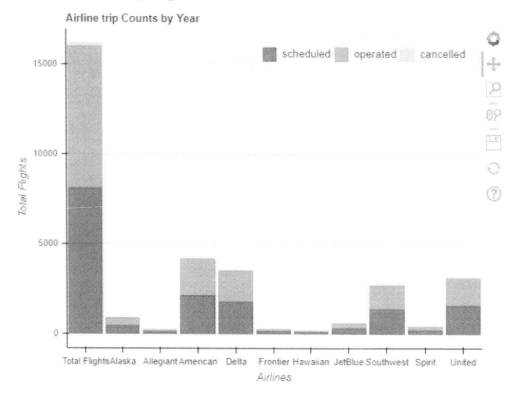

Figure 9.35*: Air travel database case study – output-4*
stacked bar chart of flights scheduled, operated, and canceled

Let us see an open case study using Altair library

Open case study – Using Altair

While we didn't cover this as a chapter, Altair is a simple library to use like seaborn, plotly, or bokeh.

Recommended exercises to try out

- **Task-1:** A bar chart using random numbers generated.

- **Task-2:** A scatter chart using the **vega_datasets.cars()** dataset.

- **Task-3:** A scatter chart using the **mark_point()** function on the **cars()** dataset.

- **Task-4:** A **mark_tick()** function-based plotting of qualitative and ordinal data.

- **Task-5:** A scatter chart using the **vega_datasets.countries()** dataset is similar to gapminder. We shall plot based on fertility and life expectancy.

- **Task-6:** An area chart using the **vega_datasets.stocks()** dataset for various stocks.

- **Task-7:** A stremgraph using the **mark_area()** function leveraging the **vega_datasets.stocks()** dataset

A sample of the expected output for this exercise is as follows:

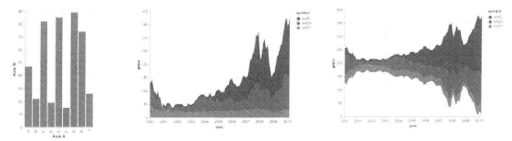

Figure 9.36: Altair case study output for a bar chart, area chart, and streamgraph

Let us take this book to a logical closure by covering the resources to enhance the knowledge needed for data visualization and approaching the explosive growth of data visualization and storytelling.

Solution file

You can use a *Jupyter Notebook* in your local instance or use a free notebook service such as *Google Research's CoLab* (**https://colab.research.google.com/**) using your Google ID to create the solution. The solution file is given with the link for all exercises in this book. The code is hidden by default if you want references, and you may view the code by clicking the button available at the top of the notebook. It gives a way to toggle on and off as well.

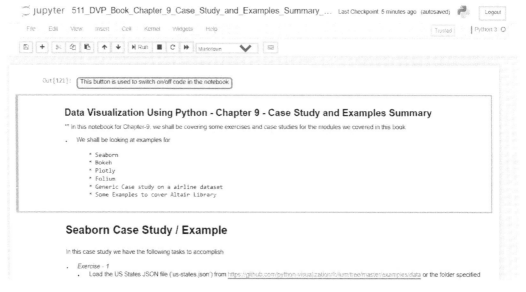

*Figure 9.37: The solution file appearance and button
for enabling/disabling the code display in a Jupyter notebook*

Resources

We are living in a digital world, and the resources available at our disposal are humongous. The wealth of knowledge and data getting added are phenomenal. To keep up with the changes, an intelligent approach is needed to learn and chisel skills needed to excel in one's career. Data visualization and data science are no-less. The depth of knowledge in one subject or a tool may become a thing of the past. To keep up with the developments, it is good to look at top knowledge sources. Some of the resources recommended for such an endeavor that is not covered already in the book are as follows:

- Kaggle tutorials, knowledge resources, datasets, problem statements, and notebooks

- GitHub for data visualization

- Medium topics on data visualization

- Courses of Udacity, Coursera, LinkedIn, edX, Udemy, and YouTube videos

- Good blog posts on visualization in general

By keeping abreast of the latest development, practicing regularly, and imbibing the leading trends and practices, one can become one of the good specialists sought after, if not the best.

Conclusion

In this chapter, we covered some good examples in the form of case studies. We tried some of the key visualization elements using python in a real hands-on manner. These examples are done using very basic coding with no need for superficial skills or world-class coding experience. Data visualization is exactly that. It should be easy to practice, easy to dissect, and map the data into beautiful insights through powerful storytelling. Python has become the swiss-army-knife for data visualization and many other aspects of data science. As we saw through hundreds of examples over the past nine chapters, it is a powerful and impactful tool to use. The growth of libraries is something to keep up with, and with good due diligence and focus, one can master the trick. For that, best wishes for a brilliant and enterprising journey ahead!

Index

Printed in Great Britain
by Amazon

85507038R00208